Advanced .NET Remoting

INGO RAMMER

apress™

ISBN (pbk): 1-59059-025-2
Printed and bound in the United States of America 12345678910
Trademarked names may appear in this book. Rather than use a trademark symbol with every occurrence of a trademarked name, we use the names only in an editorial fashion and to the benefit of the trademark owner, with no intention of infringement of the trademark.
Technical Reviewer: Kent Sharkey
Editorial Directors: Dan Appleman, Peter Blackburn, Gary Cornell, Jason Gilmore, Karen Watterson, John Zukowski
Managing Editor: Grace Wong
Project Manager: Alexa Stuart
Copy Editor: Ami Knox
Production Editor: Julianna Scott Fein
Compositor and Illustrator: Impressions Book and Journal Services, Inc.
Indexer: Valerie Haynes Perry
Cover Designer: Tom Debolski
Marketing Manager: Stephanie Rodriguez

Distributed to the book trade in the United States by Springer-Verlag New York, Inc., 175 Fifth Avenue, New York, NY, 10010 and outside the United States by Springer-Verlag GmbH & Co. KG, Tiergartenstr. 17, 69112 Heidelberg, Germany.
In the United States, phone 1-800-SPRINGER, Email orders@springer-ny.com, or visit http://www.springer-ny.com.
Outside the United States, fax +49 6221 345229, Email orders@springer.de, or visit http://www.springer.de.

For information on translations, please contact Apress directly at 2560 Ninth Street, Suite 219, Berkeley, CA 94710.
Email info@apress.com, or visit http://www.apress.com.
The information in this book is distributed on an "as is" basis, without warranty. Although every precaution has been taken in the preparation of this work, neither the author nor Apress shall have any liability to any person or entity with respect to any loss or damage caused or alleged to be caused directly or indirectly by the information contained in this work.
The source code for this book is available to readers at http://www.apress.com in the Downloads section.

To Katja
Each day that starts with you being nearby can only turn out great.
I love you.

Contents at a Glance

Contents

About the Author

INGO RAMMER is CEO and cofounder of Sycom Software, an Austrian software consulting company. He started his professional career years ago with obscure scripting languages such as Perl and Tcl/Tk on various versions of Unix. Shortly after this he converted to the Windows platform and created some large-scale distributed applications with Visual Basic and ASP. He implemented cross-platform remote procedure calls using XML and HTTP POST way before the term "Web Services" had been coined for this technology, and he still focuses on the integration of applications written in different programming languages and platforms.

About the Technical Reviewer

KENT SHARKEY is currently employed at Microsoft as a Technical Evangelist for the .NET Framework and Visual Studio .NET. He roams the land striving to smite the heretics, convert the heathens, and celebrate the faithful. In between he sleeps (far too little), bangs his head against the .NET Framework (far too often, with little result), and tries to help everyone however he can. He lives in Redmond with the three women of his life: Margaret (the wife), Squirrel (the warrior), and Cica (the princess).

Acknowledgments

I STARTED WRITING MY FIRST computer programs mostly due to my father, who was interested in computers at a time when only a few people saw the potential in this upcoming technology. His enthusiasm about computers made it possible for me to play around with such weird devices as the Commodore Plus 4, the Sinclair QL, and the Philips MSX-2 at about the age of ten or eleven. All of those computers had one thing in common—as soon as they had been powered on, you landed in the programming language, which of course was BASIC at that time (the real one, when AUTO 10 was essential). Learning to program computers therefore has been an almost natural activity for me. I really want to thank both my mother Helga and my father Willi for giving me a great childhood and for providing me with all the support I needed to quench my thirst for knowledge at this time.

The person who shaped the greatest part of my professional life was Juergen Nitsche, who dared to employ me as the lead programmer for a series of custom business applications when I was a 16-year-old high school boy. This partnership turned out so well that about four years later we founded our own company, of which we both are still CEOs and owners. Thanks for your trusting me from the beginning.

I also want to say thanks to my fellows at the NOVA framework team, especially Christian "Gumbo" Wehrl and Harald Haefele, for bearing with my absence during the course of writing this book and for all the great VB vs. Java vs. C++ vs. .NET discussions we had. Best wishes also to Robert "Stony" Steinfest, who has the most interesting developer personality I've ever come across. Your unique, friendly way of dealing with users, testers, and junior programmers alike really is legendary. You guys are brilliant!

As I sometimes get too obsessed about working with Microsoft technology, kudos go out to Edgar Hucek and Markus Gaertner for reminding me that this world is about choices. (That is, Ed is a real Open Source fan and Markus is the best Java guru I've gotten to know.)

I also want to thank Jay "Saurik" Freeman for creating the Anakrino MSIL-to-C# decompiler. This tool allowed me to understand the .NET Remoting Framework at a level that made it possible for me to write this book. If you also want or need to understand one or another part of the .NET platform, be sure to grab a free copy of this tool at http://www.anakrino.org.

Last but not least, this book would not have been possible without the great Apress team who worked with me during the last months. This starts with Dan Appleman and Gary Cornell, who gave me the opportunity to write for the best publisher when it comes to .NET books. I also want to thank Kent Sharkey from Microsoft for agreeing to tech review this book. My biggest thanks go out to Ami

Knox, who was my copy editor and who really managed to turn my manuscripts into a readable and understandable book. Possibly the most important person on this endeavor was Alexa Stuart, who mastered to "herd the cats" and kept us all on track while working on this book. Kudos also go out to all the people at Apress who did not work directly with me but whose effort definitely influenced the success of this book: Stephanie, Julianna, Grace, Doris, and everyone else who worked with us but whose name I do not yet know.

Working with all of you was great!

Introduction

WITHIN THE LAST TEN YEARS a lot of changes have happened in the way software has been designed and developed. Until about five years ago, it might have been sufficient to provide a monolithic client application that connected directly to a database server to perform its tasks.

Later, architects and managers alike demanded applications built from reusable components to provide improved abstraction, reusability, and maintainability. COM and Visual Basic did a great job of providing developers with the means to achieve these goals in an easy way.

The introduction of the Microsoft DNA concept along with MTS introduced a further layer of abstraction and enabled developers to centralize business logic on servers to develop scalable systems.

Nowadays the world starts to get connected. Architects and managers again place new demands on developers. Parts of your centralized business logic need to be "opened" and interfaces need to be provided to third parties—to other companies in your enterprise or even to business partners. On the other hand, your applications have to incorporate services provided by other companies, such as address verification or creditworthiness-rating services.

Visual Basic up to version 6.0 did a great job for the developer working in a closed LAN-environment, but can hardly be judged as a "connected" language. The SOAP Toolkit and the MSXML parser provided a first glimpse into the world of open and connected systems, but implementation still remained too labor intensive to be a practical approach for opening a lot of interfaces to third parties. Stability, security, versioning, and transfer of object-oriented structures were not supported by these technologies.

The Microsoft .NET Framework, on the other hand, has been designed with these requirements in mind. This starts with the IL and CLR, which provide an easy way to integrate different programming languages, and reaches up to .NET Remoting, which provides a comfortable way to interconnect different applications and components in an object-oriented manner. It also allows for far greater extensibility than DCOM, for example, did before.

This is what *Advanced .NET Remoting* will teach you, and I hope you will consider it a valuable resource for your work on distributed .NET applications. Read on to find out in detail what this book covers and who will benefit most from it.

What Is Covered in This Book

This book covers the means of cross-process and cross-machine interaction of applications developed with the .NET Framework. It will provide you with an in-depth understanding of the remoting capabilities that are built into the .NET Framework.

.NET Remoting is different from most other means of remote object access because it can be as easy as writing COM components in Visual Basic 6, yet also gives you the option to extend remoting to include virtually any protocol on any transportation layer you will come across.

The first part of the book gives you a thorough introduction to .NET Remoting basics and how you can use .NET Remoting "out of the box." This gives you a whole range of possibilities, from fast binary transfer protocol to a cross-platform SOAP protocol, with the potential to switch between both without changing a single line in your code. At the end of this part, you will be able to design and develop remoteable components and know just what you have to do to achieve your goals. This part also deals with objects' lifetimes, security, versioning, marshalling, and deployment.

The second part covers the advanced features of .NET Remoting and its extensibility model. At the end of the second part you will have an in-depth understanding of the inner workings of remoting and will know how to extend the framework to meet your requirements. You should not be afraid, especially as you go through the sample code in the second part of the book, to either hit F1 or to insert a breakpoint and examine the Locals window in your custom channel sink to see the exact contents of the objects that get passed as parameters to your methods.

What This Book Doesn't Cover

This book is in no way a rehash of the supplied documentation but is meant to be used in conjunction with it. You will only find a small percentage of the information that is covered in the online documentation in this book and vice versa, so it is very important for you to use the .NET Framework SDK documentation as well.

I chose this approach to writing a book for one simple reason: I assume that as an advanced developer you don't have too much time to waste going through a 1,000-page book of which 600 pages are a reproduction of the online documentation. Instead, you want to read the information that has not been covered before. If you think so as well, this book is right for you.

Who This Book Is For

This book is for the intermediate-to-advanced programmer who wants a hands-on guide to .NET Remoting. Although this book is not an introduction to .NET, the CLR, or any .NET language, you nevertheless will be able to use the knowledge and insight you'll get from this book with any of these programming languages. Because it is my opinion that C# is or will become the ".NET language of choice," all examples in this book are written in C#. But if you're a VB .NET developer, don't despair; it's not about programming languages—it's about the framework!

If you are a "use-it" developer, Chapters 1 through 6 of this book will serve you well by providing a general introduction to the possibilities of remoting and giving you in-depth information on how to use the capabilities that come with .NET Remoting "out of the box."

If you are more of an "understand-it-and-extend-it" developer, the second part of this book is for you. Chapters 7 through 11 were written for those who want to understand what's going on behind the scenes of .NET Remoting and how the framework can be customized using proxies, messages, channel sinks, and providers. It also demonstrates how a complete transport channel is implemented from scratch.

How This Book Is Structured

Advanced .NET Remoting is divided into two parts. The first part (Chapters 1 through 6) covers everything you need to know for developing distributed applications within the .NET Framework. The second part (Chapters 7 through 11) gives you a thorough technical insight that will allow you to really understand what's happening behind the scenes and how you can tap into customizing the framework to suit your exact needs. Following is a brief chapter-by-chapter summary of the topics covered in this book.

Chapter 1: Introduction to Remoting

This chapter gives you a short introduction to the world of distributed application development and the respective technologies. It presents some scenarios in which .NET Remoting can be employed and includes historical background on the progress and development of various remoting frameworks during the last ten years.

Chapter 2: .NET Remoting Basics

This chapter gets you started with your first remoting application. Before going directly into the code, I present the distinctions between .NET Remoting and other distributed application frameworks. I then introduce you to the basic types of remote objects, which are server-activated objects and client-activated objects, and show you how to pass data by value. I also give you some basic information about lifetime management issues and the generation of metadata, which is needed for the client to know about the interfaces of the server-side objects.

Chapter 3: Remoting in Action

In this chapter, I demonstrate the key techniques you'll need to know to use .NET Remoting in your real-world applications. I show you the differences between Singleton and SingleCall objects and untangle the mysteries of client-activated objects. I also introduce you to SoapSuds, which can be used to generate proxy objects containing only methods' stubs.

Chapter 4: Configuration and Deployment

This chapter introduces you to the aspects of configuration and deployment of .NET Remoting applications. It shows you how to use configuration files to avoid the hard coding of URLs or channel information for your remote object. You also learn about hosting your server-side components in Windows Services and IIS.

Chapter 5: Securing .NET Remoting

This chapter shows you how to leverage IIS' features when it comes to hosting your components in a secured environment. In this chapter you learn how to enable basic HTTP sign-on and the more secure Windows-integrated authentication scheme, which is based on a challenge/response protocol. You also see how to enable encrypted access by using standard SSL certificates at the server side.

Chapter 6: In-Depth .NET Remoting

As a developer of distributed applications using .NET Remoting, you have to consider several fundamental differences from other remoting techniques and, of course, from the development of local applications. These differences, including lifetime management, versioning, and the handling of asynchronous calls and events, are covered in this chapter.

Chapter 7: Inside the Framework

.NET provides an unprecedented extensibility for the remoting framework. The layered architecture of the .NET Remoting Framework can be customized by either completely replacing the existing functionality of a given tier or chaining new implementation with the baseline .NET features.

Before working on the framework and its extensibility, I really encourage you to get a thorough understanding of the existing layers and their inner workings in this architecture. This chapter gives you that information.

Chapter 8: Creation of Sinks

This chapter covers the instantiation of message and channel sinks and sink chains. It shows you the foundation on which to build your own sinks—something you need to know before tackling the implementation of custom sinks.

Chapter 9: Extending .NET Remoting

This chapter builds on the information from Chapters 7 and 8 and shows you how to implement custom remoting sinks. This includes channel sinks that compress or encrypt the transported information, message sinks to pass additional runtime information from a client to the server or to change the .NET Remoting programming model. This chapter concludes with showing you how to implement custom remoting proxies that forward method calls to remote objects.

Chapter 10: Developing a Transport Channel

This chapter builds on the information you gained in Chapters 7, 8, and 9 and presents the development of a custom .NET Remoting channel that transfers messages via standard Internet e-mail by using SMTP and POP3. It shows not only the implementation of this channel but also the necessary phase of analyzing the underlying protocol to combine it with the features and requirements of .NET Remoting.

Chapter 11: Context Matters

This last chapter is about message-based processing in local applications. Here you learn how you can intercept calls to objects to route them through IMessageSinks. This routing allows you to create and maintain parts of your application's business logic at the metadata level by using custom attributes. You also discover why it might be a good idea to do so.

Source Code Download

You can find all source code presented in this book at the Apress download page at http://www.apress.com. If you have further suggestions or comments or want to access more sample code on .NET Remoting, you are invited to visit my site at http://www.dotnetremoting.cc.

    I hope you will benefit from the techniques and information I provide in this book when building your distributed applications based on the .NET Framework and when extending the framework to make it suit your needs.

Ingo Rammer
Vienna, Austria

CHAPTER 1

Introduction
to Remoting

THIS CHAPTER GIVES YOU a short introduction to the world of distributed application development and its respective technologies. Here you get a chance to examine some scenarios in which .NET Remoting can be employed and learn some historical background on the progress and development of various remoting frameworks during the last ten years.

What Is Remoting?

Remoting is the process of programs or components interacting across certain boundaries. These contexts will normally resemble either different processes or machines.[1] In the .NET Framework, this technology provides the foundation for distributed applications—it simply replaces DCOM.

Remoting implementations generally distinguish between *remote objects* and *mobile objects*. The former provides the ability to execute methods on remote servers, passing parameters and receiving return values. The remote object will always "stay" at the server, and only a reference to it will be passed around among other machines.

When mobile objects pass a context boundary, they are serialized (marshaled) into a general representation—either a binary or a human readable format like XML—and then deserialized in the other context involved in the process. Server and client both hold copies of the same object. Methods executed on those copies of the object will always be carried out in the local context, and no message will travel back to the machine from which the object originated. In fact, after serialization and deserialization, the copied objects are indistinguishable from regular local objects, and there is also no distinction between a server object and a client object.

---

[1] .NET extends this concept to include the ability to define additional contexts within one running application. Object accesses crossing these boundaries will pass the .NET Remoting Framework as well.

Scenarios for .NET Remoting

At the beginning of the client/server era, remoting was mostly used for accessing a server's resources. Every database or file server is an implementation of some technique that allows code to be executed remotely. Programming these older frameworks was so difficult a task that few products except for these server-side core services implemented remoting.

Nowadays the building of distributed applications has gotten a lot easier so that it's quite feasible to distribute business applications among various machines to improve performance, scalability, and maintainability.

Centralized Business Logic

One of the key scenarios for implementing remoting is the concentration of business logic on one or more central servers. This considerably simplifies the maintainability and operability of large-scale applications. Changes in business logic do not entail your having to roll out an application to your organization's 10,000 worldwide users—you just have to update one single server.

When this centralized business logic is shared among different applications, this labor-saving effect multiplies considerably; instead of patching several applications, you just have to change the server's implementation.

Physical Separation of Layers

The security of a company's vital databases represents a common concern in this time of Web-enabled businesses. The general recommendation is against directly connecting from the Web server to the database because this setup would allow attackers easy access to critical data after they have seized control of the Web server.

Instead of this direct connection, an intermediate application server is introduced. This server is placed in a so-called demilitarized zone (DMZ), located between two firewalls. Firewall #1 only allows connections from the Web server to the app server, and Firewall #2 only allows connections from the app server to the databases.

Because the application server doesn't allow the execution of arbitrary SQL statements, yet provides object-oriented or function-based access to business logic, a security compromise of the Web server (which can only talk to the app server) is noncritical to a company's operations.

Accessing Other Platforms

In today's mid- to large-scale enterprises, you will normally encounter a heterogeneous combination of different platforms, frameworks, and programming languages. It is not uncommon to find that a bunch of tools have been implemented: Active Server Pages (ASP), Java Server Pages (JSP), PHP, or ColdFusion for Web applications, Visual Basic or Java for in-house applications, C++ for server-side batch jobs, scripting languages for customizing CRM systems, and so on.

Integrating these systems can be a daunting task for system architects. Remoting architectures like CORBA, SOAP, and .NET Remoting are an absolute necessity in large-scale enterprise application integration. (CORBA and SOAP are introduced and compared later in this chapter.)

Third-Party Access

Opening systems to third parties in a business-to-business environment is quite common nowadays. This process started with hard-to-implement EDI documents, transferred via proprietary networks, and is recently opening up for smaller companies due to the possibility of using SOAP, which is fairly easier to implement.

Order-entry applications, which allow your business partners to directly place orders from one ERP system to the other, constitute one example of an application utilizing this kind of remoting. More sophisticated applications are starting to be developed—address verification, customer creditworthiness ratings, and online price-comparison systems are just the beginning.

Evolution of Remoting

The scenarios presented thus far have only been possible due to the constant evolution of remoting frameworks. The implementation of large-scale business applications in a distributed manner has only been practicable after the technical problems have been taken care of by the frameworks. CORBA, COM+, and EJB started this process several years ago, and .NET Remoting simplifies this process even more.

To underscore how far remoting has evolved from its cumbersome beginnings, the following sections give you a brief history of the various remoting frameworks.

DCE/RPC

Distributed Computing Environment (DCE), designed by the Open Software Foundation (OSF) during the early 1990s, was created to provide a collection of tools and services that would allow easier development and administration of distributed applications. The DCE framework provides several base services such as Remote Procedure Calls (DCE/RPC), Security Services, Time Services, and so on.

Implementing DCE is quite a daunting task; the interfaces have to be specified in Interface Definition Language (IDL) and compiled to C headers, client proxies, and server stubs by an IDL compiler. When implementing the server, one has to link the binary with DCE/Threads, which are available for C/C++. The use of programming languages other than these is somewhat restricted due to the dependence on the underlying services, like DCE/Threads, with the result that one has to live with single-threaded servers when refraining from using C/C++.

DCE/RPC nevertheless is the foundation for many current higher-level protocols including DCOM and COM+. Several application-level protocols such as MS SQL Server, Exchange Server, Server Message Block (SMB), which is used for file and printer sharing, and Network File System (NFS) are also based on DCE/RPC.

CORBA

Designed by the Object Management Group (OMG), an international consortium of about 800 companies, CORBA's aim is to be the middleware of choice for heterogeneous systems. OMG's CORBA, which stands for *Common Object Request Broker Architecture*, is only a collection of standards; the implementation of object request brokers (ORBs) is done by various third parties. Because parts of the standard are optional and the vendors of ORBs are allowed to include additional features that are not in the specifications, the world has ended up with some incompatible request brokers. As a result, an application developed to make use of one vendor's features could not easily be ported to another ORB. When you buy a CORBA-based program or component, you just can't be sure if it will integrate with your CORBA applications, which probably were developed for a different request broker.

Aside from this potential problem, CORBA also has quite a steep learning curve. The standard reads like a complete wish list of everything that's possible with remoted components—sometimes it simply is too much for the "standard business." You'll probably end up reading documents for days or weeks before your first request is ever sent to a server object.

Nevertheless, when you have managed to implement your first CORBA application, you'll be able to integrate a lot of programming languages and platforms. There are even layers for COM or EJB integration, and apart from SOAP, CORBA is the only true multiplatform, multiprogramming language environment for distributed applications.

DCOM

Distributed Component Object Model (DCOM) is an "extension" that fits in the Component Object Model (COM) architecture, which is a binary interoperability standard that allows for component-oriented application development. You'll usually come in contact with COM when using ActiveX controls or ActiveX DLLs.

DCOM allows the distribution of those components among different computers. Scalability, manageability, and its use in WANs pose several issues that need to be addressed. DCOM uses a pinging process to manage the object's lifetimes; all clients that use a certain object will send messages after certain intervals. When a a server receives these messages it knows that the client is still alive; otherwise it will destroy the object.

Additionally, reliance on the binary DCE/RPC protocol poses the need for direct TCP connections between the client and its server. Use of HTTP proxies is not possible. DCOM is available for Microsoft Windows and for some UNIX dialects (ported by the German Software AG).

MTS/COM+

COM+, formerly *Microsoft Transaction Server* (MTS), was Microsoft's first serious attempt to reach into the enterprise application domain. It not only serves as a remoting platform, but also provides transaction, security, scalability, and deployment services. COM+ components can even be used via Microsoft Message Queue Server to provide asynchronous execution of methods.

Despite its advantages, COM+ does not yet support the automatic marshalling of objects to pass them by value between applications; instead you have to pass your data structures using ADO recordsets or other means of serialization. Other disadvantages that keep people from using COM+ are the somewhat difficult configuration and deployment, which complicates its use for real-world applications.

Java RMI

Traditional *Java Remote Method Invocation* (Java RMI) uses a manual proxy/stub compilation cycle. In contrast to DCE/RPC and DCOM, the interfaces are not written in an abstract IDL but in Java. This is possible due to Java being the only language for which the implementation of RMI is possible.

This limitation locked RMI out of the game of enterprise application integration. Even though all relevant platforms support a Java Virtual Machine, integration with legacy applications is not easily done.

Java EJB

Enterprise Java Beans (EJB) was Sun's answer to Microsoft's COM+. Unlike CORBA, which is only a standard, EJB comes with a reference implementation. This allows developers to check if their products run in any standard-complying EJB container. EJB has been widely accepted by the industry, and there are several container implementations ranging from free open source to commercial implementations by well-known middleware vendors.

One problem with EJB is that even though a reference implementation exists, most vendors add features to their application servers. When a developer writes a component that uses one of those features, the application will not run on another vendor's EJB container.

Former versions of EJB have been limited to the Java platform because of their internal reliance on RMI. The current version allows the use of IIOP, which is the same transfer protocol CORBA uses, and third parties already provide commercial COM/EJB bridges.

Web Services/SOAP/XML-RPC

Web Services provided the first easy to understand and implement solution to true cross-platform and cross-language interoperability. Web Services technically are stateless calls to remote components via HTTP POST with a payload encoded in some XML format.

Two different XML encodings are currently in major use: XML-RPC and SOAP. *XML-RPC* can be described as a poor man's SOAP. It defines a very lightweight protocol with a specification size of about five printed pages. Implementations are already available for a lot of programming environments, ranging from AppleScript to C/C++, COM, Java, Perl, PHP, Python, Tcl, and Zope—and of course there's also an implementation for .NET.

SOAP, or *Simple Object Access Protocol*, defines a much richer set of services; the specification covers not only remote procedure calls, but also the *Web*

Services Description Language (WSDL) and *Universal Description, Discovery, and Integration* (UDDI). WSDL is SOAP's interface definition language, and UDDI serves as a directory service for the discovery of Web Services. Those additional protocols and specifications are also based on XML, which allows all SOAP features to be implemented on a lot of platforms.

The specifications and white papers for SOAP, WSDL, UDDI, and corresponding technologies cover several hundred pages, and you can safely assume that this document will grow further when topics like routing and transactions are addressed. Fortunately for .NET developers, the .NET platform takes care of *all* issues regarding SOAP.

.NET Remoting

At first look, .NET Remoting is to Web Services what ASP has been to CGI programming. It takes care of a lot of issues for you: contrary to Web Services, for example, .NET Remoting enables you to work with stateful objects. This single fact allows it to be the base of tomorrow's distributed applications.

In addition to the management of stateful objects, .NET Remoting gives you a flexible and extensible framework that allows for different transfer mechanisms (HTTP and TCP are supported by default), encodings (SOAP and binary come with the framework), and security settings (IIS Security and SSL come out of the box).

With these options, and the possibility of extending all of them or providing completely new implementations, .NET Remoting is well suited to today's distributed applications. You can choose between HTTP/SOAP for the Internet or TCP/binary for LAN applications by literally changing a single line in a configuration file.

Interface description does not have to be manually coded in any way, even though it's supported if you like to design your applications this way. Instead, metadata can be extracted from running servers, where the WSDL is automatically generated, or from any .NET assembly.

Summary

This chapter provided a short introduction to the world of distributed application development and the respective technologies. You now know about the various scenarios in which .NET Remoting can be applied and understand how it differs from other distributed application protocols and techniques.

CHAPTER 2

.NET Remoting Basics

THIS CHAPTER GETS YOU STARTED with your first remoting application. Before going
directly into the code, I present the differences between .NET Remoting and other
distributed application frameworks. I then introduce you to the basic types of
remote objects, server-activated objects and client-activated objects, and show
you how to pass data by value. I also give you some basic information about lifetime management issues and the generation of metadata, which is needed for the
client to know about the interfaces of the server-side objects.

Advantages of .NET Remoting

As you've seen in the previous chapter, several different architectures for the
development of distributed applications already exist. You might therefore won-
der why .NET introduces another, quite different way of developing those kinds
of applications. One of the major benefits of.NET Remoting is that it's centralized
around well-known and well-defined standards like HTTP and SOAP.

Ease of Implementation

Comparing .NET Remoting to other remoting schemas is like comparing COM
development in Visual Basic to C++. Visual Basic 6 allowed developers to concen-
trate on the business needs their applications had to fulfill without having to
bother with the technical details of COM. The C++ programmers had to know the
exact specifications of COM (at least before the introduction of ATL) and implement truckloads of code for supporting them.

    With .NET this concept of absolute ease of implementation has been
extended to the development of distributed applications. There are no
proxy/stub-compilation cycles as in Java RMI. You don't have to define your
interfaces in an abstract language as you would with CORBA or DCOM. A unique
feature is that you don't have to decide up front on the encoding format of remoting requests; instead, you can switch from a fast binary format to SOAP by
changing one word in a configuration file. You can even provide both communication channels for the same objects by adding another line to the configuration.
You are not fixed on one platform or programming language as with DCOM,

COM+, and Java EJB. Configuration and deployment is a lot easier than it was in DCOM.

Even though .NET Remoting provides a lot of features, it doesn't lock you in. Quite the contrary: it can be as easy as you like or as complex as you need. The process of enabling remoting for an object can be as straightforward as writing two lines of code or as sophisticated as implementing a given transfer protocol or format on your own.

Extensible Architecture

.NET Remoting offers the developer and administrator a vastly greater choice of protocols and formats than any of the former remoting mechanisms. In Figure 2-1, you can see a simplified view of the .NET Remoting architecture. Whenever a client application holds a reference to a remote object, it will be represented by a TransparentProxy object, which "masquerades" as the destination object. This proxy will allow all of the target object's instance methods to be called upon it. Whenever a method call is placed to the proxy, it will be converted into a message, and the message will pass various layers.

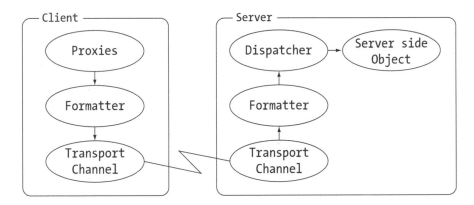

Figure 2-1. The .NET Remoting architecture (simplified)

The message will pass a serialization layer—the formatter—which converts it into a specific transfer format such as SOAP. The serialized message later reaches a transport channel, which transfers it to a remote process via a specific protocol like HTTP or TCP. On the server side, the message also passes a formatting layer, which converts the serialized format back into the original message and forwards it to the dispatcher. Finally, the dispatcher calls the target object's method and passes back the response values through all tiers. This architecture is shown in detail in Chapter 7.

In contrast to other remoting architectures, most layers can either be extended or completely replaced, and additional layers can be chained to the baseline .NET Remoting Framework to allow for custom processing of messages. (More about this in Chapters 7, 8, and 9.)

You can easily switch between implementations of the different layers without changing any source code. A remoting application that's been written using a binary TCP-based protocol can be opened for third parties using a SOAP/HTTP-based protocol by changing some lines in a configuration file to replace the .NET Remoting transport channel.

Interface Definitions

Most remoting systems like DCE/RPC, RMI, and J2EE demand a manual creation of so-called proxy/stub objects. The proxy encapsulates the connection to the remote object on the client and forwards calls to a stub object on the server, which in turn passes them on to the "real" object. In most of these environments (at least in CORBA, DCE/RPC, and DCOM) the "source code" for generating these objects has to be written in an abstract Interface Definition Language and precompiled to generate implementation headers for a certain programming language.

In comparison to this traditional approach, .NET Remoting uses a generic proxy for all kinds of remote objects. This is possible because .NET is the first framework that has been designed with remoting in mind; on other platforms these capabilities have been retrofitted and therefore have to be integrated into the given architecture and programming model.

Such ease of remoting poses the potential problem of your using an incorrect design.[1] This book will help you to make the right architectural decisions. For example, even though you don't have to write any interface definitions in IDL, you still should separate interface from implementation; you can, however, write both in the same language—in *any* .NET programming language. .NET Remoting provides several different ways of defining those interfaces, as discussed in the following sections.

Shared Assembly

In this case, the server-side object's implementation exists on the client as well. Only during instantiation is it determined whether a local object or an object on the remote server will be created. This method allows for a semitransparent

---

[1] This is partly the same as it was in Visual Basic 6. VB 6 allowed you to create applications without a lot of up-front design work. This often led to applications that were hardly maintainable in the long run.

switch between invoking the local implementation (for example, when working offline) and invoking server-side objects (for example, to make calculations on better-performing servers when connected to the network).

When using this method with "conventional" distributed applications that don't need to work in a disconnected scenario, you need to use a lot of care, because it poses some risks due to programming errors. When the object is mistakenly instantiated as a local object on the client and passed to the server (as a method's parameter, for example) you might run into serious troubles, ranging from InvalidCastExceptions to code that works in the development environment but doesn't work in the production environment due to firewall restrictions. In this case the client has in reality become the server, and further calls to the object will pass from the server to your clients.

Shared Interfaces or Base Objects

When creating a distributed application, you define the base classes or interfaces to your remote objects in a separated assembly. This assembly is used on both the client and the server. The real implementation is placed only on the server and is a class that extends the base class or implements the interface.

The advantage is that you have a distinct boundary between the server and the client application, but you have to build this intermediate assembly as well. Good object-oriented practices nevertheless recommend this approach! Unfortunately, as you will see in later chapters, this approach doesn't work in all .NET Remoting scenarios.

Generated Metadata Assembly

This approach is one of the more elegant ones. You develop the server in the same way as when using the shared assemblies method. Instead of really sharing the DLL or EXE, you later extract the necessary metadata, which contains the interface information, using SoapSuds.

SoapSuds will either need the URL to a running server or the name of an assembly as a parameter, and will extract the necessary information (interfaces, base classes, objects passed by value, and so on). It will put this data into a new assembly, which can be referenced from the client application. You can then continue to work as if you'd have separated your interfaces right from the beginning. For certain scenarios—especially when using client-activated objects—this is the way to go.

Serialization of Data

With the exception of earlier TCP/IP RPC implementations, in which you even had to worry about little-endian/big-endian conversions, all current remoting frameworks support the automatic encoding of simple data types into the chosen transfer format. The problem starts when you want to pass a copy of an object from server to client. Java RMI and EJB support these requirements, but COM+, for example, did not. The commonly used serializable objects within COM+ were PropertyBag and ADO Recordsets—but there was no easy way of passing large object structures around.

In .NET Remoting the encoding/decoding of objects is natively supported. You just need to mark such objects with the [Serializable] attribute or implement the interface ISerializable and the rest will be taken care of by the framework. This even allows you to pass your objects cross-platform via XML.

The serialization mechanism marshals simple data types and subobjects (which have to be serializable or exist as remote objects), and even ensures that circular references (which could result in endless loops when not discovered) don't do any harm.

Lifetime Management

In distributed applications there are generally three ways of managing lifetime. The first is to have an open network connection (for example, using TCP) from the client to the server. Whenever this connection is terminated, the server's memory will be freed.

Another possibility is the DCOM approach, where a combined reference counting and pinging mechanism is used. In this case the server receives messages from its clients at certain intervals. As soon as no more messages are received, it will free its resources.

In the Internet age, in which you don't know your users up front, you cannot rely on the possibility of creating a direct TCP connection between the client and the server. Your users might be sitting behind a firewall that only allows HTTP traffic to pass through. The same router will block any pings the server might send to your users. Because of those issues, the .NET Remoting lifetime service is customizable as well. By default an object will get a lifetime assigned to it, and each call from the client will increase this "time to live." The .NET Framework also allows a sponsor to be registered with a server-side object. It will be contacted just before the lifetime is over and can also increase the object's time to live.

The combination of these two approaches allows for a configurable lifetime service that does not depend on any specific connection from the server to the client.

Multiserver/Multiclient

When you use remote objects (as opposed to using copies of remotely generated objects that are passed by value), .NET automatically keeps track of where they originated. So a client can ask one server to create an object and safely pass this as a method's parameter to another server.

The second server will then directly execute its methods on the first server, without a round-trip through the client. Nevertheless, this also means there has to be a direct way of communication from the second server to the first one— that is, there must not be a firewall in between, or at least the necessary ports should be opened.

Your First Remoting Application

In the following sections, you create a sample .NET Remoting application that demonstrates some of the concepts discussed earlier in this chapter. First and foremost, there are two very different kinds of objects when it comes to remoting: objects that are passed by reference and those that are passed by value. MarshalByRefObjects[2] allow the ability to execute remote method calls on the server side. These objects will live on the server and only a so-called ObjRef will be passed around. You can think of the ObjRef as a networked pointer that shows on which server the object lives and contains an ID to uniquely identify the object. The client will usually not have the compiled objects in one of its assemblies; instead only an interface or a base class will be available. Every method, including property gets/sets, will be executed on the server. The .NET Framework's proxy objects will take care of all remoting tasks, so that the object will look just like a local one on the client.

The second kind of objects will be referred to as *ByValue objects* throughout this book. When these objects are passed over remoting boundaries (as method parameters or return values), they are serialized into a string or a binary representation and restored as a copy on the other side of the communications channel. After this re-creation, there is no notation of client or server for this kind of object; each one has its own copy, and both run absolutely independently. Methods called on these objects will execute in the same context as the origination of the method call. For example, when the client calls a function on the server that returns a ByValue object, the object's state (its instance variables) will be transferred to the client and subsequent calls of methods will be executed directly on the client. This also means that the client has to have the compiled object in one of its assemblies. The only other requirement for an object to be

---

[2] Called so because every object of this kind has to extend System.MarshalByRefObject.

passable by value is that it supports serialization. This is implemented using a class-level attribute: [Serializable]. In addition to this "standard" serialization method, you'll also be able to implement ISerializable, which I show you how to do in Chapter 6.

The First Sample

This sample remoting application exposes a server-side MarshalByRefObject in Singleton mode. You will call this object CustomerManager, and it will provide a method to load a Customer object (which is a ByValue object) from a fictitious database. The resulting object will then be passed as a copy to the client.

Architecture

When using remote objects, both client and server must have access to *the same* interface definitions and serializable objects that are passed by value. This leads to the general requirement that at least three assemblies are needed for any .NET Remoting project: a shared assembly, which contains serializable objects and interfaces or base classes to MarshalByRefObjects; a server assembly, which implements the MarshalByRefObjects; and a client assembly, which consumes them.

In most of the examples throughout this book, you will end up with these three assemblies:

- *General:* This represents the shared assembly, which contains the interface ICustomerManager and the ByValue object Customer. As the methods of a Customer object will be executed either on the client or on the server, the implementation is contained within the General assembly as well.

- *Server:* This assembly contains the server-side implementation of CustomerManager.

- *Client:* This assembly contains a sample client.

Defining the Remote Interface

As a first step, you have to define the interface ICustomerManager, which will be implemented by the server. In this interface, you'll define a single method, getCustomer(), that returns a Customer object to the caller.

```
public interface ICustomerManager
{
    Customer getCustomer(int id);
}
```

This interface will allow the client to load a Customer object by a given ID.

Defining the Data Object

Because you want to provide access to customer data, you first need to create a *Customer* class that will hold this information. This object needs to be passed as a copy (by value), so you have to mark it with the [Serializable] attribute.

In addition to the three properties FirstName, LastName and DateOfBirth, you will also add a method called getAge() that will calculate a customer's age. Next to performing this calculation, this method will write a message to the console so that you can easily see in which context (client or server) the method is executing.

```
[Serializable]
public class Customer
{
    public String FirstName;
    public String LastName;
    public DateTime DateOfBirth;

    public Customer()
    {
        Console.WriteLine("Customer.constructor: Object created");
    }

    public int getAge()
    {
        Console.WriteLine("Customer.getAge(): Calculating age of {0}, " +
            "born on {1}.",
            FirstName,
            DateOfBirth.ToShortDateString());

        TimeSpan tmp = DateTime.Today.Subtract(DateOfBirth);
        return tmp.Days / 365; // rough estimation
    }
}
```

Up to this point in the code, there's not much difference from a local application. Before being able to start developing the server, you have to put the interface and the class in the namespace General and compile this project to a separate DLL, which will later be referenced by the server and the client.

Implementing the Server

On the server you need to provide an implementation of ICustomerManager that will allow you to load a customer from a fictitious database; in the current example, this interface will only fill the Customer object with static data.

To implement the sample server, you create a new console application in Visual Studio .NET called Server and add a reference to the framework assembly System.Runtime.Remoting.dll and the newly compiled General.dll from the previous step (you will have to use the Browse button here, because you didn't copy the assembly to the global assembly cache (GAC)). The server will have to access the namespace General and System.Runtime.Remoting plus a remoting channel, so you have to add the following lines to the declaration:

```
using System.Runtime.Remoting;
using General;
using System.Runtime.Remoting.Channels;
using System.Runtime.Remoting.Channels.Http;
```

As described previously, you will have to implement ICustomerManager in an object derived from MarshalByRefObject. The getCustomer() method will just return a dummy Customer object:

```
class CustomerManager: MarshalByRefObject, ICustomerManager
{
    public CustomerManager()
    {
        Console.WriteLine("CustomerManager.constructor: Object created");
    }

    public Customer getCustomer(int id)
    {
        Console.WriteLine("CustomerManager.getCustomer): Called");
        Customer tmp = new Customer();
        tmp.FirstName = "John";
        tmp.LastName = "Doe";
        tmp.DateOfBirth = new DateTime(1970,7,4);
```

```
            Console.WriteLine("CustomerManager.getCustomer(): Returning " +
                                "Customer-Object");
            return tmp;
        }
    }
```

It still looks more or less the same as a "conventional" nonremoting class would—the only difference is that it doesn't inherit directly from Object, but from MarshalByRefObject.

Now let's have a look at the server startup code. This is a very basic variant of registering a server-side object. It doesn't yet use a configuration file, but the server's parameters are hard coded in void Main().

```
class ServerStartup
{
    static void Main(string[] args)
    {
        HttpChannel chnl = new HttpChannel(1234);
        ChannelServices.RegisterChannel(chnl);
        RemotingConfiguration.RegisterWellKnownServiceType(
                                typeof(CustomerManager),
                                "CustomerManager.soap",
                                WellKnownObjectMode.Singleton);

        // the server will keep running until keypress.
        Console.ReadLine();
    }
}
```

Now take a closer look at the startup sequence of the server:

```
HttpChannel chnl = new HttpChannel(1234);
```

A new HTTP channel (System.Runtime.Remoting.Channels.Http.HttpChannel) is created and configured to listen on port 1234. The default transfer format for HTTP is SOAP.

```
ChannelServices.RegisterChannel(chnl);
```

The channel is registered in the remoting system. This will allow incoming requests to be forwarded to the corresponding objects.

```
RemotingConfiguration.RegisterWellKnownServiceType(
        typeof(CustomerManager),
        "CustomerManager.soap",
        WellKnownObjectMode.Singleton);
```

The class CustomerManager is registered as a WellKnownServiceType (a MarshalByRefObject). The URL will be CustomerManager.soap—whereas this can be any string you like, the extension .soap or .rem should be used for consistency. This is absolutely necessary when hosting the components in IIS as it maps these two extensions to the .NET Remoting Framework (as shown in Chapter 4).

The object's mode is set to Singleton to ensure that only one instance will exist at any given time.

```
Console.ReadLine();
```

This last line is not directly a part of the startup sequence but just prevents the program from exiting while the server is running. You can now compile and start this server.

> **NOTE** *If you look closely at the startup sequence, you'll notice that the registered class is not directly bound to the channel. In fact, you'd be right in thinking that all available channels can be used to access all registered objects.*

Implementing the Client

The sample client will connect to the server and ask for a Customer object. For the client (which will be a console application in this example) you also need to add a reference to System.Runtime.Remoting.dll and the compiled General.dll from the preceding step (you will again have to use the Browse button, because you didn't copy the assembly to the GAC). The same using statements are needed as for the server:

```
using System.Runtime.Remoting;
using General;
using System;
using System.Runtime.Remoting.Channels.Http;
using System.Runtime.Remoting.Channels;
```

The void `Main()` method will register a channel, contact the server to acquire a Customer object, and print a customer's age.

```
class Client
{
   static void Main(string[] args)
   {
      HttpChannel channel = new HttpChannel();
      ChannelServices.RegisterChannel(channel);

      ICustomerManager mgr = (ICustomerManager) Activator.GetObject(
         typeof(ICustomerManager),
         "http://localhost:1234/CustomerManager.soap");
      Console.WriteLine("Client.Main(): Reference to CustomerManager acquired");

      Customer cust = mgr.getCustomer(4711);
      int age = cust.getAge();
      Console.WriteLine("Client.Main(): Customer {0} {1} is {2} years old.",
         cust.FirstName,
         cust.LastName,
         age);

      Console.ReadLine();
   }
}
```

Now let's take a detailed look at the client:

```
HttpChannel channel = new HttpChannel();
ChannelServices.RegisterChannel(channel);
```

With these two lines, the HTTP channel is registered on the client. It is not necessary to specify a port number here, because the client-side TCP port will be assigned automatically.

```
ICustomerManager mgr = (ICustomerManager) Activator.GetObject(
        typeof(ICustomerManager),
        "http://localhost:1234/CustomerManager.soap");
```

This line creates a local proxy object that will support the interface ICustomerManager.

Let's examine the call to Activator.GetObject a little closer:

```
Activator.GetObject(typeof(ICustomerManager),
                    "http://localhost:1234/CustomerManager.soap");
```

Instead of using the new operator, you have to let the Activator create an object. You need to specify the class or interface of the object—in this case, ICustomerManager—and the URL to the server. This is not necessary when using configuration files, because in that situation the new operator will know which classes will be remotely instantiated and will show the corresponding behavior.

In this example, the Activator will create a proxy object on the client side (or in reality two proxies—more on this later) but will not yet contact the server.

```
Customer cust = mgr.getCustomer(4711);
```

The getCustomer() method is executed on the TransparentProxy object. Now the first connection to the server is made and a message is transferred that will trigger the execution of getCustomer() on the server-side Singleton object CustomerManager. You can verify this because you included a Console.WriteLine() statement in the server's getCustomer() code. This line will be written into the server's console window.

The server now creates a Customer object and fills it with data. When the method returns, this object will be serialized and all public and private properties converted to an XML fragment. This XML document is encapsulated in a SOAP return message and transferred back to the client. The .NET Remoting Framework on the client now implicitly generates a new Customer object on the client and fills it with the serialized data that has been received from the server.

The client now has an exact copy of the Customer object that has been created on the server; there is *no* difference between a normal locally generated object and this serialized and deserialized one. All methods will be executed directly in the client's context! This can easily be seen in Figure 2-2, which shows the included WriteLine() statement in the Customer object's getAge() method that will be output to the client's console window. Figure 2-3 shows the corresponding output of the server application.

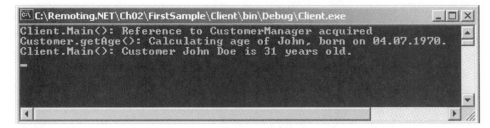

Figure 2-2. Client output for first sample

Figure 2-3. Server output for the first sample

Extending the Sample

Quite commonly, data has to be validated against several business rules. It's very convenient and maintainable to place this validation code on a central server. To allow validation of Customer data, you will extend the ICustomerManager interface to include a `validate()` method. This method will take a Customer object as a parameter and return another object by value. This returned object contains the status of the validation and explanatory text. As a sample business rule, you will check if the customer has been assigned a first name and last name and is between 0 and 120 years old.

General Assembly

In the General assembly extend the interface ICustomerManager to include the method `validate()`.

```
public interface ICustomerManager
{
    Customer getCustomer(int id);
    ValidationResult validate (Customer cust);
}
```

The ValidationResult is defined as follows. It will be a serializable (transfer by value) object with a constructor to set the necessary values.

```
[Serializable]
public class ValidationResult
{
    public ValidationResult (bool ok, String msg)
    {
        Console.WriteLine("ValidationResult.ctor: Object created");
        this.Ok = ok;
        this.ValidationMessage = msg;
    }

    public bool Ok;
    public String ValidationMessage;
}
```

Server

On the server, you have to provide an implementation of the mentioned business rule:

```
public ValidationResult validate(Customer cust)
{
    int age = cust.getAge();
    Console.WriteLine("CustomerManager.validate() for {0} aged {1}",
                        cust.FirstName, age);
    if ((cust.FirstName == null) || (cust.FirstName.Length == 0))
    {
        return new ValidationResult(false,"Firstname missing");
    }

    if ((cust.LastName == null) || (cust.LastName.Length == 0))
    {
        return new ValidationResult(false, "Lastname missing");
    }

    if (age < 0 || age > 120)
    {
        return new ValidationResult(false,"Customer must be " +
        "younger than 120 years");
    }
```

```
        return new ValidationResult(true,"Validation succeeded");
    }
```

This function just checks the given criteria and returns a corresponding ValidationResult object, which contains the state of the validation (success/failure) and some explanatory text.

Client

To run this sample, you also have to change the client to create a new Customer object and let the server validate it.

```
static void Main(string[] args)
{
    HttpChannel channel = new HttpChannel();
    ChannelServices.RegisterChannel(channel);

    ICustomerManager mgr = (ICustomerManager) Activator.GetObject(
        typeof(ICustomerManager),
        "http://localhost:1234/CustomerManager.soap");
    Console.WriteLine("Client.main(): Reference to rem. object acquired");

    Console.WriteLine("Client.main(): Creating customer");
    Customer cust = new Customer();
    cust.FirstName = "Joe";
    cust.LastName = "Smith";
    cust.DateOfBirth = new DateTime(1800,5,12);

    Console.WriteLine("Client.main(): Will call validate");
    ValidationResult res = mgr.validate (cust);
    Console.WriteLine("Client.main(): Validation finished");
    Console.WriteLine("Validation result for {0} {1}\n-> {2}: {3}",
                        cust.FirstName, cust.LastName,res.Ok.ToString(),
                        res.ValidationMessage);

    Console.ReadLine();
}
```

As you can see in Figure 2-4, the Customer object is created in the client's context and then passed to the server as a parameter of validate(). Behind the scenes the same thing happens as when getCustomer() is called in the previous example: the Customer object will be serialized and transferred to the server, which will in turn create an exact copy.

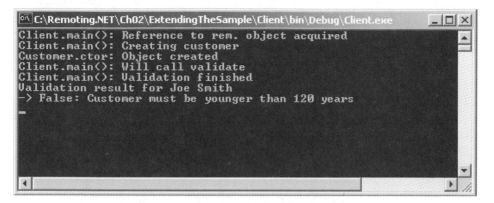

Figure 2-4. Client's output when validating a customer

This copied object is used for validation against the defined business rules. When looking at the server's output in Figure 2-5, you will see that CustomerManager.Validate() and Customer.getAge() are executed on the server. The returned ValidationResult is serialized and transferred to the client.

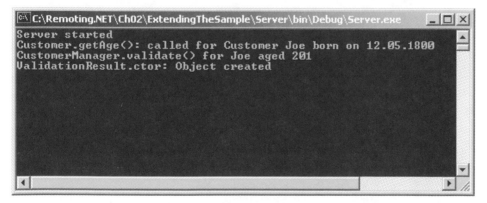

Figure 2-5. Server's output while validating a customer

Summary

In this chapter, you read about the basics of .NET Remoting. You now know the difference between MarshalByRefObjects, which allow you to call server-side methods, and ByValue objects, which have to be serializable and will be passed as copies. You read about the general structure of a remoting application and implemented a sample application that relied on shared interfaces.

Remoting in Action

IN THIS CHAPTER, I DEMONSTRATE the key techniques you'll need to know to use .NET Remoting in your real-world applications. I show you the differences between Singleton and SingleCall objects and untangle the mysteries of client-activated objects. I also introduce you to SoapSuds.exe, which can be used to generate proxy objects containing only methods' stubs. This chapter is somewhat code based, so prepare yourself to start VS .NET quite often!

Types of Remoting

As you have seen in the previous chapter's examples, there are two very different types of remote interaction between components. One uses serializable objects that are passed as a copy to the remote process. The second employs server-side (remote) objects that allow the client to call their methods.

ByValue Objects

Marshalling objects by value means to serialize their state (instance variables), including all objects referenced by instance variables, to some persistent form from which they can be deserialized in a different context. This ability to serialize objects is provided by the .NET Framework when you set the attribute [Serializable] for a class or implement ISerializable.

When passing the Customer object in the previous chapter's validation example to the server, it is serialized to XML like this:

```
<a1:Customer id="ref-4">
<FirstName id="ref-5">Joe</FirstName>
<LastName id="ref-6">Smith</LastName>
<DateOfBirth>1800-05-12T00:00:00.0000+02:00</DateOfBirth>
</a1:Customer>
```

This XML document will be read by the server and an exact copy of the object created.

> **NOTE** *An important point to know about ByValue objects is that they are not remote objects. All methods on those objects will be executed locally (in the same context) to the caller. This also means that, unlike with MarshalByRefObjects, the compiled class has to be available to the client. You can see this in the preceding snippet, where "age" is not serialized but will be recalculated at the client using the* getAge() *method.*

When a ByValue object holds references to other objects, those have to be either serializable or MarshalByRefObjects; otherwise, an exception will be thrown, indicating that those objects are not remoteable.

MarshalByRefObjects

A MarshalByRefObject is a remote object that runs on the server and accepts method calls from the client. Its data is stored in the server's memory and its methods executed in the server's AppDomain. Instead of passing around a variable that points to an object of this type, in reality only a pointer-like construct—called an ObjRef—is passed around. Contrary to common pointers, this ObjRef does not contain the memory address, rather the server name/IP address and an object identity that identifies exactly *one* object of the many that are probably running on the server. I cover this in depth later in this chapter. MarshalByRefObjects can be categorized into two groups: *server-activated objects* (SAOs) and *client-activated objects* (CAOs).

Server-Activated Objects

Server-activated objects are somewhat comparable to classic stateless Web Services. When a client requests a reference to a SAO, no message will travel to the server. Only when methods are called on this remote reference will the server be notified.

Depending on the configuration of its objects, the server then decides whether a new instance will be created or an existing object will be reused. SAOs can be marked as either *Singleton* or *SingleCall*. In the first case, one instance serves the requests of all clients in a multithreaded fashion. When using objects in SingleCall mode, as the name implies, a new object will be created for each request and destroyed afterwards.

In the following examples, you'll see the differences between these two kinds of services. You'll use the same shared interface, client- and server-side implementation of the service, and only change the object mode on the server.

The shared assembly General.dll will contain the interface to a very simple remote object that allows the storage and retrieval of stateful information in form of an int value, as shown in Listing 3-1.

Listing 3-1. The Interface Definition That Will Be Compiled to a DLL

```
using System;

namespace General
{
    public interface IMyRemoteObject
    {
        void setValue (int newval);
        int getValue();
    }
}
```

The client that is shown in Listing 3-2 provides the means for opening a connection to the server and tries to set and retrieve the instance values of the server-side remote object. You'll have to add a reference to System.Runtime.Remoting.DLL to your Visual Studio .NET project for this example.

Listing 3-2. A Simple Client Application

```
using System;
using System.Runtime.Remoting;
using General;
using System.Runtime.Remoting.Channels.Http;
using System.Runtime.Remoting.Channels;

namespace Client
{

    class Client
    {
        static void Main(string[] args)
        {
            HttpChannel channel = new HttpChannel();
            ChannelServices.RegisterChannel(channel);

            IMyRemoteObject obj = (IMyRemoteObject) Activator.GetObject(
                typeof(IMyRemoteObject),
                "http://localhost:1234/MyRemoteObject.soap");
            Console.WriteLine("Client.Main(): Reference to rem. obj acquired");
```

```
            int tmp = obj.getValue();
            Console.WriteLine("Client.Main(): Original server side value: {0}",tmp);

            Console.WriteLine("Client.Main(): Will set value to 42");
            obj.setValue(42);

            tmp = obj.getValue();
            Console.WriteLine("Client.Main(): New server side value {0}", tmp);

            Console.ReadLine();
        }
    }
}
```

The sample client will read and output the server's original value, change it to 42, and then read and output it again.

SingleCall Objects

For SingleCall objects the server will create a single object, execute the method, and destroy the object again. SingleCall objects are registered at the server using the following statement:

```
RemotingConfiguration.RegisterWellKnownServiceType(
        typeof(<YourClass>), "<URL>",
        WellKnownObjectMode.SingleCall);
```

Objects of this kind can obviously not hold any state information, as all internal variables will be discarded at the end of the method call. The reason for using objects of this kind is that they can be deployed in a very scalable manner. These objects can be located on different computers with an intermediate multiplexing/load-balancing device, which would not be possible when using stateful objects. The complete server for this example can be seen in Listing 3-3.

Listing 3-3. The Complete Server Implementation
```
using System;
using System.Runtime.Remoting;
using General;
using System.Runtime.Remoting.Channels.Http;
using System.Runtime.Remoting.Channels;
```

```
namespace Server
{

    class MyRemoteObject: MarshalByRefObject, IMyRemoteObject
    {
        int myvalue;

        public MyRemoteObject()
        {
            Console.WriteLine("MyRemoteObject.Constructor: New Object created");
        }

        public MyRemoteObject(int startvalue)
        {
            Console.WriteLine("MyRemoteObject.Constructor: .ctor called with {0}",
                              startvalue);
            myvalue = startvalue;
        }

        public void setValue(int newval)
        {
            Console.WriteLine("MyRemoteObject.setValue(): old {0} new {1}",
                              myvalue,newval);
            myvalue = newval;
        }
        public int getValue()
        {
            Console.WriteLine("MyRemoteObject.getValue(): current {0}",myvalue);
            return myvalue;
        }
    }

    class ServerStartup
    {
        static void Main(string[] args)
        {
            Console.WriteLine ("ServerStartup.Main(): Server started");

            HttpChannel chnl = new HttpChannel(1234);
            ChannelServices.RegisterChannel(chnl);
            RemotingConfiguration.RegisterWellKnownServiceType(
                    typeof(MyRemoteObject),
                    "MyRemoteObject.soap",
                    WellKnownObjectMode.SingleCall);
```

```
                // the server will keep running until keypress.
                Console.ReadLine();
            }
        }
    }
```

When the program is run, the output in Figure 3-1 will appear on the client.

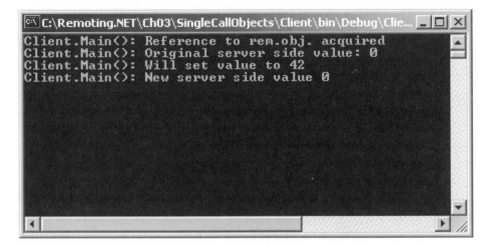

Figure 3-1. Client's output for a SingleCall object

What's happening is exactly what you'd expect from the previous description—even though it might not be what you'd normally expect from an object-oriented application. The reason for the server returning a value of 0 after setting the value to 42 is that your client is talking to a completely different object. Figure 3-2 shows the server's output.

```
C:\Remoting.NET\Ch03\SingleCallObjects\Server\bin\Debug\Se...
ServerStartup.Main(): Server started
MyRemoteObject.Constructor: New Object created
MyRemoteObject.Constructor: New Object created
MyRemoteObject.getValue(): current 0
MyRemoteObject.Constructor: New Object created
MyRemoteObject.setValue(): old 0 new 42
MyRemoteObject.Constructor: New Object created
MyRemoteObject.getValue(): current 0
```

Figure 3-2. Server's output for a SingleCall object

This indicates that the server will really create one object for each call (and an additional object during the first call as well).

Singleton Objects

Only one instance of a Singleton object can exist at any given time. When receiving a client's request, the server checks its internal tables to see if an instance of this class already exists; if not, this object will be created and stored in the table. After this check the method will be executed. The server guarantees that there will be exactly one or no instance available at a given time.

> **NOTE** *Singletons have an associated lifetime as well, so be sure to override the standard lease time if you don't want your object to be destroyed after some minutes. (More on this later in this chapter.)*

For registering an object as a Singleton, you can use the following lines of code:

```
RemotingConfiguration.RegisterWellKnownServiceType(
        typeof(<YourClass>), "<URL>",
        WellKnownObjectMode.Singleton);
```

The ServerStartup class in your sample server will be changed accordingly:

```
class ServerStartup
{
   static void Main(string[] args)
   {
      Console.WriteLine ("ServerStartup.Main(): Server started");

      HttpChannel chnl = new HttpChannel(1234);
      ChannelServices.RegisterChannel(chnl);
      RemotingConfiguration.RegisterWellKnownServiceType(
             typeof(MyRemoteObject),
             "MyRemoteObject.soap",
             WellKnownObjectMode.Singleton);

      // the server will keep running until keypress.
      Console.ReadLine();
   }
}
```

When the client is started, the output will show a behavior consistent with the "normal" object-oriented way of thinking; the value that is returned is the same value you set two lines before (see Figure 3-3).

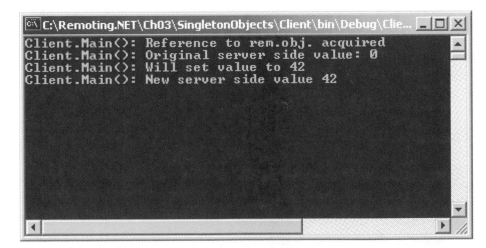

Figure 3-3. Client's output for a Singleton object

The same is true for the server, as Figure 3-4 shows.

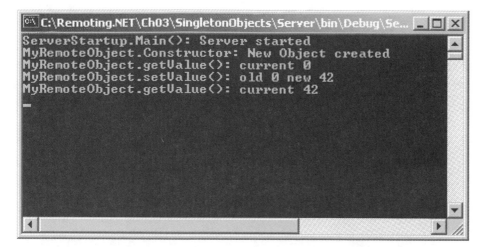

Figure 3-4. Server's output for a Singleton object

An interesting thing happens when a second client is started afterwards. This client will receive a value of 42 directly after startup without your setting this value beforehand (see Figures 3-5 and 3-6). This is because only one instance exists at the server, and the instance will stay alive even after the first client is disconnected.

> **TIP** *Use Singletons when you want to share data or resources between clients.*

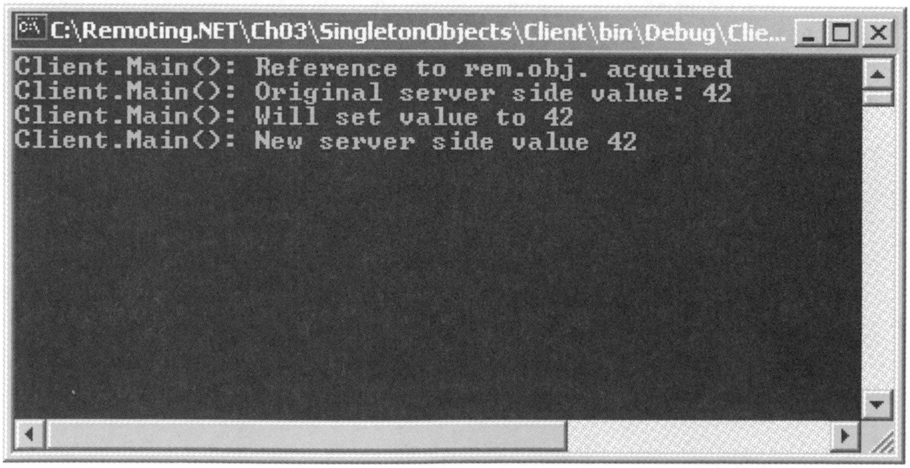

```
C:\Remoting.NET\Ch03\SingletonObjects\Client\bin\Debug\Clie...
Client.Main(): Reference to rem.obj. acquired
Client.Main(): Original server side value: 42
Client.Main(): Will set value to 42
Client.Main(): New server side value 42
```

Figure 3-5. The second client's output when calling a Singleton object

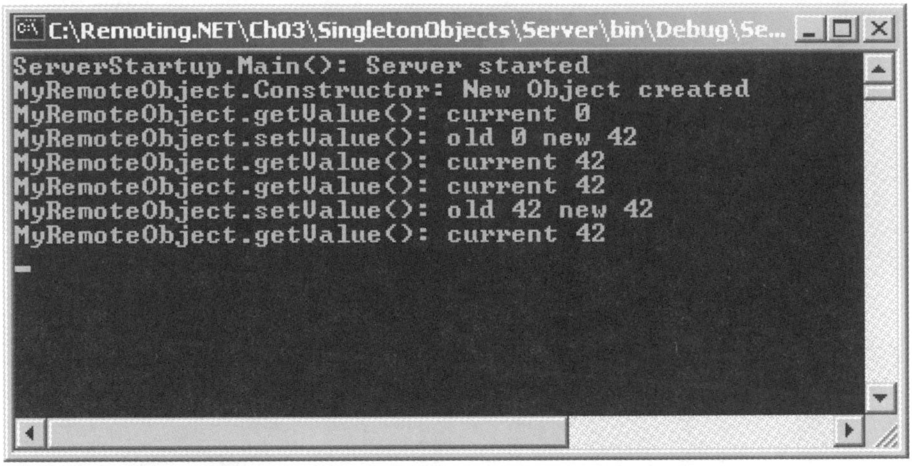

Figure 3-6. Server's output after the second call to a Singleton object

Published Objects

When using either SingleCall or Singleton objects, the necessary instances will be created dynamically during a client's request. When you want to publish a certain object instance that's been precreated on the server—for example, one using a nondefault constructor—neither alternative provides you with a solution.

In this case you can use RemotingServices.Marshal() to publish a given instance that behaves like a Singleton afterwards. The only difference is that the object has to already exist at the server before publication.

```
YourObject obj = new YourObject(<your params for constr>);
RemotingServices.Marshal(obj,"YourUrl.soap");
```

The code in the ServerStartup class will look like this:

```
class ServerStartup
{
    static void Main(string[] args)
    {
        Console.WriteLine ("ServerStartup.Main(): Server started");

        HttpChannel chnl = new HttpChannel(1234);
        ChannelServices.RegisterChannel(chnl);

        MyRemoteObject obj = new MyRemoteObject(4711);
        RemotingServices.Marshal(obj,"MyRemoteObject.soap");
```

```
        // the server will keep running until keypress.
        Console.ReadLine();
    }
}
```

When the client is run, you can safely expect to get a value of 4711 on the first request because you started the server with this initial value (see Figures 3-7 and 3-8).

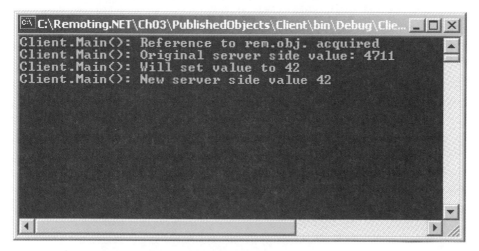

Figure 3-7. Client's output when calling a published object

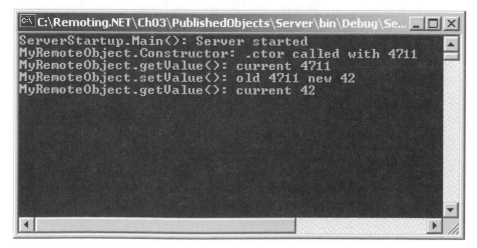

Figure 3-8. Server's output when publishing the object

Client-Activated Objects

A client-activated object (CAO) behaves mostly the same way as does a "normal" .NET object (or a COM object). When a creation request on the client is encountered (using `Activator.CreateInstance()` or the new operator), an activation message is sent to the server, where a remote object is created. On the client a proxy that holds the ObjRef to the server object is created like it is with SAOs.

A client-activated object's lifetime is managed by the same lifetime service used by SAOs, as shown later in this chapter. CAOs are so-called stateful objects; an instance variable that has been set by the client can be retrieved again and will contain the correct value.[1] These objects will store state information from one method call to the other. CAOs are explicitly created by the client, so they can have distinct constructors like normal .NET objects do.

Direct/Transparent Creation

The .NET Remoting Framework can be configured to allow client-activated objects to be created like normal objects using the new operator. Unfortunately, this manner of creation has one serious drawback: you cannot use shared interfaces or base classes. This means that you either have to ship the compiled objects to your clients or use SoapSuds to extract the metadata.

As shipping the implementation to your clients is neither feasible due to deployment and versioning issues nor in support of the general idea of distributed applications, I refrain from delving heavily into this approach here. Unfortunately, it's not currently possible to call nondefault constructors when using SoapSuds-generated metadata. When your application needs this functionality, you might choose the class factory–based approach (which is shown after this example) or rely on SoapSuds' -gc parameter to manually enhance the generated proxy (more on this parameter in Chapter 4).

In the following example, you'll use more or less the same class you did in the previous examples; it will provide your client with a `setValue()` and `getValue()` method to store and retrieve an int value as the object's state. The metadata that is needed for the client to create a reference to the CAO will be extracted with SoapSuds.exe, about which you'll read more later in this chapter.

The reliance on SoapSuds allows you to develop the server application without any need for up-front design of a shared assembly, therefore the server will simply include the CAOs implementation. You can see this in Listing 3-4.

---

[1] The only exception from this rule lies in the object's lifetime, which is managed completely differently from the way it is in .NET generally or in COM.

Listing 3-4. A Server That Offers a Client-Activated Object

```
using System;
using System.Runtime.Remoting;
using System.Runtime.Remoting.Channels.Http;
using System.Runtime.Remoting.Channels;

namespace Server
{

    public class MyRemoteObject: MarshalByRefObject
    {
        int myvalue;

        public MyRemoteObject(int val)
        {
            Console.WriteLine("MyRemoteObject.ctor(int) called");
            myvalue = val;
        }

        public MyRemoteObject()
        {
            Console.WriteLine("MyRemoteObject.ctor() called");
        }

        public void setValue(int newval)
        {
            Console.WriteLine("MyRemoteObject.setValue(): old {0} new {1}",
                                myvalue,newval);
            myvalue = newval;
        }

        public int getValue()
        {
            Console.WriteLine("MyRemoteObject.getValue(): current {0}",myvalue);
            return myvalue;
        }
    }

    class ServerStartup
    {
        static void Main(string[] args)
        {
            Console.WriteLine ("ServerStartup.Main(): Server started");
```

```
        HttpChannel chnl = new HttpChannel(1234);
        ChannelServices.RegisterChannel(chnl);

        RemotingConfiguration.ApplicationName = "MyServer";
        RemotingConfiguration.RegisterActivatedServiceType(
                        typeof(MyRemoteObject));

        // the server will keep running until keypress.
        Console.ReadLine();
    }
  }
}
```

On the server you now have the new startup code needed to register a channel and this class as a client-activated object. When adding a Type to the list of activated services, you cannot provide a single URL for each object; instead, you have to set the RemotingConfiguration.ApplicationName to a string value that identifies your server.

The URL to your remote object will be http://<hostname>:<port>/<ApplicationName>. What happens behind the scenes is that a general activation SAO is automatically created by the framework and published at the URL http://<hostname>:<port>/<ApplicationName>/RemoteActivationService.rem. This SAO will take the clients' requests to create a new instance and pass it on to the remoting framework.

To extract the necessary interface information, you can run the following SoapSuds command line in the directory where the server.exe assembly has been placed:

```
soapsuds -ia:server -nowp -oa:generated_metadata.dll
```

> **NOTE** *You should perform all command-line operations from the Visual Studio command prompt, which you can bring up by selecting Start ➤ Programs ➤ Microsoft Visual Studio .NET ➤ Visual Studio .NET Tools. This command prompt sets the correct "path" variable to include the .NET SDK tools.*

The resulting generated_metadata.dll assembly must be referenced by the client. The sample client also registers the CAO and acquires two references to (different) remote objects. It then sets the value of those objects and outputs them again, which shows that you really are dealing with two different objects.

As you can see in Listing 3-5, the activation of the remote object is done with the new operator. This is possible because you registered the Type as

ActivatedClientType before. The runtime now knows that whenever your application creates an instance of this class, it instead should create a reference to a remote object running on the server.

Listing 3-5. The Client Accesses the Client-Activated Object

```
using System;
using System.Runtime.Remoting;
using System.Runtime.Remoting.Channels.Http;
using System.Runtime.Remoting.Channels;
using System.Runtime.Remoting.Activation;
using Server;

namespace Client
{
    class Client
    {
        static void Main(string[] args)
        {
            HttpChannel channel = new HttpChannel();
            ChannelServices.RegisterChannel(channel);

            RemotingConfiguration.RegisterActivatedClientType(
                typeof(MyRemoteObject),
                "http://localhost:1234/MyServer");

            Console.WriteLine("Client.Main(): Creating first object");
            MyRemoteObject obj1 = new MyRemoteObject();
            obj1.setValue(42);

            Console.WriteLine("Client.Main(): Creating second object");
            MyRemoteObject obj2 = new MyRemoteObject();
            obj2.setValue(4711);

            Console.WriteLine("Obj1.getValue(): {0}",obj1.getValue());
            Console.WriteLine("Obj2.getValue(): {0}",obj2.getValue());

            Console.ReadLine();
        }
    }
}
```

When this code sample is run, you will see the same behavior as when using local objects—the two instances have their own state (Figure 3-9). As expected, on the server two different objects are created (Figure 3-10).

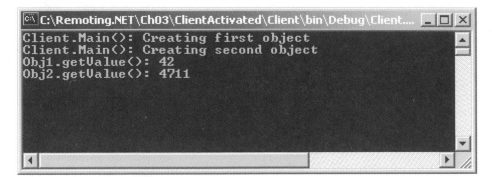

Figure 3-9. Client-side output when using CAOs

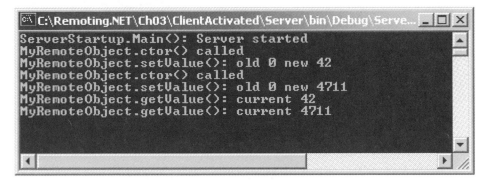

Figure 3-10. Server-side output when using CAOs

Using the Factory Design Pattern

From what you've read up to this point, you know that SoapSuds cannot extract the metadata for nondefault constructors. When your application's design relies on this functionality, you can use a factory design pattern, in which you'll include a SAO providing methods that return new instances of the CAO.

> **NOTE** *You might also just ship the server-side implementation assembly to the client and reference it directly. But as I stated previously, this is clearly against all distributed application design principles!*

Here, I just give you a short introduction to the factory design pattern. Basically you have two classes, one of which is a *factory*, and the other is the real object you want to use. Due to constraints of the real class, you will not be able to construct it directly, but instead will have to call a method on the factory, which creates a new instance and passes it to the client.

Listing 3-6 shows you a fairly simple implementation of this design pattern.

Listing 3-6. The Factory Design Pattern

```
using System;

namespace FactoryDesignPattern
{

    class MyClass
    {
    }

    class MyFactory
    {
        public MyClass getNewInstance()
        {
            return new MyClass();
        }
    }

    class MyClient
    {
        static void Main(string[] args)
        {
            // creation using "new"
            MyClass obj1 = new MyClass();

            // creating using a factory
            MyFactory fac = new MyFactory();
            MyClass obj2 = fac.getNewInstance();

        }
    }

}
```

When bringing this pattern to remoting, you have to create a factory that's running as a server-activated object (ideally a Singleton) that has a method returning a new instance of the "real class" (the CAO) to the client. This gives you a huge advantage in that you don't have to distribute the implementation to the client system or manually tweak the output from SoapSuds -gc.

> **NOTE** *Distributing the implementation to the client is not only a bad choice due to deployment issues, it also makes it possible for the client user to disassemble your object's codes using ILDASM or some other tool.*

You have to design your factory SAO using a shared assembly which contains the interface information (or abstract base classes) which are implemented by your remote objects. This is shown in Listing 3-7.

Listing 3-7. The Shared Interfaces for the Factory Design Pattern

```
using System;

namespace General
{
    public interface IRemoteObject
    {
        void setValue(int newval);
        int getValue();
    }

    public interface IRemoteFactory
    {
        IRemoteObject getNewInstance();
        IRemoteObject getNewInstance(int initvalue);
    }
}
```

On the server you now have to implement both interfaces and create a startup code that registers the factory as a SAO. You don't have to register the CAO in this case because every MarshalByRefObject can be returned by a method call; the framework takes care of the necessity to remote each call itself, as shown in Listing 3-8.

Listing 3-8. The Server-Side Factory Pattern's Implementation

```
using System;
using System.Runtime.Remoting;
using System.Runtime.Remoting.Channels.Http;
using System.Runtime.Remoting.Channels;
using System.Runtime.Remoting.Messaging;
using General;
```

```csharp
namespace Server
{
    class MyRemoteObject: MarshalByRefObject, IRemoteObject
    {
        int myvalue;

        public MyRemoteObject(int val)
        {
            Console.WriteLine("MyRemoteObject.ctor(int) called");
            myvalue = val;
        }

        public MyRemoteObject()
        {
            Console.WriteLine("MyRemoteObject.ctor() called");
        }

        public void setValue(int newval)
        {
            Console.WriteLine("MyRemoteObject.setValue(): old {0} new {1}",
                              myvalue,newval);
            myvalue = newval;
        }

        public int getValue()
        {
            Console.WriteLine("MyRemoteObject.getValue(): current {0}",myvalue);
            return myvalue;
        }
    }

    class MyRemoteFactory: MarshalByRefObject,IRemoteFactory
    {
        public MyRemoteFactory() {
            Console.WriteLine("MyRemoteFactory.ctor() called");
        }

        public IRemoteObject getNewInstance()
        {
            Console.WriteLine("MyRemoteFactory.getNewInstance() called");
            return new MyRemoteObject();
        }
```

```
            public IRemoteObject getNewInstance(int initvalue)
            {
                Console.WriteLine("MyRemoteFactory.getNewInstance(int) called");
                return new MyRemoteObject(initvalue);
            }
        }


    class ServerStartup
    {
        static void Main(string[] args)
        {
            Console.WriteLine ("ServerStartup.Main(): Server started");

            HttpChannel chnl = new HttpChannel(1234);
            ChannelServices.RegisterChannel(chnl);

            RemotingConfiguration.RegisterWellKnownServiceType(
                typeof(MyRemoteFactory),
                "factory.soap",
                WellKnownObjectMode.Singleton);

            // the server will keep running until keypress.
            Console.ReadLine();
        }
    }
}
```

The client, which is shown in Listing 3-9, works a little bit differently from the previous one as well. It creates a reference to a remote SAO using `Activator.GetObject()`, upon which it places two calls to `getNewInstance()` to acquire two different remote CAOs.

Listing 3-9. The Client Uses the Factory Pattern

```
using System;
using System.Runtime.Remoting;
using System.Runtime.Remoting.Channels.Http;
using System.Runtime.Remoting.Channels.Tcp;
using System.Runtime.Remoting.Channels;
using General;
```

```
namespace Client
{
    class Client
    {
        static void Main(string[] args)
        {
            HttpChannel channel = new HttpChannel();
            ChannelServices.RegisterChannel(channel);

            Console.WriteLine("Client.Main(): Creating factory");
            IRemoteFactory fact = (IRemoteFactory) Activator.GetObject(
                typeof(IRemoteFactory),
                "http://localhost:1234/factory.soap");

            Console.WriteLine("Client.Main(): Acquiring first object from factory");
            IRemoteObject obj1 = fact.getNewInstance();
            obj1.setValue(42);

            Console.WriteLine("Client.Main(): Acquiring second object from " +
                              "factory");
            IRemoteObject obj2 = fact.getNewInstance(4711);

            Console.WriteLine("Obj1.getValue(): {0}",obj1.getValue());
            Console.WriteLine("Obj2.getValue(): {0}",obj2.getValue());

            Console.ReadLine();
        }
    }
}
```

When this sample is running, you see that the client behaves nearly identically to the previous example, but the second object's value has been set using the object's constructor, which is called via the factory (Figure 3-11). On the server a factory object is generated, and each new instance is created using the overloaded getNewInstance() method (Figure 3-12).

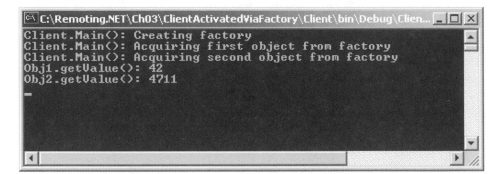

Figure 3-11. Client-side output when using a factory object

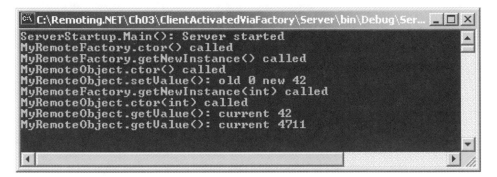

Figure 3-12. Server-side output when using a factory object

Managing Lifetime

One point that can lead to a bit of confusion is the way an object's lifetime is managed in the .NET Remoting Framework. Common .NET objects are managed using a garbage collection algorithm that checks if any other object is still using a given instance. If not, the instance will be garbage collected and disposed.

When you apply this schema (or the COM way of reference counting) to remote objects, it pings the client-side proxies to ensure that they are still using the objects and that the application is still running (this is mainly what DCOM did). The reason for this is that normally a client that has been closed unexpectedly or went offline due to a network outage might not have decremented the server-side reference counter. Without some additional measure, these server-side objects would in turn use the server's resources forever. Unfortunately, when your client is behind an HTTP proxy and is accessing your objects using SOAP remoting, the server will not be able to contact the client in any way.

This constraint leads to a new kind of lifetime service: the lease-based object lifetime. Basically this means that each server-side object is associated with a lease upon creation. This lease will have a time-to-live counter (which starts at five minutes by default) that is decremented in certain intervals. In addition to the initial time, a defined amount (two minutes in the default configuration) is added to this time to live upon every method call a client places on the remote object.

When this time reaches zero, the framework looks for any sponsors registered with this lease. A *sponsor* is an object running on the server itself, the client, or any machine reachable via a network that will take a call from the .NET Remoting Framework asking whether an object's lifetime should be renewed or not (more on this in Chapter 6).

When the sponsor decides that the lease will not be renewed or when the framework is unable to contact any of the registered sponsors, the object is marked as timed out and then garbage collected. When a client still has a reference to a timed-out object and calls a method on it, it will receive an exception.

To change the default lease times, you can override InitializeLifetimeService() in the MarshalByRefObject. In the following example, you see how to change the last CAO sample to implement a different lifetime of only ten milliseconds for this object. Normally LeaseManager only polls all leases every ten seconds, so you have to change this polling interval as well.

```
namespace Server
{
    class MyRemoteObject: MarshalByRefObject, IRemoteObject
    {
        public override object InitializeLifetimeService()
        {
            Console.WriteLine("MyRemoteObject.InitializeLifetimeService() called");
            ILease lease = (ILease)base.InitializeLifetimeService();
            if (lease.CurrentState == LeaseState.Initial)
            {
                lease.InitialLeaseTime = TimeSpan.FromMilliseconds(10);
                lease.SponsorshipTimeout = TimeSpan.FromMilliseconds(10);
                lease.RenewOnCallTime = TimeSpan.FromMilliseconds(10);
            }
            return lease;
        }

        // rest of implementation . . .
    }

    class MyRemoteFactory: MarshalByRefObject,IRemoteFactory
    {
        // rest of implementation
    }
```

```
class ServerStartup
{
    static void Main(string[] args)
    {
        Console.WriteLine ("ServerStartup.Main(): Server started");

        LifetimeServices.LeaseManagerPollTime = TimeSpan.FromMilliseconds(10);

        HttpChannel chnl = new HttpChannel(1234);
        ChannelServices.RegisterChannel(chnl);

        RemotingConfiguration.RegisterWellKnownServiceType(
            typeof(MyRemoteFactory),
            "factory.soap",
            WellKnownObjectMode.Singleton);

        // the server will keep running until keypress.
        Console.ReadLine();
    }
}
}
```

On the client side, you can add a one-second delay between creation and the first call on the remote object to see the effects of the changed lifetime. You also need to provide some code to handle the RemotingException that will get thrown because the object is no longer available at the server. The client is shown in Listing 3-10.

Listing 3-10. A Client That Calls a Timed-Out CAO

```
using System;
using System.Runtime.Remoting;
using System.Runtime.Remoting.Channels.Http;
using System.Runtime.Remoting.Channels.Tcp;
using System.Runtime.Remoting.Channels;
using General;

namespace Client
{
    class Client
    {
        static void Main(string[] args)
        {
            HttpChannel channel = new HttpChannel();
```

```
ChannelServices.RegisterChannel(channel);

Console.WriteLine("Client.Main(): Creating factory");
IRemoteFactory fact = (IRemoteFactory) Activator.GetObject(
    typeof(IRemoteFactory),
    "http://localhost:1234/factory.soap");

Console.WriteLine("Client.Main(): Acquiring object from factory");
IRemoteObject obj1 = fact.getNewInstance();

Console.WriteLine("Client.Main(): Sleeping one second");
System.Threading.Thread.Sleep(1000);

Console.WriteLine("Client.Main(): Setting value");
try
{
    obj1.setValue(42);
}
catch (Exception e)
{
    Console.WriteLine("Client.Main(). EXCEPTION \n{0}",e.Message);
}

Console.ReadLine();
        }
    }
}
```

Running this sample, you see that the client is able to successfully create a factory object and call its getNewInstance() method (Figure 3-13). When calling setValue() on the returned CAO, the client will receive an exception stating the object has timed out. The server runs normally (Figure 3-14).

Figure 3-13. The client receives an exception because the object has timed out.

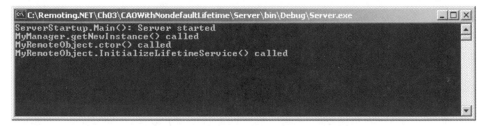

Figure 3-14. The server when overriding `InitializeLifetimeService()`

Types of Invocation

The .NET Framework provides three possibilities to call methods on remote objects (no matter if they are Singleton, SingleCall, or published objects). You can execute their methods in a synchronous, asynchronous, or asynchronous one-way fashion.

Synchronous calls are basically what I showed you in the preceding examples. The server's remote method is called like a common method, and the client blocks (waits) until the server has completed its processing. If an exception occurs during execution of the remote invocation, the exception is thrown at the line of code in which you called the server.

Asynchronous calls are executed in a two-step process. (Asynchronous calls are discussed in more detail in Chapter 6.) The first step triggers the execution but does not wait for the method's response value. The program flow continues on the client. When you are ready to collect the function's response, you have to call another function that checks if the server has already finished processing your request; if not, it blocks until finalization. Any exception thrown during the call of your method will be rethrown at the line of code where you collect the response. Even if the server has been offline, you won't be notified beforehand.

The last kind of function is a little different from the preceding ones. With asynchronous one-way methods, you don't have the option of receiving return values or getting an exception if the server has been offline or otherwise unable to fulfill your request. The .NET Remoting Framework will just *try* to call the methods on the remote server and won't do anything else.

Synchronous Calls

As I've mentioned, synchronous calls are the usual way of calling a function in the .NET Framework. The server will be contacted directly and, except when using multiple client-side threads, the client code will block until the server has finished executing its method. If the server is unavailable or an exception occurs while carrying out your request, the exception will be rethrown at the line of code where you called the remote method.

Using Synchronous Calls

In the following series of examples for the different types of invocation, you use a common server and a shared assembly called General.dll (you'll see some slight modifications in the last part). This server just provides you with a Singleton object that stores an int as its state and has an additional method that returns a String. You'll use this later to demonstrate the collection of return values when using asynchronous calls.

Defining the General.dll

In Listing 3-11, you see the shared General.dll in which the necessary interface is defined.

Listing 3-11. The Shared Assembly's Source Code

```
using System;
using System.Runtime.Remoting.Messaging;

namespace General
{
    public abstract class BaseRemoteObject: MarshalByRefObject
    {
        public abstract void setValue(int newval);
        public abstract int getValue();
        public abstract String getName();
    }
}
```

Creating the Server

The server, shown in Listing 3-12, implements the defined methods with the addition of making the setValue() and getName() functions long-running code. In both methods, a five-second delay is introduced so you can see the effects of long-lasting execution in the different invocation contexts.

Listing 3-12. A Server with Some Long-Running Methods

```
using System;
using System.Runtime.Remoting;
using General;
using System.Runtime.Remoting.Channels.Http;
using System.Runtime.Remoting.Channels;
using System.Runtime.Remoting.Messaging;
using System.Collections;
using System.Threading;

namespace Server
{
    class MyRemoteObject: BaseRemoteObject
    {
        int myvalue;

        public MyRemoteObject()
        {
            Console.WriteLine("MyRemoteObject.Constructor: New Object created");
        }

        public override void setValue(int newval)
        {
            Console.WriteLine("MyRemoteObject.setValue(): old {0} new {1}",
                                myvalue,newval);

            // simulate a long running action
            Console.WriteLine("    .setValue() -> waiting 5 sec before setting" +
                                "value");
            Thread.Sleep(5000);

            myvalue = newval;
            Console.WriteLine("    .setValue() -> value is now set");
        }

        public override int getValue()
        {
            Console.WriteLine("MyRemoteObject.getValue(): current {0}",myvalue);
            return myvalue;
        }
```

```
    public override String getName()
    {
        Console.WriteLine("MyRemoteObject.getName(): called");

        // simulate a long running action
        Console.WriteLine("      .getName() -> waiting 5 sec before continuing");
        Thread.Sleep(5000);

        Console.WriteLine("      .getName() -> returning name");
        return "John Doe";
    }
}

class ServerStartup
{
    static void Main(string[] args)
    {
        Console.WriteLine ("ServerStartup.Main(): Server started");

        HttpChannel chnl = new HttpChannel(1234);
        ChannelServices.RegisterChannel(chnl);

        RemotingConfiguration.RegisterWellKnownServiceType(
                typeof(MyRemoteObject),
                "MyRemoteObject.soap",
                WellKnownObjectMode.Singleton);

        // the server will keep running until keypress.
        Console.ReadLine();
    }
}
}
```

Creating the Client

The first client, which is shown in Listing 3-13, calls the server synchronously, as in all preceding examples. It calls all three methods and gives you statistics on how long the total execution took.

Listing 3-13. The First Client Calls the Methods Synchronously

```
using System;
using System.Runtime.Remoting;
using General;
using System.Runtime.Remoting.Channels.Http;
using System.Runtime.Remoting.Channels.Tcp;
using System.Runtime.Remoting.Channels;
using System.Runtime.Remoting.Proxies;
using System.Threading;

namespace Client
{

    class Client
    {

        static void Main(string[] args)
        {
            DateTime start = System.DateTime.Now;

            HttpChannel channel = new HttpChannel();
            ChannelServices.RegisterChannel(channel);
            BaseRemoteObject obj = (BaseRemoteObject) Activator.GetObject(
                typeof(BaseRemoteObject),
                "http://localhost:1234/MyRemoteObject.soap");
            Console.WriteLine("Client.Main(): Reference to rem.obj. acquired");

            Console.WriteLine("Client.Main(): Will set value to 42");
            obj.setValue(42);

            Console.WriteLine("Client.Main(): Will now read value");
            int tmp = obj.getValue();
            Console.WriteLine("Client.Main(): New server side value {0}", tmp);


            Console.WriteLine("Client.Main(): Will call getName()");
            String name = obj.getName();
            Console.WriteLine("Client.Main(): received name {0}",name);

            DateTime end = System.DateTime.Now;
            TimeSpan duration = end.Subtract(start);
            Console.WriteLine("Client.Main(): Execution took {0} seconds.",
                        duration.Seconds);
```

```
        Console.ReadLine();
    }
  }
}
```

As the calls to the long-running methods getName() and setValue() are
expected to take roughly five seconds each, and you have to add a little overhead
for .NET Remoting (especially for the first call on a remote object), this example
will take more than ten seconds to run.

You can see that this assumption is right by looking at the client's output in
Figure 3-15. The total client execution takes 12 seconds. When looking at the
server's output in Figure 3-16, note that all methods are called synchronously.
Every method is finished before the next one is called by the client.

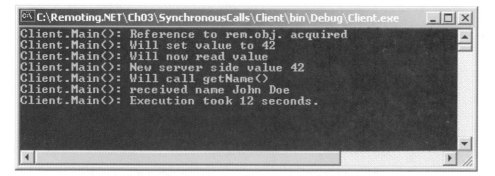

Figure 3-15. Client's output when using synchronous calls

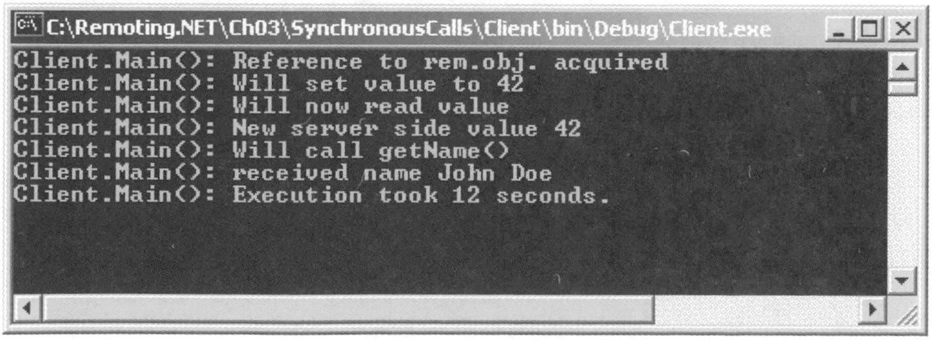

Figure 3-16. Server's output when called synchronously

Asynchronous Calls

In the synchronous calls example, you saw that waiting for every method to complete incurs a performance penalty if the calls themselves are independent; the second call doesn't need the output from the first. You could now use a separate thread to call the second method, but even though threading is quite simple in .NET, it would probably render the application more complex if you use a distinct thread for any longer lasting remote function call. The .NET Framework provides a feature, called *asynchronous delegates*, that allows methods to be called in an asynchronous fashion with only three lines of additional code.

Delegate Basics

A *delegate* is, in its regular sense, just a kind of an object-oriented function pointer. You will initialize it and pass a function to be called when the delegate is invoked. In .NET Framework, a delegate is a subclass of `System.MulticastDelegate`, but C# provides an easier way to define a delegate instead of declaring a new `Class`.

Declaring a Delegate

The declaration of a delegate looks quite similar to the declaration of a method:

```
delegate <ReturnType> <name> ([parameters]);
```

As the delegate will call a method at some point in the future, you have to provide it with a declaration that matches the method's signature. When you want a delegate to call the following method:

```
public String doSomething(int myValue)
```

you have to define it as follows:

```
delegate String doSomethingDelegate (int myValue);
```

> **NOTE** *The delegate's parameter and return types have to match those of the method.*

Remember that the delegate is in reality just another class, so you cannot define it within a method's body, only directly within a namespace or another class!

Asynchronously Invoking a Delegate

When you want to use a delegate, you first have to create an instance of it, passing the method to be called as a constructor parameter:

```
doSomethingDelegate del = new doSomethingDelegate(doSomething);
```

> **NOTE** *When passing the method to the constructor, be sure not to include an opening or closing parenthesis — (or) —as in* doSomething(). *The previous example uses a static method* doSomething *in the same class. When using static methods of other classes, you have to pass* SomeClass.someMethod, *and for instance methods, you pass* SomeObject.doSomething.

The asynchronous invocation of a delegate is a two-step process. In the first step, you have to trigger the execution using BeginInvoke(), as follows:

```
IAsyncResult ar = del.BeginInvoke(42,null,null);
```

> **NOTE** BeginInvoke() *behaves a little strangely in the IDE. You won't see it using IntelliSense, as it is automatically generated during compilation. The parameters are the same as the method parameters, according to the delegate definition, followed by two other objects; you won't be using these two objects in the following examples, instead passing null to* BeginInvoke().

BeginInvoke() then returns an IAsyncResult object that will be used later to retrieve the method's return values. When ready to do so, you call EndInvoke() on the delegate passing the IAsyncResult as a parameter. The EndInvoke() method will block until the server has completed executing the underlying method.

```
String res = del.EndInvoke(ar);
```

> **NOTE**   EndInvoke() *will not be visible in the IDE either. The method takes*
> *an IAsyncResult as a parameter, and its return type will be defined in the*
> *delegate's declaration.*

Creating an Example Delegate

In Listing 3-14, a delegate is used to asynchronously call a local function and wait
for its result. The method returns a String built from the passed int parameter.

Listing 3-14. Using a Delegate in a Local Application

```
using System;

namespace SampleDelegate
{
    class SomethingClass
    {
        delegate String doSomethingDelegate(int myValue);

        public static String doSomething(int myValue)
        {
            return "HEY:" + myValue.ToString();
        }

        static void Main(string[] args)
        {
            doSomethingDelegate del = new doSomethingDelegate(doSomething);
            IAsyncResult ar = del.BeginInvoke(42,null,null);
            // ... do something different here
            String res = del.EndInvoke(ar);

            Console.WriteLine("Got result: '{0}'",res);

            //wait for return to close
            Console.ReadLine();
        }
    }
}
```

As expected, the application outputs "HEY:42" as you can see in Figure 3-17.

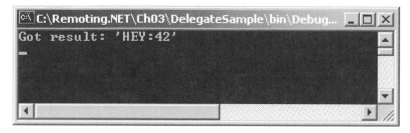

Figure 3-17. The sample delegate

Implementing the New Client

In the new remoting client, shown in Listing 3-15, you see how to change the calls to getName() and setValue() to use delegates as well. Your client then invokes both delegates and subsequently waits for their completion before synchronously calling getValue() on the server. In this instance, you use the same server application as in the preceding example.

Listing 3-15. The New Client Now Using Asynchronous Delegates

```
using System;
using System.Runtime.Remoting;
using General;
using System.Runtime.Remoting.Channels.Http;
using System.Runtime.Remoting.Channels.Tcp;
using System.Runtime.Remoting.Channels;
using System.Runtime.Remoting.Proxies;
using System.Threading;

namespace Client
{

    class Client
    {
        delegate void SetValueDelegate(int value);
        delegate String GetNameDelegate();

        static void Main(string[] args)
        {
            DateTime start = System.DateTime.Now;
```

```
HttpChannel channel = new HttpChannel();
ChannelServices.RegisterChannel(channel);
BaseRemoteObject obj = (BaseRemoteObject) Activator.GetObject(
    typeof(BaseRemoteObject),
    "http://localhost:1234/MyRemoteObject.soap");
Console.WriteLine("Client.Main(): Reference to rem.obj. acquired");


Console.WriteLine("Client.Main(): Will call setValue(42)");
SetValueDelegate svDelegate = new SetValueDelegate(obj.setValue);
IAsyncResult svAsyncres = svDelegate.BeginInvoke(42,null,null);
Console.WriteLine("Client.Main(): Invocation done");

Console.WriteLine("Client.Main(): Will call getName()");
GetNameDelegate gnDelegate = new GetNameDelegate(obj.getName);
IAsyncResult gnAsyncres = gnDelegate.BeginInvoke(null,null);
Console.WriteLine("Client.Main(): Invocation done");

Console.WriteLine("Client.Main(): EndInvoke for setValue()");
svDelegate.EndInvoke(svAsyncres);
Console.WriteLine("Client.Main(): EndInvoke for getName()");
String name = gnDelegate.EndInvoke(gnAsyncres);

Console.WriteLine("Client.Main(): received name {0}",name);

Console.WriteLine("Client.Main(): Will now read value");
int tmp = obj.getValue();
Console.WriteLine("Client.Main(): New server side value {0}", tmp);

DateTime end = System.DateTime.Now;
TimeSpan duration = end.Subtract(start);
Console.WriteLine("Client.Main(): Execution took {0} seconds.",
                duration.Seconds);

Console.ReadLine();
        }
    }
}
```

When looking in the client's output in Figure 3-18, you can see that both long-running methods have been called at nearly the same time. This results in improved runtime performance, taking the execution time down from 12 seconds to 8 at the expense of making the application slightly more complex.

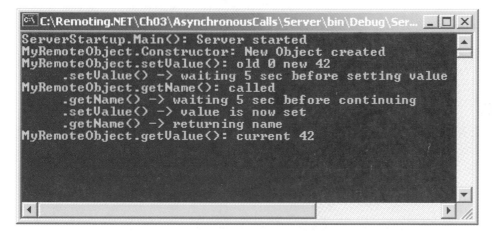

Figure 3-18. Client output when using asynchronous calls

The server output in Figure 3-19 shows that both methods have been entered on the server at the same time without blocking the client.

```
C:\Remoting.NET\Ch03\AsynchronousCalls\Server\bin\Debug\Ser...
ServerStartup.Main(): Server started
MyRemoteObject.Constructor: New Object created
MyRemoteObject.setValue(): old 0 new 42
     .setValue() -> waiting 5 sec before setting value
MyRemoteObject.getName(): called
     .getName() -> waiting 5 sec before continuing
     .setValue() -> value is now set
     .getName() -> returning name
MyRemoteObject.getValue(): current 42
```

Figure 3-19. Server's output when called asynchronously

Asynchronous One-Way Calls

One-way calls are a little different from asynchronous calls in the respect that the .NET Framework does not guarantee their execution. In addition, the methods used in this kind of call cannot have return values or out parameters. You also use delegates to call one-way methods, but the EndInvoke() function will exit immediately without checking if the server has finished processing yet. No exceptions are thrown, even if the remote server is down or the method call is malformed. Reasons for using these kind of methods (which aren't guaranteed to be executed at all) can be found in uncritical logging or tracing facilities, where the nonexistence of the server should not slow down the application.

Demonstrating an Asynchronous One-Way Call

You define one-way methods using the [OneWay] attribute. This happens in the defining metadata (in the General.dll in these examples) and doesn't need a change in the server or the client.

Defining the General.dll

The attribute [OneWay()] has to be specified in the interface definition of each method that will be called this way. As shown in Listing 3-16, you change only the setValue() method to become a one-way method; the others are still defined as earlier.

Listing 3-16. The Shared Interfaces DLL Defines the One-Way Method

```
using System;
using System.Runtime.Remoting.Messaging;

namespace General
{
    public abstract class BaseRemoteObject: MarshalByRefObject
    {
        [OneWay()]
        public abstract void setValue(int newval);
        public abstract int getValue();
        public abstract String getName();
    }
}
```

Implementing the Client

On the server side, no change is needed, so you can directly look at the client. In theory, no modification is needed for the client as well, but extend it a little here to catch the eventual exception during execution, as shown in Listing 3-17.

Listing 3-17. Try/Catch Blocks Are Added to the Client

```
using System;
using System.Runtime.Remoting;
using General;
using System.Runtime.Remoting.Channels.Http;
using System.Runtime.Remoting.Channels.Tcp;
using System.Runtime.Remoting.Channels;
using System.Runtime.Remoting.Proxies;
using System.Threading;

namespace Client
{

    class Client
    {
        delegate void SetValueDelegate(int value);

        static void Main(string[] args)
        {
            HttpChannel channel = new HttpChannel();
            ChannelServices.RegisterChannel(channel);
            BaseRemoteObject obj = (BaseRemoteObject) Activator.GetObject(
                typeof(BaseRemoteObject),
                "http://localhost:1234/MyRemoteObject.soap");
            Console.WriteLine("Client.Main(): Reference to rem.obj. acquired");

            Console.WriteLine("Client.Main(): Will call setValue(42)");
            SetValueDelegate svDelegate = new SetValueDelegate(obj.setValue);
            IAsyncResult svAsyncres = svDelegate.BeginInvoke(42,null,null);
            Console.WriteLine("Client.Main(): Invocation done");

            Console.WriteLine("Client.Main(): EndInvoke for setValue()");
            try
            {

                svDelegate.EndInvoke(svAsyncres);
                Console.WriteLine("Client.Main(): EndInvoke returned successfully");
            }
            catch (Exception e)
            {
                Console.WriteLine("Client.Main(): EXCEPTION during EndInvoke");
            }
            // wait for keypress
            Console.ReadLine();
```

```
            }
        }
    }
```

When this client is started, you will see the output in Figure 3-20 *no matter whether the server is running or not.*

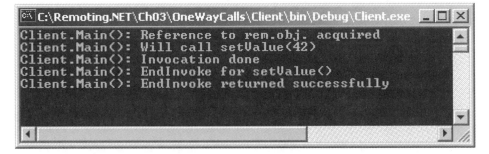

Figure 3-20. Client output when using one-way methods

As shown in Listing 3-18, you can now change the method in General.dll back to a standard method (non–one-way) by commenting out the [OneWay()] attribute.

Listing 3-18. Removing the [OneWay()] Attribute

```csharp
using System;
using System.Runtime.Remoting.Messaging;

namespace General
{
    public abstract class BaseRemoteObject: MarshalByRefObject
    {
        // no more one-way attribute [OneWay()]
public abstract void setValue(int newval);
        public abstract int getValue();
        public abstract String getName();
    }
}
```

Recompilation and a restart of the client (still without a running server) yields the result in Figure 3-21: an exception is thrown and a corresponding error message is output.

C:\Remoting.NET\Ch03\OneWayCalls\Client\bin\Debug\Client.exe
Client.Main(): Reference to rem.obj. acquired
Client.Main(): Will call setValue(42)
Client.Main(): Invocation done
Client.Main(): EndInvoke for setValue()
Client.Main(): EXCEPTION during EndInvoke

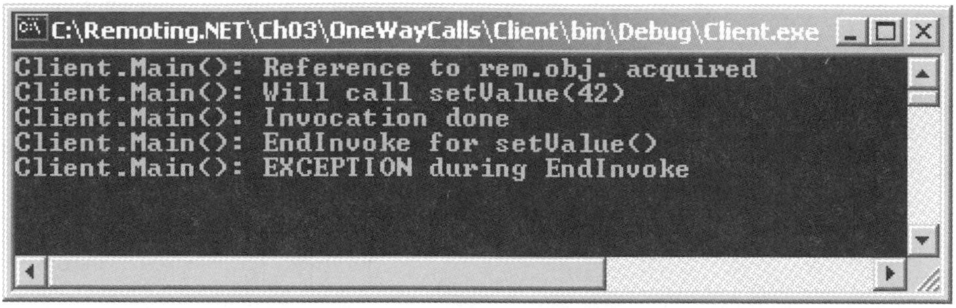

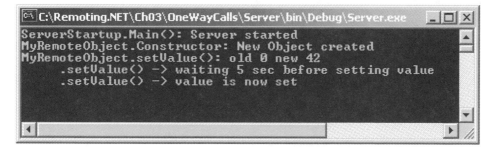

Figure 3-21. Client output when removing the [OneWay()] attribute

When you now start the server (and restart the client), you get the output shown in Figure 3-22, no matter if you used the [OneWay()] attribute or not. The interesting thing is that when using [OneWay()], the call to `EndInvoke()` finishes *before* the server completes the method. This is because in reality the client just *ignores* the server's response when using one-way method calls.

> **CAUTION** *Always remember that the client* ignores *the server's output and doesn't even check if the server is running when using one-way methods!*

C:\Remoting.NET\Ch03\OneWayCalls\Server\bin\Debug\Server.exe
ServerStartup.Main(): Server started
MyRemoteObject.Constructor: New Object created
MyRemoteObject.setValue(): old 0 new 42
.setValue() -> waiting 5 sec before setting value
.setValue() -> value is now set

Figure 3-22. Output on the server—independent of [OneWay()] attribute

Multiserver Configuration

When using multiple servers in an application in which remote objects on one server will be passed as parameters to methods of a second server's object, there are a few things you need to consider.

Before talking about cross-server execution, I show you some details of remoting with MarshalByRefObjects. As the name implies, these objects are marshaled by reference—instead of passing a copy of the object over the network, only a pointer to this object, known as an ObjRef, will travel. Contrary to common pointers in languages like C++, ObjRefs don't reference a memory address but instead contain a network address (like a TCP/IP address and TCP port) and an object ID that's employed on the server to identify which object instance is used by the calling client. (You can read more on ObjRefs in Chapter 7.) On the client side these ObjRefs are encapsulated by a proxy object (actually, by two proxies, but you also get the chance to read more on those in Chapter 7).

After creating two references to client-activated objects on a remote server, for example, the client will hold two TransparentProxy objects. These objects will both contain an ObjRef object, which will in turn point to one of the two distinct CAOs. This is shown in Figure 3-23.

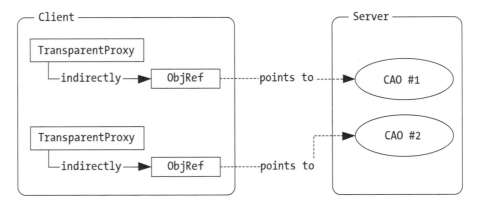

Figure 3-23. ObjRefs are pointing to server-side objects.

When a variable referencing a MarshalByRefObject is passed as a parameter to a remote function, the following happens: the ObjRef is taken from the proxy object, gets serialized (ObjRef is [Serializable]), and is passed to the remote machine (the second server in this example). On this machine, new proxy objects are generated from the deserialized ObjRef. Any calls from the second machine to the remote object are placed *directly* on the first server without any intermediate steps via the client.

NOTE   *As the second server will contact the first one directly, there has to be a means of communication between them; that is, if there is a firewall separating the two machines, you have to configure it to allow connections from one server to the other.*

Examining a Sample Multiserver Application

In the following example, I show you how to create a multiserver application in which Server 1 will provide a Singleton object that has an instance variable of type int. The client will obtain a remote reference to this object and pass it to a "worker object" located on a secondary server. This worker object is a SingleCall service providing a doSomething() method, which takes an instance of the first object as a parameter. Figure 3-24 shows the Unified Modeling Language (UML) diagram for this setup.

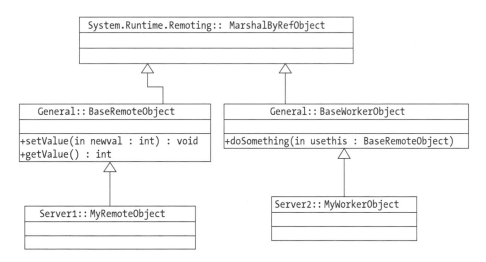

Figure 3-24. UML diagram of the multiserver example

> **NOTE** *For this example, I change the approach from using interfaces in General.dll to using abstract base classes. The reason for the change is that, upon passing a MarshalByRefObject to another server, the ObjRef is serialized and deserialized. On the server side, during the deserialization, the .NET Remoting Framework will generate a new proxy object and afterwards will try to downcast it to the correct type (cast from MarshalByRefObject to BaseRemoteObject in this example). This is possible because the ObjRef includes information about the type and its class hierarchy. Unfortunately, the .NET Remoting Framework does not also serialize the interface hierarchy in the ObjRef, so these interface casts would not succeed.*

Figures 3-25 to 3-27 illustrate the data flow between the various components. In Figure 3-25, you see the situation after the first method call of the client on the first server object. The client holds a proxy object containing the ObjRef that points to the server-side Singleton object.

> **NOTE** *I use IDs like MRO#1 for an instance of MyRemoteObject not because that's .NET-like, but because it allows me to more easily refer to a certain object instance when describing the architecture.*

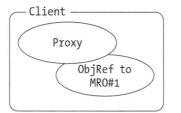 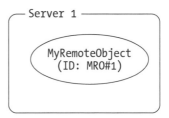

Figure 3-25. Client and single server

In the next step, which you can see in Figure 3-26, the client obtains a reference to the MarshalByRefObject called MyWorkerObject on the second server. It calls a method and passes its reference to the first server's object as a parameter. The ObjRef to this object (MRO#1) is serialized at the client and deserialized at the server, and a new proxy object is generated that sits on the second server and points to the object on the first. (Figure 3-27.) When MWO#1 now calls a method on MRO#1, the call will go directly from Server 2 to Server 1.

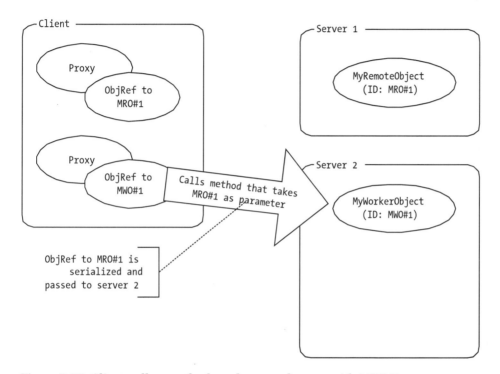

Figure 3-26. Client calls a method on the second server with MRO#1 as parameter.

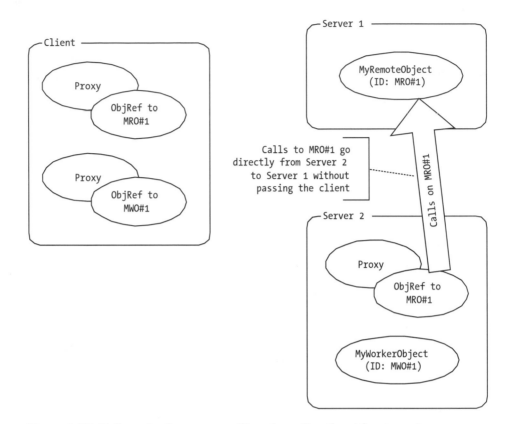

Figure 3-27. Calls to the first server will go there directly without passing the client.

Implementing the Shared Assembly

In the shared assembly, which is shown in Listing 3-19, you have to change the approach from using interfaces (which have been used in the prior examples) to abstract base classes because of the reasons stated previously. These are the superclasses of the classes you will implement in the two servers, therefore they have to descend from MarshalByRefObject as well.

Listing 3-19. Using Abstract Base Classes in the Shared Assembly
```
using System;

namespace General
{
    public abstract class BaseRemoteObject: MarshalByRefObject
```

```
   {
       public abstract void setValue(int newval);
       public abstract int getValue();
   }

   public abstract class BaseWorkerObject: MarshalByRefObject
   {
       public abstract void doSomething(BaseRemoteObject usethis);
   }
}
```

The BaseRemoteObject's descendant is a Singleton located on the first server, and it allows the client to set and read an int as state information. The BaseWorkerObject's implementation is placed in Server 2 and provides a method that takes an object of type BaseRemoteObject as a parameter.

Implementing the First Server

The first server very closely resembles the servers from the other examples. The only difference is that MyRemoteObject is no direct child of MarshalByRefObject, but instead is a descendant of BaseRemoteObject, defined in the shared assembly.

This object, implemented as a Singleton, is shown in Listing 3-20.

Listing 3-20. The First Server

```
using System;
using System.Runtime.Remoting;
using General;
using System.Runtime.Remoting.Channels.Http;
using System.Runtime.Remoting.Channels;

namespace Server
{
    class MyRemoteObject: BaseRemoteObject
    {
        int myvalue;

        public MyRemoteObject()
        {
            Console.WriteLine("MyRemoteObject.Constructor: New Object created");
        }
```

```
        public override void setValue(int newval)
        {
            Console.WriteLine("MyRemoteObject.setValue(): old {0} new {1}",
                              myvalue,newval);
            myvalue = newval;
        }


        public override int getValue()
        {
            Console.WriteLine("MyRemoteObject.getValue(): current {0}",myvalue);
            return myvalue;
        }
    }


    class ServerStartup
    {
        static void Main(string[] args)
        {
            Console.WriteLine ("ServerStartup.Main(): Server [1] started");

            HttpChannel chnl = new HttpChannel(1234);
            ChannelServices.RegisterChannel(chnl);
            RemotingConfiguration.RegisterWellKnownServiceType(
                    typeof(MyRemoteObject),
                    "MyRemoteObject.soap",
                    WellKnownObjectMode.Singleton);

            // the server will keep running until keypress.
            Console.ReadLine();
        }
    }
}
```

Implementing the Second Server

The second server works differently from those in prior examples. It provides
a SingleCall object that accepts a BaseRemoteObject as a parameter. The SAO
will contact this remote object, read and output its state, and change it
before returning.

The server's startup code is quite straightforward and works the same as in
the preceding examples. It opens an HTTP channel on port 1235 and registers the
well-known object. This second server is shown in Listing 3-21.

> **NOTE** *When running two servers on one machine, you have to give the servers different port numbers. Only one application can occupy a certain port at any given time. When developing production-quality applications, you should always allow the user or system administrator to configure the port numbers in a configuration file, via the registry or using a GUI.*

Listing 3-21. The Second Server

```
using System;
using System.Runtime.Remoting;
using General;
using System.Runtime.Remoting.Channels.Http;
using System.Runtime.Remoting.Channels;
using System.Collections;

namespace Server
{

    class MyWorkerObject: BaseWorkerObject
    {

        public MyWorkerObject()
        {
            Console.WriteLine("MyWorkerObject.Constructor: New Object created");
        }

        public override void doSomething(BaseRemoteObject usethis)
        {
            Console.WriteLine("MyWorkerObject.doSomething(): called");
            Console.WriteLine("MyWorkerObject.doSomething(): Will now call" +
                        "getValue() on the remote obj.");

            int tmp = usethis.getValue();
            Console.WriteLine("MyWorkerObject.doSomething(): current value of " +
                        "the remote obj.; {0}", tmp);

            Console.WriteLine("MyWorkerObject.doSomething(): changing value to 70");
            usethis.setValue(70);
        }
    }
}
```

```
class ServerStartup
{
    static void Main(string[] args)
    {
        Console.WriteLine ("ServerStartup.Main(): Server [2] started");

        HttpChannel chnl = new HttpChannel(1235);
        ChannelServices.RegisterChannel(chnl);

        RemotingConfiguration.RegisterWellKnownServiceType(
                typeof(MyWorkerObject),
                "MyWorkerObject.soap",
                WellKnownObjectMode.SingleCall);

        // the server will keep running until keypress.
        Console.ReadLine();
    }
}
}
```

Running the Sample

When the client is started, it first acquires a remote reference to MyRemoteObject running on the first server. It then changes the object's state to contain the value 42 and afterwards reads the value from the server and outputs it in the console window (see Figure 3-28).

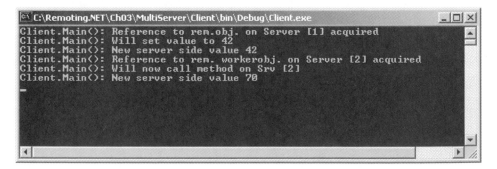

Figure 3-28. The client's output

Next it fetches a remote reference to MyWorkerObject running on the second server. The client calls the method doSomething() and passes its reference to MyRemoteObject as a parameter. When Server 2 receives this call, it contacts Server 1 to read the current value from MyRemoteObject and afterwards changes it to 70. (See Figures 3-29 and 3-30.)

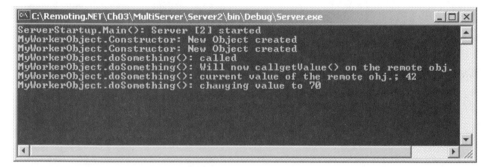

```
C:\Remoting.NET\Ch03\MultiServer\Server1\bin\Debug\Server.exe
ServerStartup.Main(): Server [1] started
MyRemoteObject.Constructor: New Object created
MyRemoteObject.setValue(): old 0 new 42
MyRemoteObject.getValue(): current 42
MyRemoteObject.getValue(): current 42
MyRemoteObject.setValue(): old 42 new 70
MyRemoteObject.getValue(): current 70
```

Figure 3-29. The first server's output

```
C:\Remoting.NET\Ch03\MultiServer\Server2\bin\Debug\Server.exe
ServerStartup.Main(): Server [2] started
MyWorkerObject.Constructor: New Object created
MyWorkerObject.Constructor: New Object created
MyWorkerObject.doSomething(): called
MyWorkerObject.doSomething(): Will now callgetValue() on the remote obj.
MyWorkerObject.doSomething(): current value of the remote obj.; 42
MyWorkerObject.doSomething(): changing value to 70
```

Figure 3-30. The second server's output

When the call from client to the second server returns, the client again contacts MyRemoteObject to obtain the current value, 70, which shows that your client really has been talking to the same object from both processes.

Shared Assemblies

As you've seen in this chapter, .NET Remoting applications need to share common information about remoteable types between server and client. Contrary to other remoting schemas like CORBA, Java RMI, and J2EE EJBs, with which you don't have a lot of choice for writing these shared interfaces, base classes, and metadata, the .NET Framework gives you at least four possible ways to do so, as I discuss in the following sections.

Shared Implementation

The first way to share information about remoteable types is to implement your server-side objects in a shared assembly and deploy this to the client as well. The main advantage here is that you don't have any extra work. Even though this might save you some time during implementation, I really recommend against this approach. Not only does it violate the core principles of distributed application development, but it also allows your clients, which are probably third parties accessing your ERP system to automate order entry, to use ILDASM or one of the upcoming MSIL-to-C# decompilers to disassemble and view your business logic. Unfortunately, this approach is shown in several MSDN examples.

Nevertheless, there are application scenarios that depend on this way of sharing the metadata. When you have an application that can be used either connected or disconnected and will access the same logic in both cases, this might be the way to go. You can then "switch" dynamically between using the local implementation and using the remote one.

Shared Interfaces

In the first examples in this book, I show the use of shared interfaces. With this approach, you create an assembly that is copied to both the server and the client. The assembly contains the interfaces that will be implemented by the server. The disadvantage to using this process of sharing the metadata is that you won't be able to pass those objects as parameters to functions running in a different context (either on the same or another server or on another client) because the resulting MarshalByRefObject cannot be downcast to these interfaces.

Shared Base Classes

Instead of sharing interfaces between the client and the server, you can also create abstract base classes in a shared assembly. The server-side object will inherit from these classes and implement the necessary functionality. The big advantage here is that abstract base classes are, contrary to the shared interfaces, capable of being passed around as parameters for methods located in different AppDomains. Still, this approach has one disadvantage: you won't be able to use those objects without `Activator.GetObject()` or a factory. Normally when the .NET Framework is configured correctly on the client side, it is possible to use the new operator to create a reference to a remote object. Unfortunately, you can never create a new instance of an abstract class or an interface, so the compiler will block this functionality.

SoapSuds-Generated Metadata

As each of the other approaches has a drawback, let's see what SoapSuds can do for you. This program's functionality is to extract the metadata (that is, the type definition) from a running server or an implementation assembly and generate a new assembly that contains only this meta information. You will then be able to reference this assembly in the client application without manually generating any intermediate shared assemblies.

Calling SoapSuds

SoapSuds is a command-line utility, therefore the easiest way to start it is to bring up the Visual Studio .NET Command Prompt by selecting Start ➣ Programs ➣ Microsoft Visual Studio .NET ➣ Visual Studio .NET Tools. This command prompt will have the path correctly set so that you can execute all .NET Framework SDK tools from any directory.

Starting SoapSuds without any parameters will give you detailed usage information. To generate a metadata DLL from a running server, you have to call SoapSuds with the -url parameter:

```
soapsuds -url:<URL> -oa:<OUTPUTFILE>.DLL -nowp
```

> **NOTE** *You normally have to append ?wsdl to the URL your server registered for a SOA to allow SoapSuds to extract the metadata.*

To let SoapSuds extract the information from a compiled DLL, you use the -ia parameter:

```
soapsuds -ia:<assembly> -oa:<OUTPUTFILE>.DLL -nowp
```

Wrapped Proxies

When you run SoapSuds in its default configuration (without the -nowp parameter) by passing only a URL as an input parameter and telling it to generate an assembly, it will create what is called a *wrapped proxy*. The wrapped proxy can only be used on SOAP channels and will directly store the path to your server. Normally you do not want this.

> **NOTE** *This behavior is useful when you want to access a third-party Web Service whose application URL you happen to have.*

I normally recommend using wrapped proxies only when you want to quickly test a SOAP remoting service. As an example, in the next section I show you how to implement a server without previously specifying any shared interfaces or base classes.

Implementing the Server

The server in this example will be implemented without any up-front definition of interfaces. You only need to create a simplistic SAO and register an HTTP channel to allow access to the metadata and the server-side object, as shown in Listing 3-22.

Listing 3-22. Server That Presents a SAO

```
using System;
using System.Runtime.Remoting;
using System.Runtime.Remoting.Channels.Http;
using System.Runtime.Remoting.Channels;

namespace Server
{

    class SomeRemoteObject: MarshalByRefObject
    {
        public void doSomething()
        {
            Console.WriteLine("SomeRemoteObject.doSomething() called");
        }
    }

    class ServerStartup
    {
        static void Main(string[] args)
        {
            Console.WriteLine ("ServerStartup.Main(): Server started");

            HttpChannel chnl = new HttpChannel(1234);
            ChannelServices.RegisterChannel(chnl);
            RemotingConfiguration.RegisterWellKnownServiceType(
```

```
            typeof(SomeRemoteObject),
            "SomeRemoteObject.soap",
            WellKnownObjectMode.SingleCall);

        // the server will keep running until keypress.
        Console.ReadLine();
    }
  }
}
```

Generating the SoapSuds Wrapped Proxy

To generate a wrapped proxy assembly, use the SoapSuds command line shown
in Figure 3-31. The resulting meta.dll should be copied to the client directory, as
you will have to reference it when building the client-side application.

Figure 3-31. SoapSuds command line used to generate a wrapped proxy

Implementing the Client

Assuming you now want to implement the client application, you first have to set
a reference to the meta.dll in the project's References dialog box in VS .NET or
employ the /r:meta.dll parameter to the command-line compiler. You can then
use the Server namespace and directly instantiate a SomeRemoteObject using
the new operator, as shown in Listing 3-23.

Listing 3-23. Wrapped Proxies Simplify the Client's Source Code
```
using System;
using Server;

namespace Client
{
    class Client
    {
        static void Main(string[] args)
        {
```

```
Console.WriteLine("Client.Main(): creating rem. reference");
SomeRemoteObject obj = new SomeRemoteObject();
Console.WriteLine("Client.Main(): calling doSomething()");
obj.doSomething();
Console.WriteLine("Client.Main(): done ");

Console.ReadLine();
    }
  }
}
```

Even though this code looks intriguingly simply, I recommend against using a wrapped proxy for several reasons: the server's URL is hard coded, and you can only use an HTTP channel and not a TCP channel.

When you start this client, it will generate the output shown in Figure 3-32. Check the server's output in Figure 3-33 to see that doSomething() has really been called on the server-side object.

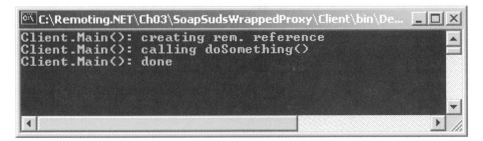

Figure 3-32. Client's output when using a wrapped proxy

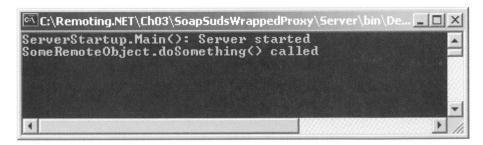

Figure 3-33. The server's output shows that doSomething() *has been called.*

Wrapped Proxy Internals

Starting SoapSuds with the parameter -gc instead of -oa:<assemblyname> will
generate C# code in the current directory. You can use this code to manually
compile a DLL or include it directly in your project.

Looking at the code in Listing 3-24 quickly reveals why you can use it without
any further registration of channels or objects. (I strip the SoapType attribute,
which would normally contain additional information on how to remotely call
the object's methods.)

Listing 3-24. A SoapSuds-Generated Wrapped Proxy

```csharp
using System;
using System.Runtime.Remoting.Messaging;
using System.Runtime.Remoting.Metadata;
using System.Runtime.Remoting.Metadata.W3cXsd2001;


namespace Server {

    public class SomeRemoteObject :
            System.Runtime.Remoting.Services.RemotingClientProxy
    {
        // Constructor
        public SomeRemoteObject()
        {
            base.ConfigureProxy(this.GetType(),
                "http://localhost:1234/SomeRemoteObject.soap");
        }

        public Object RemotingReference
        {
            get{return(_tp);}
        }

[SoapMethod(SoapAction="http://schemas.microsoft.com/clr/nsassem/
Server.SomeRemoteObject/Server#doSomething")]
        public void doSomething()
        {
            ((SomeRemoteObject) _tp).doSomething();
        }


    }
}
```

What this wrapped proxy does behind the scenes is provide a custom imple-mentation/extension of RealProxy (which is the base for RemotingClientProxy) so that it can be used transparently. This architecture is shown in detail in Chapter 7.

Nonwrapped Proxy Metadata

Fortunately, SoapSuds allows the generation of nonwrapped proxy metadata as well. In this case, it will only generate empty class definitions, which can then be used by the underlying .NET Remoting TransparentProxy to generate the true method calls—no matter which channel you are using.

This approach also gives you the huge advantage of being able to use config-uration files for channels, objects, and the corresponding URLs (more on this in the next chapter) so that you don't have to hard code this information. In the fol-lowing example, you can use the same server as in the previous example, only changing the SoapSuds command and implementing the client in a different way.

Generating the Metadata with SoapSuds

As you want to generate a metadata-only assembly, you have to pass the -nowp parameter to SoapSuds to keep it from generating a wrapped proxy (see Figure 3-34).

Figure 3-34. SoapSuds command line for a metadata-only assembly

Implementing the Client

When using metadata-only output from SoapSuds, the client looks a lot different from the previous one. In fact, it closely resembles the examples I show you at the beginning of this chapter.

First you have to set a reference to the newly generated meta.dll from the current SoapSuds invocation and indicate that your client will be using this namespace. You can then proceed with the standard approach of creating and registering a channel and calling `Activator.GetObject()` to create a reference to the remote object. This is shown in Listing 3-25.

Listing 3-25. The Client with a Nonwrapped Proxy

```csharp
using System;
using System.Runtime.Remoting;
using System.Runtime.Remoting.Channels.Http;
using System.Runtime.Remoting.Channels;
using Server;

namespace Client
{
   class Client
   {
      static void Main(string[] args)
      {
         HttpChannel chnl = new HttpChannel();
         ChannelServices.RegisterChannel(chnl);

         Console.WriteLine("Client.Main(): creating rem. reference");
         SomeRemoteObject obj = (SomeRemoteObject) Activator.GetObject (
            typeof(SomeRemoteObject),
            "http://localhost:1234/SomeRemoteObject.soap");

         Console.WriteLine("Client.Main(): calling doSomething()");
         obj.doSomething();

         Console.WriteLine("Client.Main(): done ");
         Console.ReadLine();
      }
   }
}
```

When this client is started, both the client-side and the server-side output will be the same as in the previous example (see Figures 3-35 and 3-36).

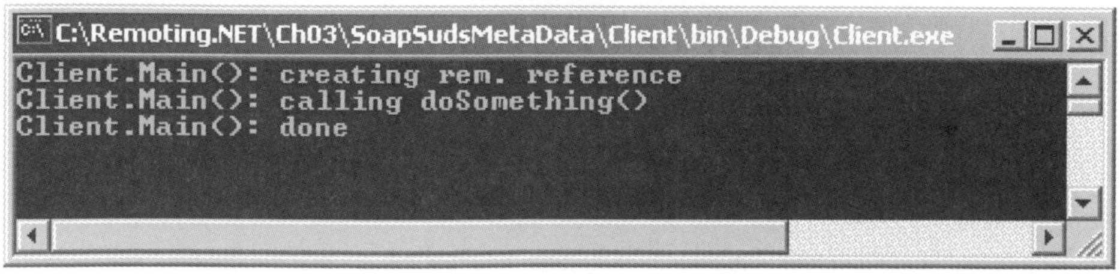

Figure 3-35. The client's output when using a metadata-only assembly

85

Figure 3-36. The server's output is the same as in the previous example.

Summary

In this chapter you read about the basics of distributed .NET applications using .NET Remoting. You now know the difference between ByValue objects and MarshalByRefObjects, which can be either server-activated objects (SAO) or client-activated objects (CAO). You can call remote methods asynchronously, and you know about the dangers and benefits of one-way methods. You also learned about the different ways in which a client can receive the necessary metadata to access remote objects, and that you should normally use the -nowp parameter with SoapSuds.

It seems that the only thing that can keep you from developing your first real-world .NET Remoting application is that you don't yet know about various issues surrounding configuration and deployment of such applications. These two topics are covered in the following chapter.

CHAPTER 4

Configuration and Deployment

THIS CHAPTER INTRODUCES YOU to the aspects of configuration and deployment of .NET Remoting applications. It shows you how to use configuration files to avoid the hard coding of URLs or channel information for your remote object.

You also learn about hosting your server-side components in Windows services or Internet Information Server (IIS)—the latter of which gives you the possibilities to deploy your components for authenticated or encrypted connections, which is covered in detail in Chapter 5.

To configure your applications, you can choose to either implement all channel and object registrations on your own or employ the standard .NET Remoting configuration files. These files are XML documents, and they allow you to configure nearly every aspect of remoting, ranging from various default and custom channels (including custom properties for your own channels) to the instantiation behavior of your objects.

The big advantage, and the main reason you should always use configuration files in production applications, is that you can change the application's remoting behavior without the need to recompile. For example, you could create a configuration file for users located directly within your LAN who might use a direct TCP channel, and another file for WAN users who will use a secured HTTP channel with SSL encryption. All this can be done without changing a single line in your application's source code.

With other remoting architectures, the choice of deployment and configuration is largely determined when choosing the framework. With Java EJBs, for example, the "container," which can be compared to an application server, defines the means of configuration and locks you into a single means of deployment. The same is true for the COM+ component, which has to be hosted in Windows Component services.

In the .NET Remoting Framework, you have several possibilities for operation: you can run your remote objects in a distinct stand-alone application (as shown in the previous examples in this book), run them in a Windows service, or host them in IIS.

Configuration Files

.NET Remoting configuration files allow you to specify parameters for most aspects of the remoting framework. These files can define tasks as simple as registering a channel and specifying a Type as a server-activated object, or can be as complex as defining a whole chain of IMessageSinks with custom properties.

Instead of writing code like this on the server:

```
HttpChannel chnl = new HttpChannel(1234);
ChannelServices.RegisterChannel(chnl);
RemotingConfiguration.RegisterWellKnownServiceType(
                typeof(CustomerManager),
                "CustomerManager.soap",
                WellKnownObjectMode.Singleton);
```

you can use a configuration file that contains the following XML document to specify the same behavior:

```
<configuration>
  <system.runtime.remoting>
    <application>
      <channels>
        <channel ref="http" port="1234" />
      </channels>
      <service>
        <wellknown mode="Singleton"
                   type="Server.CustomerManager, Server"
                   objectUri="CustomerManager.soap" />
      </service>

    </application>
  </system.runtime.remoting>
</configuration>
```

To employ this configuration file in your application, you have to call RemotingConfiguration.Configure() and pass the filename of your *.config file to it.

```
String filename = "server.exe.config";
RemotingConfiguration.Configure(filename);
```

> **NOTE** *As a convention for .NET applications, the configuration filename should be <applicationname>.config, whereas an application filename includes the extension .exe or .dll.*

When using this code in the IDE, remember to put the *.config files in the directory where the application will be built!

Watch for the Metadata!

Instead of using `Activator.GetObject()` and passing a URL to it, you can use the new operator after loading the configuration file with `RemotingConfiguration.Configure()`.

In terms of the sample application in Chapter 2, this means that instead of the following call:

```
ICustomerManager mgr = (ICustomerManager) Activator.GetObject(
        typeof(ICustomerManager),
        "http://localhost:1234/CustomerManager.soap");
```

you might simply use this statement after the configuration file has been loaded:

```
CustomerManager mgr = new CustomerManager()
```

And here the problem starts: you need the definition of the class CustomerManager on the client. The interface is not sufficient anymore, because you cannot use `IInterface x = new IInterface()`, as this would represent the instantiation of an interface, which is not possible.

In Chapter 3, I show you several tools for supplying the necessary metadata in a shared assembly: interfaces, abstract base classes, and SoapSuds-generated metadata-only assemblies. When using configuration files, you won't be able to employ abstract base classes or interfaces—you simply have to resort to SoapSuds-generated metadata.

When your application includes only SAOs/CAOs (and no [Serializable] objects), you're fine with using `soapsuds -ia:<assembly> -nowp -oa:<meta_data.dll>` to generate the necessary metadata. However, when you are using [Serializable] objects, which not only hold some data but also have methods defined, you need to provide the implementation (the General.dll in the examples) to the client as well.

To see the problem and its solution, take a look at Listing 4-1. This code shows you a [Serializable] class in a shared assembly that will be called General.dll.

Listing 4-1. A Shared [Serializable] Class

```
using System;
namespace General
{

    [Serializable]
    public class Customer
    {
        public String FirstName;
        public String LastName;
        public DateTime DateOfBirth;

        public int getAge()
        {
            TimeSpan tmp = DateTime.Today.Subtract(DateOfBirth);
            return tmp.Days / 365; // rough estimation
        }
    }
}
```

On the server side you use the following configuration file, which allows you to write `CustomerManager obj = new CustomerManager` to acquire a reference to the remote object.

```
<configuration>
  <system.runtime.remoting>
    <application>
      <channels>
        <channel ref="http" port="1234" />
      </channels>
      <service>
        <wellknown mode="Singleton"
                   type="Server.CustomerManager, Server"
                   objectUri="CustomerManager.soap" />
      </service>

    </application>
  </system.runtime.remoting>
</configuration>
```

The server itself, which is shown in Listing 4-2, implements a MarshalByRefObject that provides a getCustomer() method, which will return a Customer object by value.

Listing 4-2. The Server-Side Implementation of CustomerManager

```
using System;
using System.Runtime.Remoting;
using General;

namespace Server
{

    class CustomerManager: MarshalByRefObject
    {
        public Customer getCustomer(int id)
        {
            Customer tmp = new Customer();
            tmp.FirstName = "John";
            tmp.LastName = "Doe";
            tmp.DateOfBirth = new DateTime(1970,7,4);
            return tmp;
        }
    }

    class ServerStartup
    {
        static void Main(string[] args)
        {
            Console.WriteLine ("ServerStartup.Main(): Server started");

            String filename = "server.exe.config";
            RemotingConfiguration.Configure(filename);

            // the server will keep running until keypress.
            Console.WriteLine("Server is running, Press <return> to exit.");
            Console.ReadLine();
        }
    }
}
```

After compiling, starting the server, and running the SoapSuds command shown in Figure 4-1, you'll unfortunately end up with a little bit more output than expected.

Figure 4-1. SoapSuds command line for extracting the metadata

The Generated_General.dll file (which you can see in Figure 4-2) contains not only the metadata for Server.CustomerManager, but also the definition for General.Customer. This is because SoapSuds generates metadata-only assemblies for all classes and assemblies that are referenced by your server. You'll run into the same problems when referencing parts from mscorlib.dll or other classes from the System.* namespaces.

Comparing Generated_Meta.dll to the original General.Customer in General.dll (the one that has been created by compiling the shared project) in Figure 4-3, you can see that although the generated Customer class contains all defined fields, it does not include the getAge() method.

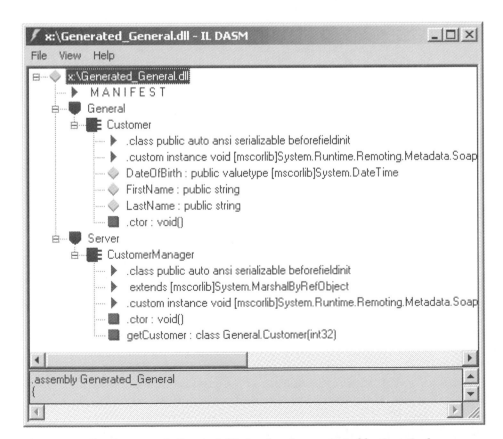

Figure 4-2. The Generated_General.dll that has been created by SoapSuds

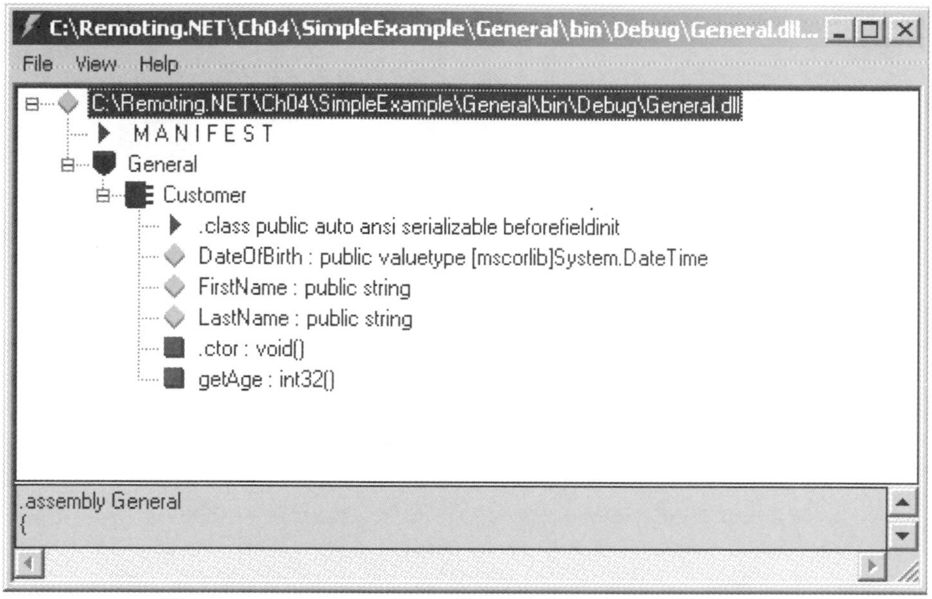

Figure 4-3. The original General.dll contains the method `Customer.GetAge()`.

You can now safely assume that using the Generated_General.dll will not be sufficient for the application; after all, you *want* access to the getAge() method.

If you try to reference both General.dll and Generated_General.dll in your client application, you will end up with a namespace clash. Both assemblies contain the same namespace and the same class (General.Customer). Depending on the order of referencing the two DLLs, you'll end up with either a compile-time error message telling you that the getAge() method is missing *or* an InvalidCastException when calling `CustomerManager.getCustomer()`.

Using SoapSuds to Generate Source Code

To further convince you that shipping the implementation to the client is not the best idea, even if it does solve the preceding problems posed by sharing metadata, I present an alternative solution.

Although SoapSuds can be used to generate DLLs from the WSDL information provided by your server, it can also generate C# code files, including not only the definition but also the required SoapMethodAttributes, so that the remoting framework will know the server's namespace identifier.

To generate code instead of DLLs, you have to specify the parameter -gc instead of -oa:<someassembly>.dll. This command, shown in Figure 4-4, generates one C# source code file for each server-side assembly. You will therefore end up with one file called general.cs and another called server.cs (both are placed in the current directory). The generated server.cs file is shown in Listing 4-3.

Figure 4-4. SoapSuds command line for generating C# code

Listing 4-3. The SoapSuds-Generated server.cs File

```
using System;
using System.Runtime.Remoting.Messaging;
using System.Runtime.Remoting.Metadata;
using System.Runtime.Remoting.Metadata.W3cXsd2001;
namespace Server {

    [Serializable, SoapType(XmlNamespace="http://schemas.microsoft.com/clr/n
sassem/Server/Server%2C%20Version%3D1.0.678.38058%2C%20Culture%3Dneutral%2C%
20PublicKeyToken%3Dnull", XmlTypeNamespace="http://schemas.microsoft.com/clr
/nsassem/Server/Server%2C%20Version%3D1.0.678.38058%2C%20Culture%3Dneutral%2
C%20PublicKeyToken%3Dnull")]
    public class CustomerManager : System.MarshalByRefObject
    {
        [SoapMethod(SoapAction="http://schemas.microsoft.com/clr/nsassem/Ser
ver.CustomerManager/Server#getCustomer")]
        public General.Customer getCustomer(Int32 id)
        {
            return((General.Customer) (Object) null);
        }


    }
}
```

Generally speaking, these lines represent the interface and the attributes necessary to clearly resolve this remoting call to the server.

Instead of including the Generated_General.dll file (which also contains the namespace General), you can include this C# file in the client-side project or compile it (using the csc.exe stand-alone command line compiler) to a DLL.

> **NOTE** *When using the command-line compiler csc.exe,*
> *you have to specify the /r parameter to add a reference*
> *to General.dll. A possible compilation command might be*
> csc /t:library /out:new_generated_meta.dll /r:general server.cs.

You can now safely reference the shared General.dll, without any namespace clashes, in your project to have access to the Customer class' implementation.

Porting the Sample to Use Configuration Files

Taking the first sample application in Chapter 2 (the CustomerManager SAO that returns a Customer object by value), I'll show you here how to enhance it to use configuration files.

Assume that on the server side of this application you want an HTTP channel to listen on port 1234 and provide remote access to a well-known Singleton object. You can do this with the following configuration file:

```
<configuration>
  <system.runtime.remoting>
    <application>

      <channels>
        <channel ref="http" port="1234" />
      </channels>

      <service>
        <wellknown mode="Singleton"
                   type="Server.CustomerManager, Server"
                   objectUri="CustomerManager.soap" />
      </service>

    </application>
  </system.runtime.remoting>
</configuration>
```

The server-side implementation will simply load the configuration file and wait for <Return> to be pressed before exiting the application. The implementation of CustomerManager is the same as shown previously, and only the server's startup code is reproduced here:

```
using System;
using System.Runtime.Remoting;
using General;
```

```
namespace Server
{
   class ServerStartup
   {
      static void Main(string[] args)
      {
         String filename = "server.exe.config";
         RemotingConfiguration.Configure(filename);

         Console.WriteLine("Server is running. Press <Return> to exit.");
         Console.ReadLine();
      }
   }
}
```

Creating the Client

The client will consist of two source files, one of them being the previously mentioned SoapSuds-generated server.cs and the second will contain the real client's implementation. It will also have a reference to the shared General.dll.

To allow the client to access the server-side Singleton, you can use the following configuration file to avoid hard coding of URLs:

```
<configuration>
  <system.runtime.remoting>
    <application>

      <client>
        <wellknown type="Server.CustomerManager, Client"
                   url="http://localhost:1234/CustomerManager.soap" />
      </client>

    </application>
  </system.runtime.remoting>
</configuration>
```

Even before I get to the details of configuration files, I want to mention what the attribute "type" in the XML tag <wellknown> contains. In the previous example, you can see that on the server side the tag includes "Server.CustomerManager, Server" and on the client-side it includes "Server.CustomerManager, Client".

The format is generally "<namespace>.<class>, <assembly>", so when a call to the remote object is received at the server, it will create the class Server.CustomerManager from its Server assembly.

> **CAUTION** *Make sure you do not include the .dll or .exe extension here as the .NET Remoting Framework will not give you any error messages in this case. Instead, your application just won't work as expected. If you want to be sure that you're dealing with a remote object, you can call your object's IsTransparentProxy() method right after creation of the remote reference.*

On the client side the format is a little bit different. The preceding entry, translated into plain English, more or less reads, "If someone creates an instance of the class Server.CustomerManager, which is located in the Client assembly, then generate a remote reference pointing to http://localhost:1234/CustomerManager.soap." You therefore have to specify the client's assembly name in the type attribute of this tag. This differs when using a SoapSuds-generated DLL, in which case you would have to include the name of this generated assembly there.

> **CAUTION** *When a typo occurs in your configuration file, such as when you misspell the assembly name or the class name, there won't be an exception during "x = new Something()". Instead, you will get a reference to the local object. When you subsequently call methods on it, they will return null.*

The C# code of the client application (excluding the SoapSuds-generated server.cs) is shown in Listing 4-4.

Listing 4-4. The Working Client Application (Excluding server.cs)

```csharp
using System;
using System.Runtime.Remoting;
using General;  // from General.DLL
using Server; // from server.cs

namespace Client
{
    class Client
    {
        static void Main(string[] args)
        {
            String filename = "client.exe.config";
            RemotingConfiguration.Configure(filename);
```

```
CustomerManager mgr = new CustomerManager();

Console.WriteLine("Client.Main(): Reference to CustomerManager" +
                  " acquired");

Customer cust = mgr.getCustomer(4711);
int age = cust.getAge();
Console.WriteLine("Client.Main(): Customer {0} {1} is {2} years old.",
    cust.FirstName,
    cust.LastName,
    age);

Console.ReadLine();
        }
    }
}
```

When server and client are started, you will see the familiar output shown in Figures 4-5 and 4-6.

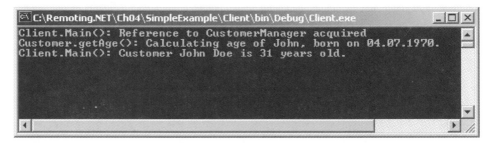

Figure 4-5. Client's output when using the configuration file

Figure 4-6. Servers's output when using the configuration file

Standard Configuration Options

All .NET configuration files start with <configuration>, and this applies to remoting configuration files as well.

A remoting configuration file basically contains the following structure:

```
<configuration>
    <system.runtime.remoting>
        <application>
            <lifetime />
            <channels />
            <service />
            <client />
        </application>
    </system.runtime.remoting>
</configuration>
```

Lifetime

Use the <lifetime> tag to configure your object's default lifetime (as discussed in Chapter 3). Valid attributes for the <lifetime> tag are listed here:

ATTRIBUTE	DESCRIPTION
leaseTime	The initial time to live (TTL) for your objects (default is 5 minutes)
sponsorshipTimeout	The time to wait for a sponsor's reply (default is 2 minutes)
renewOnCallTime	The time to add to an object's TTL when a method is called (default is 2 minutes)
leaseManagerPollTime	The interval in which your object's TTL will be checked (default is 10 seconds)

All attributes are optional and may be specified in different time units. Valid units are D for days, H for hours, M for minutes, S for seconds, and MS for milliseconds. When no unit is specified, the system will default to S. Combinations such as 1H5M are *not* supported.

Here is an example for a very short-lived object:

```
<lifetime
    leaseTime="90MS"
    renewOnCallTime="90MS"
    leaseManagerPollTime="100MS"
/>
```

Channels

The <channels> tag contains one or more channel entries. It only serves as a collection for these and doesn't have any XML attributes assigned to it.

To register a server-side TCP channel that listens on port 1234, you can specify the following configuration section:

```
<channels>
    <channel ref="tcp" port="1234">
</channels>
```

Channel

The <channel> tag allows you to specify a port number for the server application, to reference custom channels, and to set additional attributes on channels. When you want to use the default HTTP channel or TCP channel, this tag does not have to be specified on the client because these channels will be registered automatically by the framework. On the server, you have to specify at least a port number on which the server-side channel will listen.

You have basically two ways of referencing channels: using a named reference for a predeclared channel or specifying the exact type (namespace, classname, and assembly) for the channel's implementation. Valid attributes for the <channel> tag are as follows:

ATTRIBUTE	DESCRIPTION
ref	Reference for a predefined channel ("tcp" or "http") or reference to a channel that has been defined in a configuration file.
displayName	Attribute only used for the .NET Framework Configuration Tool.
type	Attribute that is mandatory when ref has not been specified. Contains the exact type (namespace, classname, assembly) of the channel's implementation. When the assembly is in the GAC, you have to specify version, culture, and public key information as well. For an example of this, see the default definition of HTTP channel in your machine.conf file (which is located in %WINDIR%\Microsoft.NET\Framework\v1.0.3705\CONFIG).
port	Server side port number. When using this attribute on a client, 0 should be specified if you want your client-side objects to be able to receive callbacks from the server.

In addition to the preceding configuration properties, the HTTP channel, which is created by specifying <channel ref="http">, supports the following entries:

ATTRIBUTE	DESCRIPTION
name	Name of the channel (default is "http"). When registering more than one channel, these names have to be unique or an empty string ("") has to be specified. The value of this attribute can be used when calling `ChannelServices.GetChannel()`.
priority	Indicator of the likelihood for this channel to be chosen by the framework to transfer data (default is 1). The higher the integer, the greater the possibility. Negative numbers are allowed.
clientConnectionLimit	Number of connections that can be simultaneously opened to a given server (default is 2).
proxyName	Name of the proxy server.
proxyPort	Port number for your proxy server.
suppressChannelData	Directive specifying whether the channel will contribute to the ChannelData that is used when creating an ObjRef. Takes a value of true or false (default is false).

(continued)

101

ATTRIBUTE	DESCRIPTION
useIpAddress	Directive specifying whether the channel shall use IP addresses in the given URLs instead of using the hostname of the server computer. Takes a value of true or false (default is true).
listen	Directive specifying whether activation shall be allowed to hook into the listener service. Takes a value of true or false (default is true).
bindTo	IP address on which the server will listen. Used only on computers with more than one IP address.
machineName	A string that specifies the machine name used with the current channel. This property overrides the useIpAddress property.

The TCP channel, which is created by specifying <channel ref="tcp"> supports the same properties as the HTTP channel and the following additional property:

ATTRIBUTE	DESCRIPTION
rejectRemoteRequests	Indicator specifying whether the server will accept requests from remote systems. When set to true, the server will not accept such requests, only allowing interapplication communication from the local machine.

On the server side, the following entry can be used to specify an HTTP channel listening on port 1234:

```
<channels>
   <channel ref="http" port="1234">
</channels>
```

On the client, you can specify an increased connection limit using the following section:

```
<channels>
   <channel ref="http" port="0" clientConnectionLimit="100">
</channels>
```

ClientProviders/ServerProviders

Underneath each channel property, you can configure nondefault client-side and server-side sink providers and formatter providers.

> **CAUTION**   *When any of these elements are specified, it's important to note that* no *default providers will be created by the system. This means that appending ?WSDL to the URL will only work if you explicitly specify* `<provider ref="wsdl" />`.

The .NET Remoting Framework is based on messages that travel through various layers. Those layers can be extended or replaced and additional layers can be added. (I discuss layers in more detail in Chapter 7.)

These layers are implemented using so-called message sinks. A message will pass a chain of sinks, each of which will have the possibility to work with the message's content or to even change the message.

Using the ClientProviders and ServerProviders properties in the configuration file, you can specify this chain of sinks through which you want a message to travel and the formatter with which a message will be serialized.

The structure for this property for the server side is as follows:

```
<channels>
  <channel ref="http" port="1234">
    <serverProviders>
        <formatter />
        <provider />
    </serverProviders>
  </channel>
</channels>
```

You may only have one formatter entry but several provider properties. Also note that sequence *does* matter.

The following attributes are common between formatters and providers:

ATTRIBUTE	DESCRIPTION
ref	Reference for a predefined SinkProvider ("soap", "binary", or "wsdl") or reference to a SinkProvider that has been defined in a configuration file.
type	Attribute that is mandatory when ref has not been specified. Contains the exact type (namespace, classname, assembly) of the SinkProvider's implementation. When the assembly is in the GAC, you have to specify version, culture, and public key information as well.

Here are additional attributes that are optional for formatters:

ATTRIBUTE	DESCRIPTION
includeVersions	Indicator of whether version information should be included in the requests. Takes a value of true or false (defaults to true for built-in formatters). This attribute changes behavior on the client side.
strictBinding	Indicator of whether the server will look for the exact type (including version) or any type with the given name. Takes a value of true or false (defaults to false for built-in formatters).

In addition to these attributes, both formatters and providers can accept custom attributes, as shown in the following example. You have to check the documentation of your custom sink provider for the names and possible values of such properties:

```
<channels>
  <channel ref="http" port="1234">
    <serverProviders>
      <provider type="MySinks.SampleProvider, Server" myAttribute="myValue" />
          <sampleProp>This is a Sample</sampleProp>
          <sampleProp>This is another Sample</sampleProp>
      </provider>
      <formatter ref="soap" />
    </serverProviders>
  </channel>
</channels>
```

Versioning Behavior

Depending on the setting of the includeVersion attribute on the client-side formatter and the strictBinding attribute on the server-side formatter, different methods for creating instances of the given types are employed:

INCLUDEVERSIONS	STRICTBINDING	RESULTING BEHAVIOR
true	true	The exact type is loaded, or a TypeLoadException is thrown.
false	true	The type is loaded using only the type name and the assembly name. A TypeLoadException is thrown if this type doesn't exist.
true	false	The exact type is loaded if present; if not, the type is loaded using only the type name and the assembly name. If the type doesn't exist, a TypeLoadException is thrown.
false	false	The type is loaded using only the type name and the assembly name. A TypeLoadException is thrown if this type doesn't exist.

Binary Encoding via HTTP

As you already know, the default HTTP channel will use a SoapFormatter to encode the messages. Using configuration files and the previously mentioned properties, you can easily switch to a BinaryFormatter for an HTTP channel.

On the server side, you use the following section in your configuration file:

```
<channels>
  <channel ref="http" port="1234">
    <serverProviders>
        <formatter ref="binary" />
    </serverProviders>
  </channel>
</channels>
```

Not necessary. See next page. [handwritten annotation]

And on the client side, you can take the following configuration file snippet:

```
<channels>
  <channel ref="http">
    <clientProviders>
        <formatter ref="binary" />
    </serverProviders>
  </channel>
</channels>
```

> **NOTE** *The server-side entry is not strictly necessary, because the server-side HTTP channel automatically uses both formatters and detects which encoding has been chosen at the client side.*

Service

The <service> property in the configuration file allows you to register SAOs and CAOs that will be made accessible by your server application. This section may contain a number of <wellknown> and <activated> properties.

The main structure of these entries is as follows:

```
<configuration>
    <system.runtime.remoting>
        <application>
            <service>
                <wellknown />
                <activated />
            </service>
        </application>
    </system.runtime.remoting>
</configuration>
```

Wellknown

Using the <wellknown> property in the server-side configuration file, you can specify SingleCall and Singleton objects that will be provided by your server. This property supports the same attributes that can also be specified when calling RemotingConfiguration.RegisterWellKnownServiceType(), as listed here:

ATTRIBUTE	DESCRIPTION
type	The type information of the published class in the form "<namespace>.<classname>, <assembly>". When the assembly is in the GAC, you have to specify version, culture, and public key information as well.
mode	Indicator specifying object type. Can take "Singleton" or "SingleCall".
objectUri	The endpoint URI for calls to this object. When the object is hosted in IIS (shown later in this chapter), the URI has to end with .soap or .rem to be processed correctly, as those extensions are mapped to the .NET Remoting Framework in the IIS metabase.
displayName	Optional attribute that specifies the name that will be used inside the .NET Framework Configuration Tool.

Using the following configuration file, the server will allow access to a CustomerManager object via the URI http://<host>:1234/CustomerManager.soap.

```
<configuration>
  <system.runtime.remoting>
    <application>
      <channels>
        <channel ref="http" port="1234" />
      </channels>
      <service>
        <wellknown mode="Singleton"
                   type="Server.CustomerManager, Server"
                   objectUri="CustomerManager.soap" />
      </service>

    </application>
  </system.runtime.remoting>
</configuration>
```

Activated

The <activated> property allows you to specify CAOs in the server-side configuration file. As the full URI to this object is determined by the application name, the only attribute that has to be specified is the type to be published.

ATTRIBUTE	DESCRIPTION
type	The type information of the published class in the form "<namespace>.<classname>, <assembly>". When the assembly is in the GAC, you have to specify version, culture, and public key information as well.

The following example allows a client to create an instance of MyClass at http://<hostname>:1234/.

```
<configuration>
    <system.runtime.remoting>
        <application>
            <channels>
                <channel ref="http" port="1234" />
            </channels>
            <service>
                <activated type="MyObject, MyAssembly"/>
            </service>
        </application>
    </system.runtime.remoting>
</configuration>
```

Client

The client-side counterpart to the <service> property is the <client> configuration entry. Its primary structure is designed to look quite similar to the <service> entry:

```
<configuration>
    <system.runtime.remoting>
        <application>
            <client>
                <wellknown />
                <activated />
            </client>
        </application>
    </system.runtime.remoting>
</configuration>
```

When using CAOs, the <client> property has to specify the URI to the server for all underlying <activated> entries.

> **NOTE** *When using CAOs from more than one server, you have to create several <client> properties in your configuration file.*

ATTRIBUTE	DESCRIPTION
url	The URL to the server, mandatory when using CAOs.
displayName	Attribute that is used in the .NET Framework Configuration Tool.

Wellknown

The <wellknown> property is used to register SAOs on the client and allows you to use the new operator to instantiate references to remote objects. The client-side <wellknown> entry has the same attributes as the call to Activator.GetObject(), as listed here:

ATTRIBUTE	DESCRIPTION
url	The full URL to the server's registered object.
type	Type information in the form "<namespace>.<classname>, <assembly>". When the target assembly is registered in the GAC, you have to specify version, culture, and public key information as well.
displayName	Optional attribute that is used in the .NET Framework Configuration Tool.

When registering a type to be remote, the behavior of the new operator will be changed. The framework will intercept each call to this operator and check if it's for a registered remote object. If this is the case, a reference to the server will be created instead of an instance of the local type.

When the following configuration file is in place, you can simply write CustomerManager x = new CustomerManager() to obtain a remote reference.

```
<configuration>
  <system.runtime.remoting>
    <application>

      <client>
        <wellknown type="Server.CustomerManager, Client"
                    url="http://localhost:1234/CustomerManager.soap" />
      </client>

    </application>
  </system.runtime.remoting>
</configuration>
```

Activated

This is the client-side counterpart to the <activated> property on the server. As the URL to the server has already been specified in the <client> entry, the only attribute to specify is the type of the remote object.

ATTRIBUTE	DESCRIPTION
type	The type information in the form "<namespace>.<classname>, <assembly>". When the target assembly is registered in the GAC, you have to specify version, culture, and public key information as well.

Data from this entry will also be used to intercept the call to the new operator. With a configuration file like the following, you can just write MyRemote x = new MyRemote() to instantiate a server-side CAO.

```
<configuration>
  <system.runtime.remoting>
    <application>

      <client url="http://localhost:1234/MyServer">
        <activated type="Server.MyRemote, Client" />
      </client>

    </application>
  </system.runtime.remoting>
</configuration>
```

Deployment

In contrast to some other frameworks (Java RMI, J2EE EJB, COM+, and so on), .NET Remoting allows you to choose quite freely how you want to deploy your server application. You can publish the objects in any kind of managed application—console, Windows Forms, and Windows services—or host them in IIS.

Console Applications

Deploying servers as .NET console applications is the easiest way to get started; every example up to this point has been designed to run from the console. The features are easily observable: instant debug output, and starting, stopping, and debugging is possible using the IDE.

Production applications nevertheless have different demands: when using console applications, you need to start the program after logging onto a Windows session. Other possible requirements such as logging, authentication, and encryption are hard to implement using this kind of host.

Windows Services

If you don't want to host the objects in IIS, classic Windows services are the way to go. Visual Studio .NET (and the .NET Framework in general) makes it easy for you to develop a Windows service application. It takes care of most issues, starting from the installation of the service to encapsulating the communication between the service control manager and your service application.

Integrating remoting in Windows services can also be viewed from another standpoint: when your primary concern is to write a Windows service—for example, to provide access to privileged resources, you can easily implement the communication with your clients using .NET Remoting. This is somewhat different from conventional approaches in the days before .NET, which forced you to define distinct communication channels using named pipes, sockets, or the COM ROT.

Cross-process remoting on a local machine using a TCP channel ought to be fast enough for most applications.

Porting to Windows Services

In the .NET Framework, a Windows service simply is a class that extends System.ServiceProcess.ServiceBase. You basically only have to override onStart() to do something useful.

A baseline Windows service is shown in Listing 4-5.

Listing 4-5. A Baseline Windows Service

```
using System;
using System.Diagnostics;
using System.ServiceProcess;

namespace WindowsService
{
    public class DummyService : System.ServiceProcess.ServiceBase
    {
        public static String SVC_NAME = "Some dummy service";

        public DummyService ()
        {
            this.ServiceName = SVC_NAME;
        }

        static void Main()
        {
            // start the service
            ServiceBase.Run(new DummyService());
        }

        protected override void OnStart(string[] args)
        {
            // do something meaningful
        }

        protected override void OnStop()
        {
            // stop doing anything meaningful ;)
        }
    }
}
```

A service like this will not be automatically installed in the service manager, so you have to provide a special Installer class that will be run during the execution of installutil.exe (from the .NET command prompt).

Listing 4-6 shows a basic service installer that registers the service to be run using the System account and started automatically during boot-up.

Listing 4-6. A Basic Windows Service Installer

```
using System;
using System.Collections;
using System.Configuration.Install;
using System.ServiceProcess;
using System.ComponentModel;
using WindowsService;

[RunInstallerAttribute(true)]
public class MyProjectInstaller: Installer
{
    private ServiceInstaller serviceInstaller;
    private ServiceProcessInstaller processInstaller;

    public MyProjectInstaller()
    {
        processInstaller = new ServiceProcessInstaller();
        serviceInstaller = new ServiceInstaller();

        processInstaller.Account = ServiceAccount.LocalSystem;
        serviceInstaller.StartType = ServiceStartMode.Automatic;
        serviceInstaller.ServiceName = DummyService.SVC_NAME;

        Installers.Add(serviceInstaller);
        Installers.Add(processInstaller);
    }
}
```

The installer has to be in your main assembly and has to have [RunInstallerAttribute(true)] set. After compiling the preceding C# files, you will have created a baseline Windows service that can be installed with installutil.exe.

When porting the Remoting server to become a Windows service, you might want to extend the base service to also allow it to write to the Windows event log. Therefore you have to add a static variable of type EventLog to hold an instance acquired during void Main(). As an alternative, you could also set the AutoLog property of the service and use the static method EventLog.WriteEntry().You will also have to extend onStart() to configure remoting to allow the handling of requests as specified in the configuration file. The complete source code for the Windows service–based remoting server is shown in Listing 4-7.

Listing 4-7. A Simple Windows Service to Host Your Remote Components

```
using System;
using System.Diagnostics;
using System.ServiceProcess;
using System.Runtime.Remoting;

namespace WindowsService
{
    public class RemotingService : System.ServiceProcess.ServiceBase
    {
        private static EventLog evt = new EventLog("Application");
        public static String SVC_NAME = ".NET Remoting Sample Service";

        public RemotingService()
        {
            this.ServiceName = SVC_NAME;
        }

        static void Main()
        {
            evt.Source = SVC_NAME;
            evt.WriteEntry("Remoting Service intializing");
            ServiceBase.Run(new RemotingService());
        }

        protected override void OnStart(string[] args)
        {
            evt.WriteEntry("Remoting Service started");
            String filename = "windowsservice.exe.config";
            RemotingConfiguration.Configure(filename);
        }

        protected override void OnStop()
        {
            evt.WriteEntry("Remoting Service stopped");
        }
    }
}
```

In two separate classes, you'll then provide the implementation of the MarshalByRefObject CustomerManager and an installer, following the preceding sample.

When this program is run in the IDE, you'll see the biggest disadvantage to developing windows services, the message box that will pop up, telling you that you won't get automatic debugging support from Visual Studio .NET IDE (see Figure 4-7).

Figure 4-7. Trying to start a Windows service from the IDE

> **TIP** *You can change* void Main() *to not start this application as a service, but instead call* onStart() *while debugging within the IDE.*

To install this application as a Windows service so that it can be started and stopped via the Services MMC snap-in or Server Explorer, you have to run installutil.exe, which is best done from a .NET command prompt. Running this application without the option /LogToConsole=false will produce a lot of information in case something goes wrong. You can see the command line for installing the service in Figure 4-8.

Figure 4-8. Installing a service using installutil.exe

When using configuration files with Windows services, those files have to be placed in <%WINDIR%>\System32 (normally c:\winnt\system32) to be readable by the application, as this is the service's startup directory. Alternatively you can access the configuration file from the application's installation directory using the following line of code:

```
RemotingConfiguration.Configure(
    AppDomain.CurrentDomain.SetupInformation.ConfigurationFile)
```

After successfully installing the service, you will be able to start it using the Microsoft Management Console, as shown in Figure 4-9.

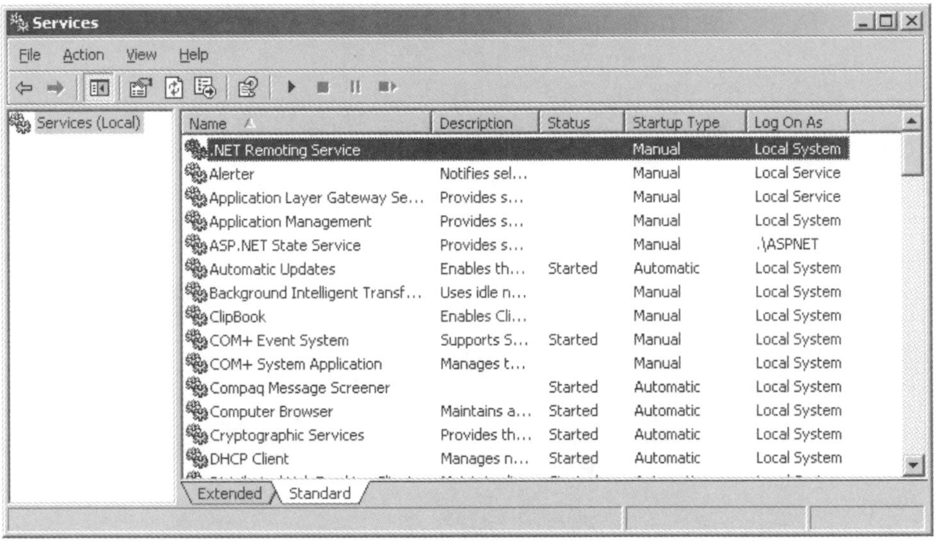

Figure 4-9. The service has been installed successfully.

After starting the service, you can see the output in the EventLog viewer, which is shown in Figure 4-10.

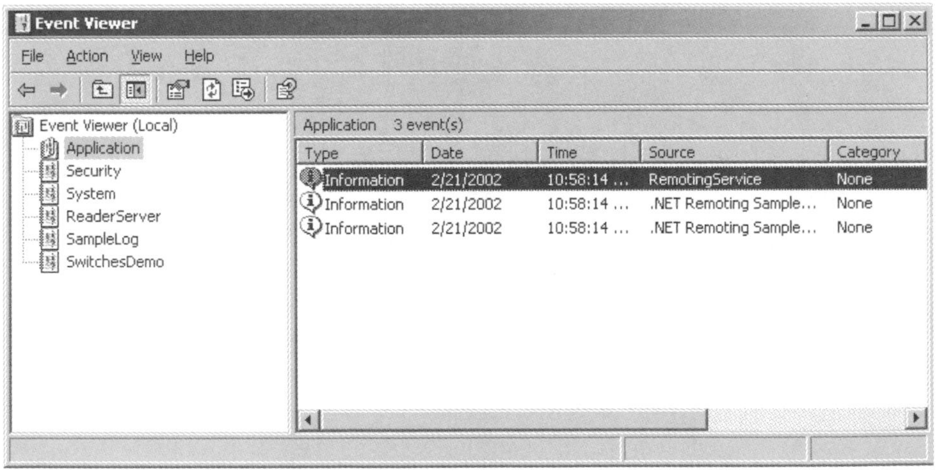

Figure 4-10. The server's output in the EventLog

You can now use the same client as in the previous example to connect to the server. After stopping it in the MMC, you can uninstall the service with the installutil.exe /U option, as show in Figure 4-11.

> **TIP** *After starting or stopping the service via MMC, the internal handle to it is not freed. When you deinstall the service, it will not be removed from the list of available services until after you close and reopen the MMC.*

Figure 4-11. Uninstalling a service using installutil.exe

Deployment Using IIS

Choosing IIS to host .NET Remoting components allows you to focus closely on application design without wasting any time with developing your own servers, authentication, and security channels, because IIS will take care of these features for you.

IIS can be configured to take care of a lot of aspects of real-world remoting. Authentication, including the use of Thread.CurrentPrincipal to employ role-based security checks, can be provided with standard Web-based methods. Depending on your architecture and security needs, either basic authentication or NT challenge/response can be chosen. Encryption can be implemented in a secure and simple way using SSL certificates, which need to be installed in IIS.

But hosting in IIS comes at a price; in particular, the performance counters won't give as high numbers as with other solutions. You'll also have to live with HTTP channel and abandon the option to switch to TCP channel, but you can still use either SOAP or binary encoding when hosting in IIS, as it is automatically configured this way!

Of course, your needs will dictate the solution to choose. If you expect several thousand calls per second, be sure to check if any version will meet your demands on the given hardware. If you're going to use the same server-side classes in your in-house LAN application and for publishing Web Services via SOAP, you can still set up a different server application using TCP channel for local use and handle the public access via IIS.

Nothing beats hosting of remote objects in IIS in terms of time to market. You just implement a MarshalByRefObject in a class library project, create a virtual directory in IISAdmin (MMC), create a virtual subdirectory called bin, and put your DLL there. You then have to create a configuration file called web.config and put this in your virtual directory. You don't even need to restart IIS when deploying your remoting components. When you want to update your server-side assembly, you can just overwrite it in the bin subdirectory, as neither the DLL nor the configuration file is locked by IIS.

When the configuration is changed by updating web.config, IIS will automatically reread this information and adopt its behavior. Moving from a staging or testing server to your production machine only involves copying this subdirectory from one host to the other. This is what Microsoft means when talking about xcopy deployment!

Designing and Developing Server-Side Objects for IIS

For the following examples, I employ the metadata approach, which I've shown you previously. I use SoapSuds with the -gc parameter to avoid namespace clashes between remote and local objects.

The server-side implementation is a little bit easier than the former ways of deployment because you only have to implement the MarshalByRefObject without any startup code for the server.

Listing 4-8 shows everything you need to code when using IIS to host your components.

Listing 4-8. Server-Side Implementation of the SAO

```
using System;
using General;

namespace Server
{
    class CustomerManager: MarshalByRefObject
    {
        public Customer getCustomer(int id)
        {
            Customer tmp = new Customer();
            tmp.FirstName = "John";
            tmp.LastName = "Doe";
```

```
        tmp.DateOfBirth = new DateTime(1970,7,4);
        return tmp;
    }
  }
}
```

After compiling this assembly to a DLL, you can proceed with setting up Internet Information Server.

Preparing Internet Information Server

Before being able to use IIS as a container for server-side objects, you have to configure several aspects of IIS. At the very least you have to create a new virtual root and set the corresponding permissions and security requirements.

Creating a Virtual Root

An IIS virtual root will allow a certain directory to be accessed using an URL. You can basically specify that the URL http://yourhost/yourdirectory will be served from c:\somedirectory, whereas the standard base URL http://yourhost/ is taken from c:\inetpub\wwwroot by default.

You create virtual roots using the MMC, which you bring up by selecting Start ➤ Programs ➤ Administrative Tools ➤ Internet Services Manager. In the Internet Services Manager you will see Default Web Site if you're running workstation software (when using server software, you'll probably see more Web sites).

Right-click Default Web Site and choose New ➤ Virtual Directory. The Virtual Directory Creation Wizard appears. Use this wizard to specify an alias and the directory it will point to. For usage as a remoting container, the default security permissions (Read and Run scripts) are sufficient.

In the directory to which the new IIS virtual directory points, you have to place your .NET Remoting configuration file. As the server will automatically watch for this file and read it, you have to call it web.config—you cannot specify a custom name.

Below this directory you can now create a folder called bin\ and place your assemblies there. As an alternative, you can place your assemblies in the GAC using gacutil.exe, but remember that you have to specify the SAO assemblies' strong names in the configuration file in this case. This is normally not recommended if your server-side DLL is just used by a single application, but is needed to provide versioning services for CAOs, as you'll see in Chapter 6.

Deployment for Anonymous Use

Before being able to convert the former example to IIS-based hosting, you have to create a new directory and an IIS virtual directory called MyServer (this will be used in the URL to the remote objects) according to the description previously given.

In the Internet Services Manager MMC, open the properties by right-clicking the newly created virtual directory, choose the Directory Security tab, and click Edit. The window shown in Figure 4-12 will open, enabling you to set the allowed authentication methods. Make sure that Allow Anonymous Access is checked.

In the configuration file, it's important that you don't specify an application name, as this property will be automatically determined by the name of the virtual directory.

> **NOTE** *When specifying channel information in a configuration file that will be used in IIS—for example, to provide a different sink chain—be sure not to include port numbers, as they will interfere with IIS' internal connection handling. When the server's load reaches a certain point, IIS may start more than one instance for handling remote object. If you have bound to a secondary port in your configuration file, this port will already be locked by the previous instance.*

```
<configuration>
  <system.runtime.remoting>
    <application>
      <service>
        <wellknown mode="Singleton"
                   type="Server.CustomerManager, Server"
                   objectUri="CustomerManager.soap" />

      </service>
    </application>
  </system.runtime.remoting>
</configuration>
```

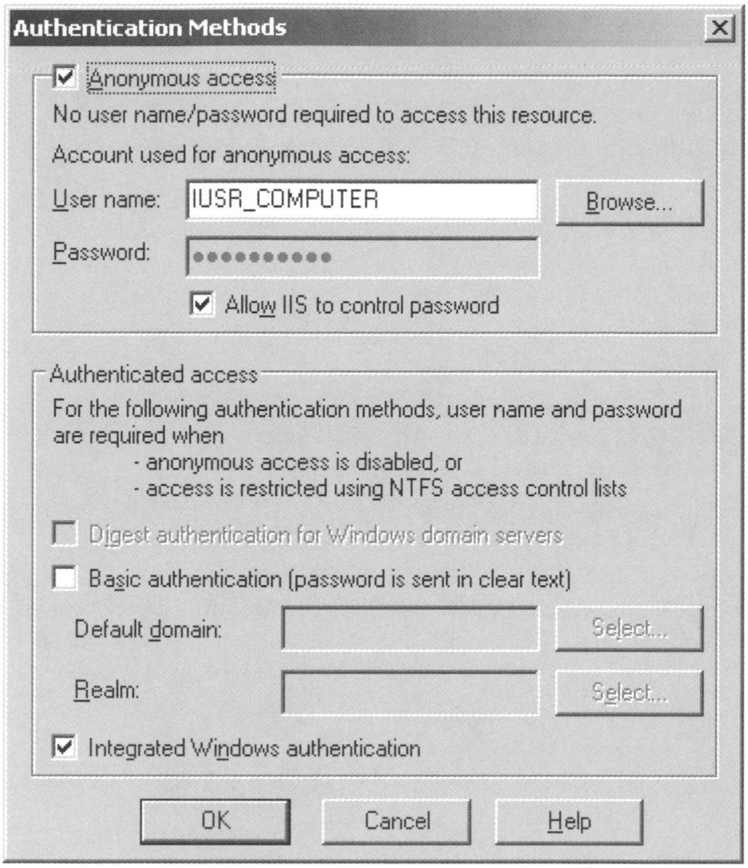

Figure 4-12. Configuring authentication methods

After putting the configuration file in your virtual directory, you have to copy the assemblies (both the shared one and the server's implementation) into its bin subdirectory. The resulting structure should be like this:

DIRECTORY	CONTENTS
x:\<path_to_your_virtual_dir>	web.config
x:\<path_to_your_virtual_dir>\bin	Assemblies that contain your remote objects and assemblies upon which your objects depend if they are not in the GAC.

The client is basically the same as in the previous examples. I use SoapSuds with the -gc and -nowp parameters to generate code for a nonwrapped proxy. From this output, I only took the server.cs and included it in the VS .NET solution.

The client itself is quite simple, as shown in Listing 4-9.

Listing 4-9. An Anonymous Client

```
using System;
using System.Runtime.Remoting;
using General;  // from General.DLL
using Server; // from server.cs

namespace Client
{
    class Client
    {
        static void Main(string[] args)
        {
            String filename = "client.exe.config";
            RemotingConfiguration.Configure(filename);

            CustomerManager mgr = new CustomerManager();

            Console.WriteLine("Client.Main(): Reference to CustomerManager " +
                              "acquired");

            Customer cust = mgr.getCustomer(4711);
            int age = cust.getAge();
            Console.WriteLine("Client.Main(): Customer {0} {1} is {2} years old.",
                cust.FirstName,
                cust.LastName,
                age);

            Console.ReadLine();
        }
    }
}
```

In contrast to the examples earlier in this chapter, the client's configuration file needs to be changed to contain the correct URL to the newly deployed components.

```
<configuration>
  <system.runtime.remoting>
    <application>

      <client>
        <wellknown type="Server.CustomerManager, Client"
                   url="http://localhost/MyServer/CustomerManager.soap" />
      </client>

    </application>
  </system.runtime.remoting>
</configuration>
```

Summary

In this chapter, you learned about the different settings that can be employed in a configuration file. You now also know why configuration files are important and why you shouldn't hard code the connection information in your .NET Remoting clients.

You know that SoapSuds -ia:<input assembly> -nowp -oa:<outputfile.DLL> will generate the necessary metadata to allow for transparent use of configuration files for all types of remote objects. I also demonstrated a possible workaround for some problems that you might encounter when using [Serializable] objects in combination with SoapSuds-generated metadata.

I showed you different deployment scenarios, including managed applications such as a console application or a windows service. You also read about the benefits of using IIS to host your remote objects.

In the next chapter, I show you how you can also use IIS to provide authenticated and encrypted access to your remote components.

Securing .NET Remoting

THIS CHAPTER SHOWS YOU HOW to leverage IIS' features when it comes to hosting your components in a secured environment. In this chapter you learn how to enable either basic HTTP sign-on or the more secure Windows-integrated authentication scheme, which is based on a challenge/response protocol. You also see how to enable encrypted access by using standard SSL certificates at the server side.

Deployment for Authenticated Use

A general problem of .NET Remoting is that the framework does not incorporate a standard means of authentication. Instead, Microsoft opened the interfaces so that any authentication (and encryption) variant can be used by implementing custom sinks and sink providers. The effort to implement these sinks may be reasonable when developing large-scale distributed applications that have to integrate with already installed third-party sign-on solutions.

For most other applications, you can use IIS to authenticate requests against Windows user accounts. This functionality is not tailored to remoting, but applies to all IIS applications, including static HTML pages and ASP.NET Web applications.

The security properties can be specified in the IIS snap-in to the MMC. You can see a "locked-down" version of the previous server in Figure 5-1.

> **CAUTION** *The* Basic Authentication *scheme, which is usable for remoting components, is* not at all secure. *Using a TCP/IP packet sniffer, one can easily capture the authentication tokens and resend them with their own requests to "impersonate" the original user. For really secure applications, encryption using SSL is highly recommended, and may even be a necessity.*

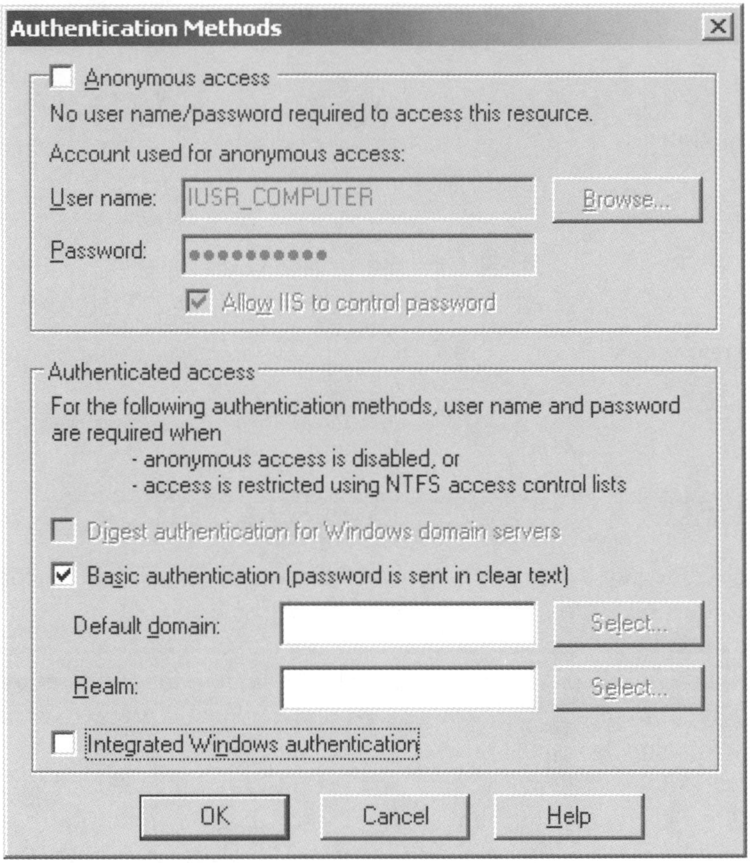

Figure 5-1. Authentication is necessary when accessing the remote objects.

When using authentication within IIS, a change in the client code is necessary to send usernames and passwords to your server. Before running the following example, you have to create a new local user called DummyRemotingUser with the password 12345 on your system.

To transfer the logon information to the server, you have to set properties on the channel sink. Unfortunately, there is no direct way to specify a valid username/password combination for a given hostname (but I'll show you how to do this using a custom sink in Chapter 9). In the meantime, you have to call the static method ChannelServices.GetChannelSinkProperties(), which takes the proxy to the remote object as a parameter. This function returns an IDictionary that allows you to set extended properties including username and password.

```
IDictionary props = ChannelServices.GetChannelSinkProperties(mgr);
props["username"] = "dummyremotinguser";
props["password"] = "12345";
```

You should also extend the client to contain code to catch possible exceptions. These can occur due to misconfigurations on the server side or when passing an incorrect username/password combination. The complete source code for an authenticated client is shown in Listing 5-1.

Listing 5-1. Client That Uses IIS' Built-In Authentication Methods

```
using System;
using System.Runtime.Remoting;
using System.Runtime.Remoting.Channels;
using System.Collections;
using System.Runtime.Remoting.Services;
using General;  // from General.DLL
using Server; // from server.cs

namespace Client
{
    class Client
    {
        static void Main(string[] args)
        {

            try
            {
                String filename = "client.exe.config";
                RemotingConfiguration.Configure(filename);

                CustomerManager mgr = new CustomerManager();

                Console.WriteLine("Client.Main(): Reference to CustomerManager " +
                            " acquired");

                IDictionary props = ChannelServices.GetChannelSinkProperties(mgr);
                props["username"] = "dummyremotinguser";
                props["password"] = "12345";

                Customer cust = mgr.getCustomer(4711);
                int age = cust.getAge();
```

```
                    Console.WriteLine("Client.Main(): Customer {0} {1} is {2} " +
                                      "years old.",
                cust.FirstName,
                cust.LastName,
                age);
        }
        catch (Exception e)
        {
            Console.WriteLine("EX: {0}",e.Message);
        }

        Console.ReadLine();
    }
  }
}
```

This client now connects to the server and authenticates the user against the specified Windows user account on the server machine. You can see in Figure 5-2 what happens when you change the password for DummyRemotingUser.

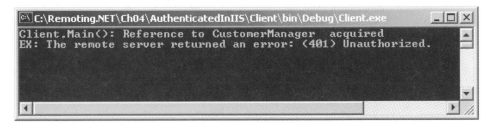

Figure 5-2. Incorrect username/password combination

Checking Roles

The approach shown in the preceding section does not yet increase security that much. Every user registered on your system or your domain will be able to access the server. What you probably want to do is only allow certain users to use your service or even assign different privileges to different users.

Using the IPrincipal interface from System.Security.Principal, you can verify the group membership of a given user. To get access to a thread's current principal, you can call System.Threading.Thread.CurrentPrincipal, as IIS sets this property when using authenticated calls. The IPrincipal's method IsInRole() allows you to check the membership of the current user in a specified Windows group.

> **TIP** *Be sure to pass not only the name of the group but also the name of your machine or domain, as in IsInRole(@"YOURMACHINE\ThisGroup") or IsInRole(@"YOURDOMAIN\ThisGroup"). You can get the name of the current computer from Environment.MachineName.*

In Listing 5-2, I show you how to extend the server to check if the remote user is in the group RemotingUsers.

> **NOTE** *You can create a group and assign users to it using the MMC (access this by right-clicking My Computer and selecting ➤ Manage, System Tools ➤ Local Users and Groups).*

Listing 5-2. Checking the Membership in Windows Groups When Hosting in IIS

```
using System;
using General;
using System.Security.Principal;

namespace Server
{
    class CustomerManager: MarshalByRefObject
    {
        public CustomerManager()
        {
            Console.WriteLine("CustomerManager.constructor: Object created");
        }

        public Customer getCustomer(int id)
        {
            String machinename = Environment.MachineName;

            IPrincipal principal =
                    System.Threading.Thread.CurrentPrincipal;

            if (! principal.IsInRole(machinename + @"\RemotingUsers"))
            {
                throw new UnauthorizedAccessException(
                        "The user is not in group RemotingUsers");
            }
```

```
Console.WriteLine("CustomerManager.getCustomer): Called");
Customer tmp = new Customer();
tmp.FirstName = "John";
tmp.LastName = "Doe";
tmp.DateOfBirth = new DateTime(1970,7,4);
Console.WriteLine("CustomerManager.getCustomer(): Returning " +
    "Customer-Object");
return tmp;
    }
  }

}
```

You can use the same client as in the earlier example with this server. Depending on the group membership of the user, you will see the output in Figure 5-3 when DummyRemotingUser is a member of RemotingUsers, or Figure 5-4 when DummyRemotingUser is not a member of this group.

> **NOTE** *Updates to group membership or users' passwords are not reflected online in IIS. You might have to either wait a little or restart IIS before such changes will take effect.*

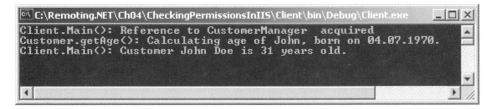

Figure 5-3. The user is in the correct group.

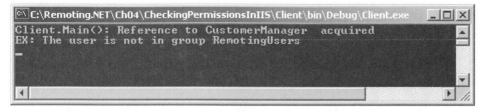

Figure 5-4. The user is not a member of the required group.

Securing the Sign-On Process

In the preceding examples, I used the so-called HTTP Basic Authentication. This enables a great deal of interoperability between various Web servers and proxies. Unfortunately, this type of authentication allows a *playback attack*, which means that someone who uses a device to monitor all network traffic can later incorporate the transferred username/password combination in his or her own requests.

When both the client and the server are based on Windows XP, 2000, or NT, you can use the Windows NT challenge/response authentication. This is a nonstandard mechanism that unfortunately does not work with all HTTP proxies. However, if it is supported by the proxies of your users, it nevertheless provides considerably higher security against playback attacks.

In this authentication scheme, the server passes a random value to the client, and this value is incorporated in its response. A playback of the password, which has been captured by watching the network packets, is therefore not possible, simply because the random value will be different.

You can switch to this authentication scheme using Internet Services Manager MMC, as shown in Figure 5-5. Neither the client's code nor the server's code has to be changed after this switch.

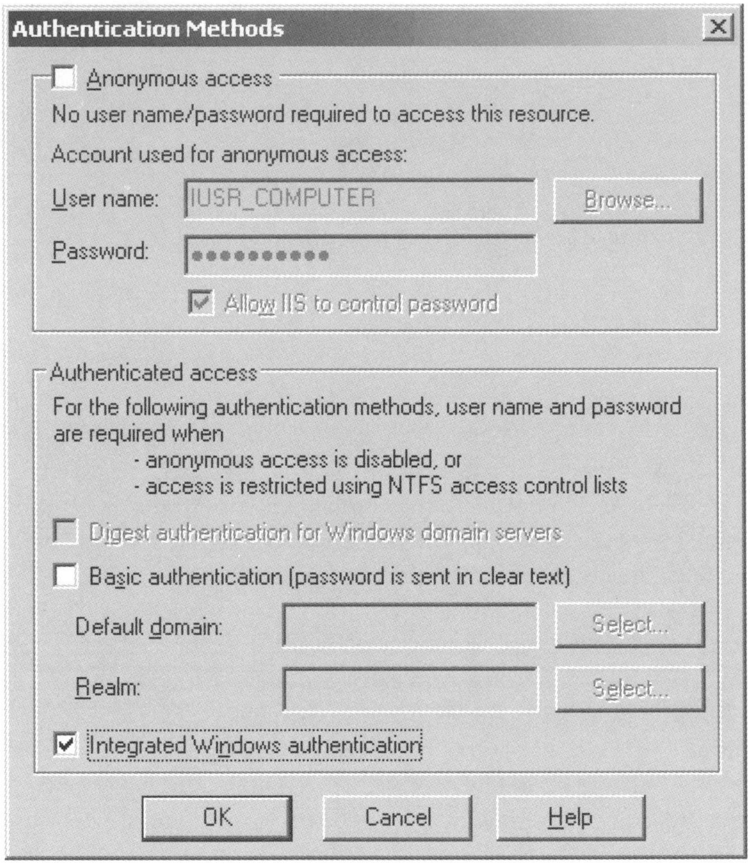

Figure 5-5. Enabling Windows authentication

> **NOTE** *You can also enable both Basic and Windows authentication at the same time. The remoting framework (as well as standard Internet Explorer) will choose the most secure method that has been announced by the server.*

Enabling Single Sign-On

When your user is authenticated against the same Windows domain in which your server is located, you finally can use integrated security. This will log your users onto the server without further need of specifying usernames or passwords.

The HTTP channel has a property called `useDefaultCredentials`. When this property is set to true via the configuration file and no username or password is specified within the ChannelSink's properties, the credentials of the currently logged-on user will be passed to the server. Because Windows 2000 can't get to a user's cleartext password, this scheme is only possible when using Windows authentication on your Web server.

When you want to switch to this authentication scheme, you just have to remove all calls to the channel sink's properties, which set the username or password, and instead include the following configuration file:

```
<configuration>
  <system.runtime.remoting>
    <application>
      <channels>
        <channel ref="http" useDefaultCredentials="true" />
      </channels>

      <client>
        <wellknown type="Server.CustomerManager, Client"
              url="http://localhost:8080/MyAuthServer/CustomerManager.soap" />
      </client>

    </application>
  </system.runtime.remoting>
</configuration>
```

Deployment for Encrypted Use

Using authentication, especially the Windows NT challenge/response authentication method, will give you a somewhat secured environment. Nevertheless, when transferring sensitive data over the Internet, authentication is just not enough—encryption needs to be applied as well.

Hosting your components in IIS gives you a head start when it comes to encryption, as you can easily leverage the built-in SSL capabilities. All it takes is installing a server-side certificate[1] and changing the URL in the client-side configuration file. After making an edit to just one line (changing "http:" to "https:"), all traffic will be secured—including the HTTP headers, authentication information, and, of course, the transferred data.

---

[1] Hint: You can get free certificates for development purposes from Verisign (www.verisign.com).

The changed configuration file looks like this:

```
<configuration>
  <system.runtime.remoting>
    <application>
      <client>
        <wellknown type="Server.CustomerManager, Client"
                   url="https://localhost/MyAuthServer/CustomerManager.soap" />
      </client>
    </application>
  </system.runtime.remoting>
</configuration>
```

SSL encryption is sometimes accused of imposing a somewhat huge overhead. This is not always true, because the "real" asymmetric cryptography only takes place during the process of establishing the secured HTTP connection. This secure connection will be reused, and the overhead thus minimized.

When testing the example in Chapter 2 using both HTTPS and HTTP, you'll see that a binary formatter via HTTPS/SSL is *faster*, and fewer bytes are transferred over the network than when using a SOAP formatter via conventional HTTP.

Summary

In this chapter, I showed you how to leverage IIS' built-in authentication and encryption feature. You now know how to set up the IIS virtual root to allow certain authentication protocols and how to check a user's role membership in your components. I also showed you how to encrypt the HTTP traffic using SSL certificates.

In the next chapter, you'll learn about some specialties of .NET Remoting. The chapter covers more advanced lifetime management issues, versioning, asynchronous calls, and events.

CHAPTER 6

In-Depth .NET Remoting

As you've already seen in the previous chapters, developers of distributed applications using .NET Remoting have to consider several fundamental differences from other remoting techniques and, of course, from the development of local applications. One of the major issues you face in any distributed object framework is the decision of how to manage an object's lifetime. Generally you have two possibilities: using distributed reference counting/garbage collection or using time-to-live counters associated with each object.

Managing an Object's Lifetime

Both CORBA and DCOM have employed distributed reference counting. With DCOM, for example, the server's objects keep counters of referrers that rely on the AddRef() and Release() methods in the same way as it's done for common COM objects. Unfortunately this has some serious drawbacks: each call to increase or decrease the reference counter has to travel to the remote object without any "real" application benefit (that is, the remote call does not do any "real" work). In DCOM, the clients will also ping the server at certain intervals to signal that they are still alive.

Both pinging and the calls to change the reference counter result in an increased network load, and the former will very likely not work with some firewalls or proxies that only allow stateless HTTP connections to pass through.

Because of those implications, Java RMI introduced a lease-based lifetime service that bears a close resemblance to what you can see in .NET Remoting today. The lease-based concept essentially assigns a time-to-live (TTL) count to each object that's created at the server. A LeaseManager then polls all server-side objects at certain intervals and decrements this TTL. As soon as this time reaches zero, the object is marked as timed out and will be marked for garbage collection. Additionally, for each method call placed on the remote object, the TTL is incremented again to ensure that objects currently in use will not time out.

In reality, though, there are applications in which objects may exist that are not used all the time. A pure TTL-based approach would time-out these objects too soon. Because of this, the .NET Remoting framework also supports a concept called *sponsorship*. For each object, one or more sponsors might be registered. Upon reaching zero TTL, the LeaseManager contacts each sponsor and asks if it wants to increase the object's lifetime. Only when none of them responds positively in a given time is the object marked for garbage collection.

A sponsor itself is a MarshalByRefObject as well. It can therefore be located on the client, the server, or any other machine that is reachable via .NET Remoting.

Understanding Leases

A *lease* holds the time-to-live information for a given object. It is therefore directly associated with a certain MarshalByRefObject's instance. At the creation of a lease, the following information is set (all of the following are of type TimeSpan):

PROPERTY	DEFAULT	DESCRIPTION
InitialLeaseTime	5 minutes	The initial TTL after an object's creation.
RenewOnCallTime	2 minutes	The grace time for a method call that is placed on the object. Mind, though, that these times are not additive—for instance, calling a method a thousand times will not result in a TTL of 2,000 minutes, but one of 2 minutes.
SponsorShipTimeout	2 minutes	When sponsors are registered for this lease, they will be contacted upon expiration of the TTL. They then can contact the LeaseManager to request additional lease time for the sponsored object. When no sponsor reacts during the time defined by this property, the lease will expire and the object will be garbage collected.

Both the ILease interface and the Lease class that provides the standard implementation are located in System.Runtime.Remoting.Lifetime. Whenever a MarshalByRefObject is instantiated (either as a CAO or as a SAO—even when using Singleton mode), the framework calls the object's `InitializeLifetimeService()` method, which will return an ILease object. In the default implementation (that is, when you don't override this method), the framework calls `LifetimeServices.GetLeaseInitial()`, which returns a Lease object containing the defaults shown in the preceding table.

> **TIP** *Whenever I mention some class for which you don't know the containing namespace, you can use WinCV.exe, which is in the Framework SDK, to locate the class and get some information about its public interface.*

The Role of the LeaseManager

The LeaseManager runs in the background of each server-side application and checks all remoted objects for their TTL. It uses a timer and a delegate that calls its LeaseTimeAnalyzer() method at certain intervals.

The initial value for this interval is set to 10 seconds. You can change this interval by using either the following line of code:

```
LifetimeServices.LeaseManagerPollTime = TimeSpan.FromSeconds(1);
```

or, when using configuration files, you can add the following settings to it:

```
<configuration>
    <system.runtime.remoting>
        <application>
            <lifetime leaseManagerPollTime="1s" />
        </application>
    </system.runtime.remoting>
</configuration>
```

You may specify different time units for the leaseManagerPollTime attribute. Valid units are D for Days, H for hours, M for minutes, S for seconds, and MS for milliseconds. When nothing is specified, the system will default to S; combinations such as "1H5M" are *not* supported.

Changing the Default Lease Time

You can easily change the default TTL for all objects in a given server-side app-domain in two ways. First, you can use the following code fragment to alter the application-wide initial lease times:

```
LifetimeServices.LeaseTime = System.TimeSpan.FromMinutes(10);
LifetimeServices.RenewOnCallTime = System.TimeSpan.FromMinutes(5);
```

As the preferred alternative, you can add the following sections to your configuration files:

```
<configuration>
    <system.runtime.remoting>
        <application>
            <lifetime
                leaseTimeout="10M"
                renewOnCallTime="5M"
            />
        </application>
    </system.runtime.remoting>
</configuration>
```

However, you have to be aware of the fact that this change affects each and every remote object that is published by this server. Increasing the TTL therefore can have negative effects toward the memory and resource utilization of your application, whereas decreasing it can lead to objects being prematurely destroyed.

> **CAUTION** *Whenever a client places a method call to a remote object with an expired TTL, an exception will be thrown.*

Changing the Lease Time on a Per-Class Basis

For certain MarshalByRefObjects (especially Singleton-mode services or objects published by `RemotingServices.Marshal()`), it is desirable to have either an "unlimited" TTL or a different lease time from that of other objects on the same server.

You can implement this functionality by overriding MarshalByRefObject's `InitializeLifetimeService()`. This method is defined to return an object, but later uses in the framework will cast this object to Lease, so make sure not to return anything else. For example, to provide, a Singleton with unlimited lifetime, implement the following:

```
class InifinitelyLivingSingleton: MarshalByRefObject
{
    public override object InitializeLifetimeService()
    {
        return null;
    }
    // . . .
}
```

To set a custom lifetime different from "infinity," you can call
base.InitializeLifetimeService() to acquire the reference to the standard
ILease object and set the corresponding values afterwards.

```
class LongerLivingSingleton: MarshalByRefObject
{

    public override object InitializeLifetimeService()
    {
        ILease tmp = (ILease) base.InitializeLifetimeService();
        if (tmp.CurrentState == LeaseState.Initial)
        {
            tmp.InitialLeaseTime = TimeSpan.FromSeconds(5);
            tmp.RenewOnCallTime = TimeSpan.FromSeconds(1);
        }
        return tmp;
    }
}
```

Examining a Basic Lifetime Example

In the following example, I show you how to implement the different changes in
an object's lifetime in one application. The server will therefore export three
MarshalByRefObjects as Singletons: DefaultLifeTimeSingleton, which will use the
"base" lifetime set by a configuration file; LongerLivingSingleton, which will override InitializeLifetimeService() to return a different lease time; and finally
InfinitelyLivingSingleton, which will just return null from
InitializeLifetimeServices().

As you can see in the following configuration file, I change the default lifetime to a considerable lower value so that you can observe the effects without having to wait five minutes until the objects time out:

```
<configuration>
  <system.runtime.remoting>
    <application>

      <channels>
        <channel ref="http" port="1234" />
      </channels>

      <lifetime
        leaseTime="10MS"
        renewOnCallTime="10MS"
        leaseManagerPollTime = "5MS"
      />

      <service>

        <wellknown mode="Singleton"
                   type="Server.DefaultLifeTimeSingleton, Server"
                   objectUri="DefaultLifeTimeSingleton.soap" />

        <wellknown mode="Singleton"
                   type="Server.LongerLivingSingleton, Server"
                   objectUri="LongerLivingSingleton.soap" />

        <wellknown mode="Singleton"
                   type="Server.InfinitelyLivingSingleton, Server"
                   objectUri="InfinitelyLivingSingleton.soap" />

      </service>
    </application>
  </system.runtime.remoting>
</configuration>
```

In the server-side implementation shown in Listing 6-1, I just include some `Console.WriteLine()` statements so that you can see when new objects are created by the framework.

Listing 6-1. Implementation Showing the Effects of Different Lifetime Settings

```
using System;
using System.Runtime.Remoting.Lifetime;
using System.Runtime.Remoting;

namespace Server
{
    class DefaultLifeTimeSingleton: MarshalByRefObject
    {

        public DefaultLifeTimeSingleton()
        {
            Console.WriteLine("DefaultLifeTimeSingleton.CTOR called");
        }

        public void doSomething()
        {
            Console.WriteLine("DefaultLifeTimeSingleton.doSomething called");
        }
    }


    class LongerLivingSingleton: MarshalByRefObject
    {

        public override object InitializeLifetimeService()
        {
            ILease tmp = (ILease) base.InitializeLifetimeService();
            if (tmp.CurrentState == LeaseState.Initial)
            {
                tmp.InitialLeaseTime = TimeSpan.FromSeconds(5);
                tmp.RenewOnCallTime = TimeSpan.FromSeconds(1);
            }
            return tmp;
        }

        public LongerLivingSingleton()
         {
            Console.WriteLine("LongerLivingSingleton.CTOR called");
        }
```

```
        public void doSomething()
        {
            Console.WriteLine("LongerLivingSingleton.doSomething called");
        }
    }

    class InfinitelyLivingSingleton: MarshalByRefObject
    {
        public override object InitializeLifetimeService()
        {
            return null;
        }
        public InfinitelyLivingSingleton()
        {
            Console.WriteLine("InfinitelyLivingSingleton.CTOR called");
        }

        public void doSomething()
        {
            Console.WriteLine("InfinitelyLivingSingleton.doSomething called");
        }
    }

    class ServerStartup
    {
        public static void Main(String[] args)
        {
            RemotingConfiguration.Configure("Server.exe.config");
            Console.WriteLine("Press <enter> to exit");
            Console.ReadLine();
        }
    }
}
```

To develop the client, you can use
soapsuds -ia:server -nowp -oa:generated_meta.dll to generate
a metadata assembly that will be referenced by the client application.
In the example shown in Listing 6-2, the different Singletons will be
called several times with varying delays.

Listing 6-2. The Client Calling the Various SAOs with Different Delays

```
using System;
using System.Runtime.Remoting;
using System.Threading;
using Server; // from generated_meta.dll

namespace Client
{
    class Client
    {
        static void Main(string[] args)
        {
            String filename = "client.exe.config";
            RemotingConfiguration.Configure(filename);

            DefaultLifeTimeSingleton def = new DefaultLifeTimeSingleton();
            LongerLivingSingleton lng = new LongerLivingSingleton();
            InfinitelyLivingSingleton inf = new InfinitelyLivingSingleton();

            /*** FIRST BLOCK ***/
            Console.WriteLine("Calling DefaultLifeTimeSingleton");
            def.doSomething();
            Console.WriteLine("Sleeping 100 msecs");
            Thread.Sleep(100);
            Console.WriteLine("Calling DefaultLifeTimeSingleton (will be new)");
            def.doSomething(); // this will be a new instance


            /*** SECOND BLOCK ***/
            Console.WriteLine("Calling LongerLivingSingleton");
            lng.doSomething();
            Console.WriteLine("Sleeping 100 msecs");
            Thread.Sleep(100);
            Console.WriteLine("Calling LongerLivingSingleton (will be same)");
            lng.doSomething(); // this will be the same instance
            Console.WriteLine("Sleeping 6 seconds");
            Thread.Sleep(6000);
            Console.WriteLine("Calling LongerLivingSingleton (will be new)");
            lng.doSomething(); // this will be a new same instance
```

```
            /*** THIRD BLOCK ***/
            Console.WriteLine("Calling InfinitelyLivingSingleton");
            inf.doSomething();
            Console.WriteLine("Sleeping 100 msecs");
            Thread.Sleep(100);
            Console.WriteLine("Calling InfinitelyLivingSingleton (will be same)");
            inf.doSomething(); // this will be the same instance
            Console.WriteLine("Sleeping 6 seconds");
            Thread.Sleep(6000);
            Console.WriteLine("Calling InfinitelyLivingSingleton (will be same)");
            inf.doSomething(); // this will be a new same instance

            Console.ReadLine();
        }
    }
}
```

In the first block, the client calls DefaultLifetimeSingleton twice. As the delay between both calls is 100 milliseconds and the object's lifetime is 10 milliseconds, a new instance of the SAO will be created.

The second block calls LongerLivingSingleton three times. Because of the increased lifetime of 5 seconds, the first two calls will be handled by the same instance. A new object will be created for the third call, which takes place after a 6-second delay.

In the last block, the client executes methods on InfinitelyLivingSingleton. Regardless of which delay is used here, the client will always talk to the same instance due to the fact that InitializeLifetimeService() returns null, which provides infinite TTL. Figures 6-1 and 6-2 prove these points.

Figure 6-1. Client-side output when dealing with different lifetimes

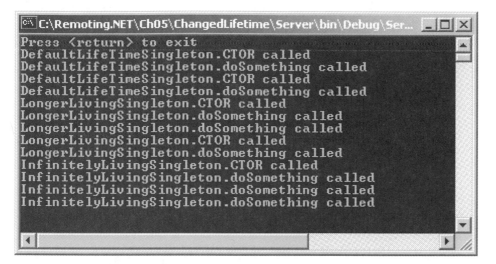

Figure 6-2. Server-side output when dealing with different lifetimes

Extending the Sample

The .NET Remoting Framework only allows the default lifetime to be changed for all objects, which might invite you to hard code changes for class-specific TTLs. The problem here is that you might not necessarily know about each possible deployment scenario when developing your server-side components, so non-default lifetimes should in reality be customizable by configuration files as well.

You can therefore change your applications to not directly derive from MarshalByRefObjects, but instead from an enhanced subtype that will check the application's configuration file to read and set changed lifetime values.

> **TIP** *I think it's good practice to use an extended form of MarshalByRefObject for your applications, as you might not always know which kind of common functionality you'll want to implement later.*

The ExtendedMBRObject, which is shown in Listing 6-3, will override `InitializeLifetimeService()` and check the appSetting entries in the configuration file for nondefault lifetime information on a class-by-class basis.

Listing 6-3. This Class Is the Base for the Following Examples

```
using System;
using System.Configuration;
using System.Runtime.Remoting.Lifetime;

namespace Server
{

    public class ExtendedMBRObject: MarshalByRefObject
    {
        public override object InitializeLifetimeService()
        {
            String myName = this.GetType().FullName;

            String lifetime =
                ConfigurationSettings.AppSettings[myName + "_Lifetime"];

            String renewoncall =
                ConfigurationSettings.AppSettings[myName + "_RenewOnCallTime"];

            String sponsorshiptimeout =
                ConfigurationSettings.AppSettings[myName + "_SponsorShipTimeout"];

            if (lifetime == "infinity")
            {
                return null;
            }
            else
            {
                ILease tmp = (ILease) base.InitializeLifetimeService();
                if (tmp.CurrentState == LeaseState.Initial)
                {
                    if (lifetime != null)
                    {
                        tmp.InitialLeaseTime =
                            TimeSpan.FromMilliseconds(Double.Parse(lifetime));
                    }

                    if (renewoncall != null)
                    {
                        tmp.RenewOnCallTime =
                            TimeSpan.FromMilliseconds(Double.Parse(renewoncall));
                    }
```

```
            if (sponsorshiptimeout != null)
            {
                tmp.SponsorshipTimeout =
                    TimeSpan.FromMilliseconds(Double.Parse(sponsorshiptimeout));
            }
        }
        return tmp;
    }
  }
}
```

In the following example, all server-side objects are changed to inherit from ExtendedMBRObject instead of MarshalByRefObject. You'll also have to remove the calls to `InitializeLifetimeService()`, as this is currently done by the super-class. You can now add the following properties for each class (all of them are optional) to the server-side configuration file:

PROPERTY	DESCRIPTION
<Typename>_Lifetime	Initial TTL in milliseconds, or "infinity"
<Typename>_RenewOnCallTime	Time to add to a method call in milliseconds
<Typename>_SponsorshipTimeout	Maximum time to react for sponsor objects

To make this example behave the same as the previous one, you can use the following server-side configuration file:

```
<configuration>
  <system.runtime.remoting>
    <application>

      <channels>
        <channel ref="http" port="5555" />
      </channels>

      <lifetime
            leaseTime="10MS"
            renewOnCallTime="10MS"
            leaseManagerPollTime = "5MS"
      />

      <service>
```

```
            <wellknown mode="Singleton"
                        type="Server.DefaultLifeTimeSingleton, Server"
                        objectUri="DefaultLifeTimeSingleton.soap" />


            <wellknown mode="Singleton"
                        type="Server.LongerLivingSingleton, Server"
                        objectUri="LongerLivingSingleton.soap" />


            <wellknown mode="Singleton"
                        type="Server.InfinitelyLivingSingleton, Server"
                        objectUri="InfinitelyLivingSingleton.soap" />


        </service>
      </application>
    </system.runtime.remoting>
    <appSettings>
      <add key="Server.LongerLivingSingleton_LifeTime" value="5000" />
      <add key="Server.LongerLivingSingleton_RenewOnCallTime" value="1000" />
      <add key="Server.InfinitelyLivingSingleton_LifeTime" value="infinity" />
    </appSettings>
</configuration>
```

When the new server is started (the client doesn't need any changes for this), you'll see the server-side output shown in Figure 6-3, which demonstrates that the changes were successful and the newly created server objects really read their lifetime settings from the configuration file.

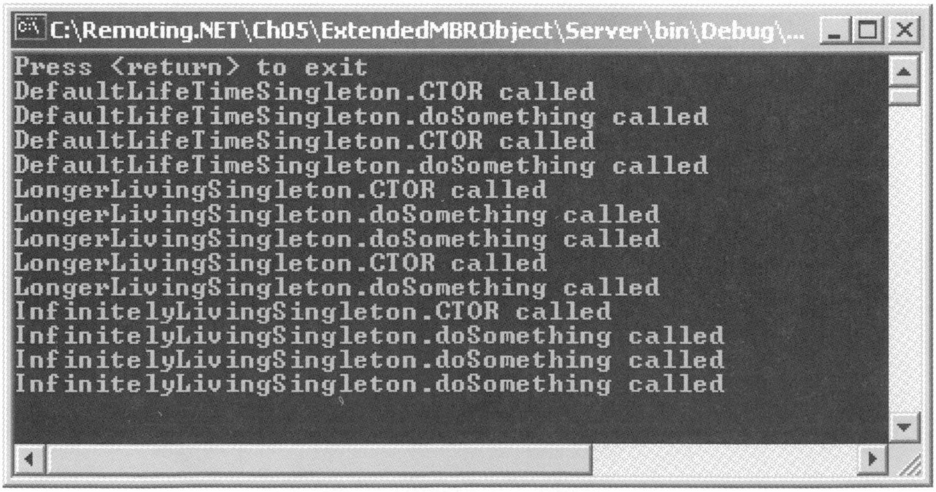

Figure 6-3. The configured server behaves as expected.

Working with Sponsors

Now that I've covered the primary aspects of lifetime management in the .NET Remoting Framework, I next show you the probably most confusing (but also most powerful) part of it: the sponsorship concept.

Whenever a remote object is created, a sponsor can be registered with it. This sponsor is contacted by the LeaseManager as soon as the object's time to live is about to expire. It then has the option to return a TimeSpan, which will be the new TTL for the remote object. When a sponsor doesn't want to extend an object's lifetime, it can simply return `TimeSpan.Zero`.

The sponsor object itself is a MarshalByRefObject that has to implement the interface ISponsor. The only other requisite for a sponsor is to be reachable by the .NET Remoting Framework. It can therefore be located either on the remoting server itself, on another server application, or on the client application.

> **CAUTION** *Beware, though, that when using client-side sponsors, the server has to be able to contact the client directly (the client becomes a server itself in this case, as it's hosting the sponsor object). When you are dealing with clients behind firewalls, this approach will not work.*

Implementing the ISponsor Interface

Sponsors have to implement the ISponsor interface, which is defined in System.Runtime.Remoting.Lifetime. It contains just one method, which will be called by the LeaseManager upon expiration of a lease's time to live.

```
public interface ISponsor
{
      TimeSpan Renewal(System.Runtime.Remoting.Lifetime.ILease lease)
}
```

The sponsor has to return a TimeSpan that specifies the new TTL for the object. If the sponsor decides not to increase the LeaseTime, it can return `TimeSpan.Zero`. A basic sponsor can look like the following:

```
public class MySponsor: MarshalByRefObject, ISponsor
{
   private bool NeedsRenewal()
   {

      // check some internal conditions
```

```
        return true;
    }

    public TimeSpan Renewal(System.Runtime.Remoting.Lifetime.ILease lease)
    {
        if (NeedsRenewal())
        {
            return TimeSpan.FromMinutes(5);
        }
        else
        {
            return TimeSpan.Zero;
        }
    }
}
```

Using Client-Side Sponsors

When using client-side sponsors, you are basically mimicking the DCOM behavior of pinging, although you have more control over the process here. After acquiring the reference to a remote object (you'll do this mostly for CAOs, as for SAOs the lifetime should normally be managed only by the server), you contact its lifetime service and register the sponsor with it.

You can get an object's LifetimeService, which will be an ILease object, using the following line of code:

```
ILease lease = (ILease) obj.GetLifetimeService();
```

The ILease interface supports a Register() method to add another sponsor for the underlying object. When you want to hold a reference to an object for an unspecified amount of time (maybe while your client application is waiting for some user input), you can register a client-side sponsor with it and increase the TTL on demand.

Calling an Expired Object's Method

In the example shown in Listing 6-4, you see the result of calling an expired object's method. This happens because the server-side lifetime is set to one second, whereas the client uses a five-second delay between two calls to the CAO. The output is shown in Figure 6-4.

Listing 6-4. Catching the Exception When Calling an Expired Object

```
using System;
using System.Runtime.Remoting;
using System.Threading;
using Server; // from generated_meta.dll

namespace Client
{

    class Client
    {
        static void Main(string[] args)
        {
            String filename = "client.exe.config";
            RemotingConfiguration.Configure(filename);

            SomeCAO cao = new SomeCAO();

            try
            {
                Console.WriteLine("{0} CLIENT: Calling doSomething()", DateTime.Now);
                cao.doSomething();
            }
            catch (Exception e)
            {
                Console.WriteLine(" -> EX: Timeout in first call\n{0}",e.Message);
            }

            Console.WriteLine("{0} CLIENT: Sleeping for 5 seconds", DateTime.Now);
            Thread.Sleep(5000);

            try
            {
                Console.WriteLine("{0} CLIENT: Calling doSomething()", DateTime.Now);
                cao.doSomething();
            }
            catch (Exception e)
            {
                Console.WriteLine(" -> EX: Timeout in second call\n{0}",e.Message );
            }
```

```
            Console.WriteLine("Finished ... press <return> to exit");
            Console.ReadLine();
        }
    }
}
```

```
C:\Remoting.NET\Ch05\ClientSideSponsoring\ProblematicClient\bin\Debug\Client.exe          _ □ ×
09.12.2001 15:46:34 CLIENT: Calling doSomething()
09.12.2001 15:46:34 CLIENT: Sleeping for 5 seconds
09.12.2001 15:46:39 CLIENT: Calling doSomething()
 --> EX: Timeout in second call
Object </a02b8c9a_9f00_47cd_a8c2_6ca4c105ab26/13039499_1.rem> has been disconnec
ted or does not exist at the server.
Finished ... press <return> to exit
```

Figure 6-4. You've been calling an expired object's method.

There are two ways of correcting this application's issues. First, you can simply increase the object's lifetime on the server as shown in the previous examples. In a lot of scenarios, however, you won't know which TTL will be sufficient. Just imagine an application that acquires a reference to a CAO and will only call another method of this object after waiting for user input. In this case, it might be desirable to add a client-side sponsor to your application and register it with the CAO's lease.

As the first step in enabling your application to work with client side sponsors, you have to include a port="" attribute in the channel section of the configuration file. Without this attribute, the channel will not accept callbacks from the server.

Because you might not know which port will be available at the client, you can supply a value of 0, which allows the .NET Remoting Framework to choose a free port on its own. When the sponsor is created and passed to the server, the channel information that gets passed to the remote process will contain the correct port number.

```
<configuration>
  <system.runtime.remoting>
    <application>
      <channels>
        <channel ref="http" port="0" />
      </channels>
```

```
        <client url="http://localhost:5555/SomeServer" >
                <activated type="Server.SomeCAO, generated_meta" />
        </client>

    </application>
  </system.runtime.remoting>
</configuration>
```

In the client's code, you then add another class that implements ISponsor. To see the exact behavior of the client-side sponsor, you might also want to add a boolean flag that indicates whether the lease time should be extended or not.

```
public class MySponsor: MarshalByRefObject, ISponsor
{

    public bool doRenewal = true;

    public TimeSpan Renewal(System.Runtime.Remoting.Lifetime.ILease lease)
    {
        Console.WriteLine("{0} SPONSOR: Renewal() called", DateTime.Now);

        if (doRenewal)
        {
            Console.WriteLine("{0} SPONSOR: Will renew (10 secs)", DateTime.Now);
            return TimeSpan.FromSeconds(10);
        }
        else
        {
            Console.WriteLine("{0} SPONSOR: Won't renew further", DateTime.Now);
            return TimeSpan.Zero;
        }
    }
}
```

In Listing 6-5 you can see a client application that registers this sponsor with the server object's lease. When the application is ready to allow the server to destroy the instance of the CAO, it will tell the sponsor to stop renewing. Normally you would call Lease.Unregister() instead, but in this case I want to show you that the sponsor won't be contacted further after returning TimeSpan.Zero to the lease manager.

Listing 6-5. Registering the Sponsor to Avoid Premature Termination of the Object

```csharp
using System;
using System.Runtime.Remoting;
using System.Runtime.Remoting.Lifetime;
using System.Threading;
using Server; // from generated_meta.dll

class Client
{
    static void Main(string[] args)
    {
        String filename = "client.exe.config";
        RemotingConfiguration.Configure(filename);

        SomeCAO cao = new SomeCAO();
        ILease le = (ILease) cao.GetLifetimeService();
        MySponsor sponsor = new MySponsor();
        le.Register(sponsor);

        try
        {
            Console.WriteLine("{0} CLIENT: Calling doSomething()", DateTime.Now);
            cao.doSomething();
        }
        catch (Exception e)
        {
            Console.WriteLine(" -> EX: Timeout in first call\n{0}",e.Message);
        }

        Console.WriteLine("{0} CLIENT: Sleeping for 5 seconds", DateTime.Now);
        Thread.Sleep(5000);

        try
        {
            Console.WriteLine("{0} CLIENT: Calling doSomething()", DateTime.Now);
            cao.doSomething();
        }
        catch (Exception e)
        {
            Console.WriteLine(" -> EX: Timeout in second call\n{0}",e.Message );
        }

        Console.WriteLine("{0} CLIENT: Telling sponsor to stop", DateTime.Now);
        le.UnRegister(sponsor);
```

```
        Console.WriteLine("Finished ... press <return> to exit");
        Console.ReadLine();
    }
}
```

When you run this application, you will see the output in Figure 6-5 at the client.

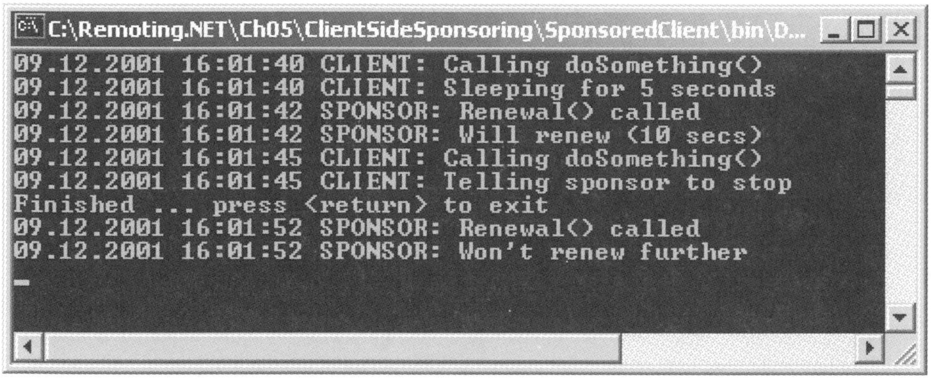

Figure 6-5. Client-side output when using a sponsor

As you can see in this figure, during the time the main client thread is sleeping for five seconds, the sponsor is contacted by the server. It renews the lease for another ten seconds. Later the sponsor is contacted again but denies the renewal (because the doRenewal field has been set to false). At this time the server-side object will expire.

Instead of telling the sponsor to stop the renewal with a flag, you normally "unregister" it from the lease. You can do this using the following line of code at the point where you're ready to allow the server to destroy the object:

```
le.Unregister(sponsor);
```

> **CAUTION** *When you decide to use client-side sponsors, you have to make sure that the client is reachable by the server. Whenever you are dealing with clients that may be located behind firewalls or proxies, you have to choose another approach!*

Using Server-Side Sponsors

Server-side sponsors that are running in the same process as the target CAOs can constitute a solution to the preceding problem, but you have keep in mind several things to make your application run stably.

First, remote sponsors are MarshalByRefObjects themselves. Therefore, they also have an assigned lifetime, and you may want to manage this yourself to provide a consistent behavior. Generally you will want your server-side sponsor to be active as long as the client application is "online." You nevertheless will have to make sure that the resources will be freed as soon as possible after the client application is ended.

One possible approach is to continuously send a command to the sponsors so that they stay alive. This can be accomplished with a simple KeepAlive() method that is called periodically from a background thread of the client application.

Another thing to watch out for is that the sponsor will be called from the .NET Remoting framework's LeaseManager. This call might well *increase* the time to live of your sponsor, depending on the RenewOnCallTime set in the configuration file. Without taking special care here, you might end up with sponsors that keep running forever when Unregister() has not been called correctly for each and every sponsored object. This could happen, for example, when the client application crashes or experiences a network disconnect.

To remove this potential problem, I suggest you add a DateTime instance variable that holds the time of the last call to the sponsor's KeepAlive() method. When the LeaseManager calls Renew(), the difference between the current time and the last time KeepAlive() has been called will be checked, and the sponsored object's lease will only be renewed when the interval is below a certain limit. As soon as all objects that are monitored by this sponsor are timed out, no further calls will be placed to the sponsor itself, and its own lease will therefore expire as well.

In the following example, I used very short lease times to show you the implications in greater detail. In production applications, you should probably keep this in the range of the default TTL, which is five minutes. The source code in Listing 6-6 shows you the implementation of a sponsor that supports the described functionality.

Listing 6-6. The Server-Side Sponsor That Is Pinged by the Client

```
using System;
using System.Runtime.Remoting.Lifetime;
using System.Runtime.Remoting;
using Server; // for ExtendedMBRObject

namespace Sponsors
{
    public class InstanceSponsor: ExtendedMBRObject, ISponsor
    {
        public DateTime lastKeepAlive;

        public InstanceSponsor()
        {
            Console.WriteLine("{0} SPONSOR: Created ", DateTime.Now);
            lastKeepAlive = DateTime.Now;
        }

        public void KeepAlive()
        {
            Console.WriteLine("{0} SPONSOR: KeepAlive() called", DateTime.Now);
            // tracks the time of the last keepalive call
            lastKeepAlive = DateTime.Now;
        }

        public TimeSpan Renewal(System.Runtime.Remoting.Lifetime.ILease lease)
        {
            Console.WriteLine("{0} SPONSOR: Renewal() called", DateTime.Now);

            // keepalive needs to be called at least every 5 seconds
            TimeSpan duration = DateTime.Now.Subtract(lastKeepAlive);
            if (duration.TotalSeconds < 5)
            {
                Console.WriteLine("{0} SPONSOR: Will renew (10 secs) ",
                        DateTime.Now);
                return TimeSpan.FromSeconds(10);
            }
            else
            {
                Console.WriteLine("{0} SPONSOR: Won't renew further", DateTime.Now);
                return TimeSpan.Zero;
            }
        }
    }
}
```

When employing the following configuration file, the sponsor will act like this: a call to KeepAlive() is needed at least every five seconds (determined from the call's time of arrival at the server, so you better call it more often from your client). When this call is received, lastKeepAlive is set to the current time using DateTime.Now and (due to the RenewOnCall time set in the configuration file) its own lease time will be increased to five seconds as well.

Whenever the LeaseManager asks for a renewal, the sponsor will compare the current time to lastKeepAlive, and only when the difference is fewer than five seconds will it extend the sponsored object's lease.

```
<configuration>
  <system.runtime.remoting>
    <application name="SomeServer">

      <channels>
        <channel ref="http" port="5555" />
      </channels>

      <lifetime
          leaseTime="1S"
          renewOnCallTime="1S"
          leaseManagerPollTime = "100MS"
      />

      <service>
        <activated type="Server.SomeCAO, Server" />
        <activated type="Sponsors.InstanceSponsor, Server" />
      </service>

    </application>
  </system.runtime.remoting>
  <appSettings>
    <add key="Sponsors.InstanceSponsor_Lifetime" value="5000" />
    <add key="Sponsors.InstanceSponsor_RenewOnCallTime" value="5000" />
  </appSettings>
</configuration>
```

> **NOTE** *The preceding sample only works with the ExtendedMBRObject shown earlier in this chapter.*

As this sponsor's KeepAlive() method needs to be called at regular intervals, you have to add another class to the client application. It will spawn a new thread that periodically calls the sponsor. This class takes an InstanceSponsor object as a constructor parameter and will call the server every three seconds until its StopKeepAlive() method is called.

```
class EnsureKeepAlive
{
    private bool _keepServerAlive;
    private InstanceSponsor _sponsor;

    public EnsureKeepAlive(InstanceSponsor sponsor)
    {
        _sponsor = sponsor;
        _keepServerAlive = true;
        Console.WriteLine("{0} KEEPALIVE: Starting thread()", DateTime.Now);
        Thread thrd = new Thread(new ThreadStart(this.KeepAliveThread));
        thrd.Start();
    }

    public void StopKeepAlive()
    {
        _keepServerAlive= false;
    }

    public void KeepAliveThread()
    {
        while (_keepServerAlive)
        {
            Console.WriteLine("{0} KEEPALIVE: Will KeepAlive()", DateTime.Now);
            _sponsor.KeepAlive();
            Thread.Sleep(3000);
        }
    }
}
```

When implementing this concept in a client application, you again have to run soapsuds -ia:server -nowp -oa:generated_meta.dll and add the newly created CAO to your client-side configuration file:

```
<activated type="Sponsors.InstanceSponsor, generated_meta" />
```

In the application itself, you have to add calls to create the server-side sponsor and to start the client-side keepalive thread:

```
SomeCAO cao = new SomeCAO();

ILease le = (ILease) cao.GetLifetimeService();
InstanceSponsor sponsor = new InstanceSponsor();

// starting the keepalive thread
EnsureKeepAlive keepalive = new EnsureKeepAlive(sponsor);

// registering the sponsor
le.Register((ISponsor) sponsor);

// ... rest of implementation removed
```

When you are finished using the CAO, you have to unregister the sponsor using `ILease.Unregister()` and stop the keepalive thread:

```
((ILease) cao.GetLifetimeService()).Unregister((ISponsor) sponsor);
keepalive.StopKeepAlive();
```

Even though in the preceding example I just used a single CAO, you can register this sponsor with multiple leases for different CAOs at the same time. When you run this application, you'll see the output shown in Figures 6-6 and 6-7 on the client and the server, respectively.

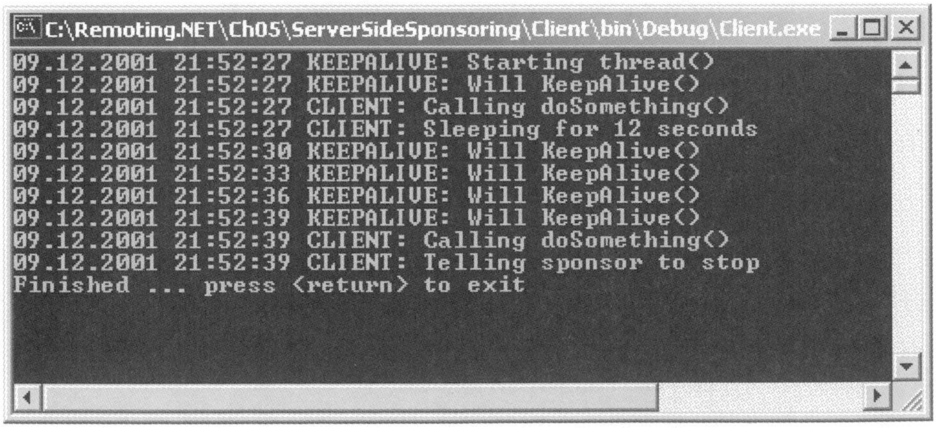

Figure 6-6. Client-side output when running with server-side sponsors

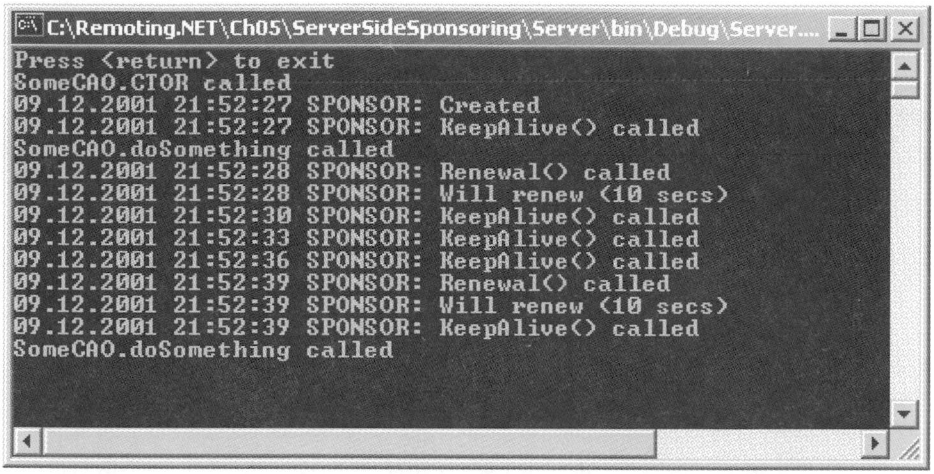

Figure 6-7. Server side output when running with server-side sponsors

In both figures, you can see that KeepAlive() is called several times while the client's main thread is sleeping. The server-side sponsor renews the lease two times before it's finally about to expire.

To see if the application behaves correctly when a client "crashes" while holding instances of the remote object, you can just kill the client after some calls to KeepAlive() and look at the server-side output, which is shown in Figure 6-8.

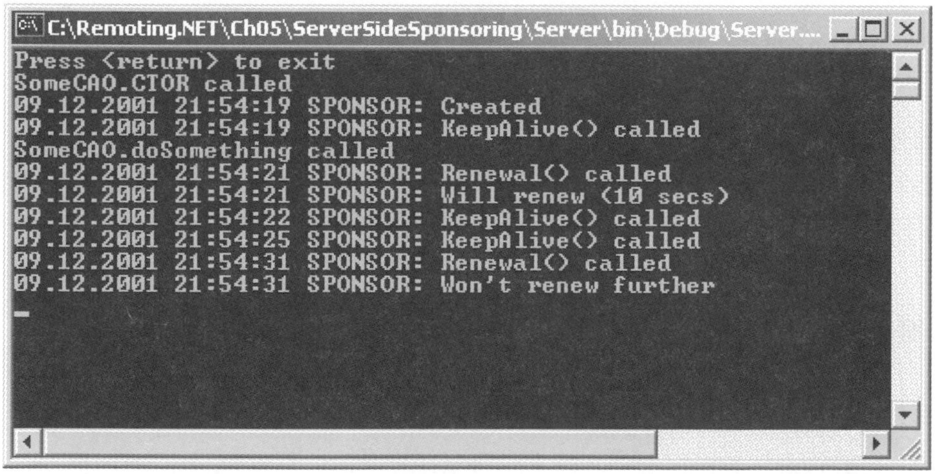

Figure 6-8. Server-side output when the client is stopped during execution

Here you can see that the sponsor processed three calls to KeepAlive() before the client stopped pinging. It received the call to Renewal() more than five seconds later than the last call to KeepAlive(), and therefore refused to further prolong the object's lease time. Hence you can be sure that both objects (the CAO and its sponsor) are timed out and correctly marked for garbage collection.

The Ins and Outs of Versioning

In most distributed applications, it's of uttermost importance to look at the application's lifecycle right from the beginning. You might have to ensure that your already deployed clients will keep working, even when your server is available in newer versions and will be providing more functionality.

Generally speaking, .NET Remoting supports the base .NET versioning services, which also implies that you have to use strong names for versioning of CAOs or serializable objects, for example. Nevertheless, in details the means of lifecycle management differ quite heavily between .NET Remoting and common .NET versioning and also differ between the various types of remoteable objects.

Versioning of Server-Activated Objects

As SAOs are instantiated on demand by the server itself, there is no direct way of managing their lifecycle. The client cannot specify to which version of a given SAO a call should be placed. The only means for supporting different versions of a SAO is to provide different URLs for them. In this case, you would have to tell your users about the new URL in other ways, as no direct support of versioning is provided in the framework.

Depending on your general architecture, you may want to place SAOs in a different assembly *or* have them in two strong named assemblies that differ only in the version number. In the remoting configuration file, you can specify which version of a SAO is published using which URL.

A Short Introduction to Strong Naming

The .NET Framework can resolve assemblies in two different ways: by assembly name, in which case the DLL has to be in the application's directory (xcopy deployed); or by a *strong name* used when the assembly is installed in the Global Assembly Cache (GAC).

A strong name consists of the assembly's name, version, culture information, and a *fingerprint* from the publisher's public/private key pair. This scheme is used to identify an assembly "without doubt," because even though another person could possibly create an assembly having the same name, version, and culture information, only the owner of the correct key pair can *sign* the assembly and provide the correct fingerprint.

Creation of a Strong Named Assembly

To generate a key pair to later sign your assemblies with, you have to use sn.exe with the following syntax:

```
sn.exe -k <keyfile>
```

> **NOTE** *All command-line tools should be accessed from the Visual Studio .NET command prompt, which is located in Start ➤ Programs ➤ Microsoft Visual Studio .NET ➤ Visual Studio.NET Tools. This version of the command prompt will set the environment variables that are needed for the use of these tools.*

For example, to create a key pair that will be stored in the file mykey.key, you can run sn.exe as shown in Figure 6-9.

> **CAUTION** *You absolutely* have to keep this key secret. If someone else *acquires your key, he or she can sign assemblies in your name. When using a publisher-based security scheme, this might compromise your enterprise security measures.*

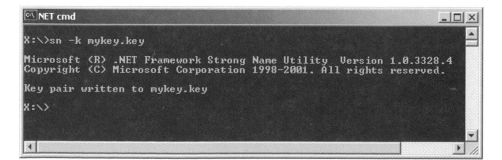

Figure 6-9. Running sn.exe to generate a key pair

When you want to generate a strong named assembly, you have to put some attributes in your source files (or update them when using VS.NET, which already includes those attributes in the file AssemblyInfo.cs, which is by default added to every project):

```
using System.Reflection;
using System.Runtime.CompilerServices;

[assembly: AssemblyCulture("")]
[assembly: AssemblyVersion("1.0.0.1")]
[assembly: AssemblyDelaySign(false)]
[assembly: AssemblyKeyFile("mykey.key")]
```

As the `AssemblyVersion` attribute defaults to "1.0.*"[1] in VS .NET, you'll have to change this to allow for definite assignment of version numbers for your components. Make sure, though, to change it whenever you distribute a new version of your DLL.

The attribute `AssemblyKeyFile` has to point to the file generated by sn.exe. When using Visual Studio .NET you have to place it in the directory that contains your project file (<project>.csproj for C# projects).

Upon compilation of this project, no matter whether you're using VS .NET or the command-line compilers, the keyfile will be used to sign the assembly, and you'll end up with a strong named assembly that can be installed in the GAC.

Installation in the GAC

To manipulate the contents of the GAC, you can either use Explorer to drag and drop your assemblies to %WINDOWS%\Assembly or use GacUtil from the .NET Framework SDK. Here are the parameters you'll use most:

PARAMETER	DESCRIPTION
/i <assemblyname>	Installs the specified assembly in the GAC. <Assemblyname> has to include the extension (.DLL or .EXE).
/l [<filter>]	Lists the contents of the GAC. If <filter> is present, only assemblies matching the filter will be listed.
/u <assembly>	Unregisters and removes a given assembly from the GAC. When <Assembly> contains a *weak name* (that is, it contains only the assembly's name), *all* versions of this assembly will be uninstalled. When using a strong name, only the matching assembly will be removed from the GAC.

---

[1] The * in this case means that this part of the version number is assigned automatically.

Lifecycle of a Versioned SAO

Lifecycle management for a SAO becomes an issue as soon as you change some of its behavior and want currently available clients that use the older version to continue working.

In the following example, I show you how to create a SAO that's placed in a strong named assembly. You then install the assembly in the GAC and host the SAO in IIS. The implementation of the first Version 1.0.0.1, shown in Listing 6-7, returns a string that later shows you which version of the SAO has been called.

Listing 6-7. Version 1.0.0.1 of the Server

```csharp
using System;
using System.Runtime.Remoting.Lifetime;
using System.Runtime.Remoting;
using System.Reflection;
using System.Runtime.CompilerServices;

[assembly: AssemblyCulture("")] // default
[assembly: AssemblyVersion("1.0.0.1")]
[assembly: AssemblyDelaySign(false)]
[assembly: AssemblyKeyFile("mykey.key")]

namespace VersionedSAO
{
    public class SomeSAO: MarshalByRefObject
    {
        public String getSAOVersion()
        {
            return "Called Version 1.0.0.1 SAO";
        }
    }
}
```

After compilation, you have to put the assembly in the GAC using gacutil.exe /i as shown in Figure 6-10.

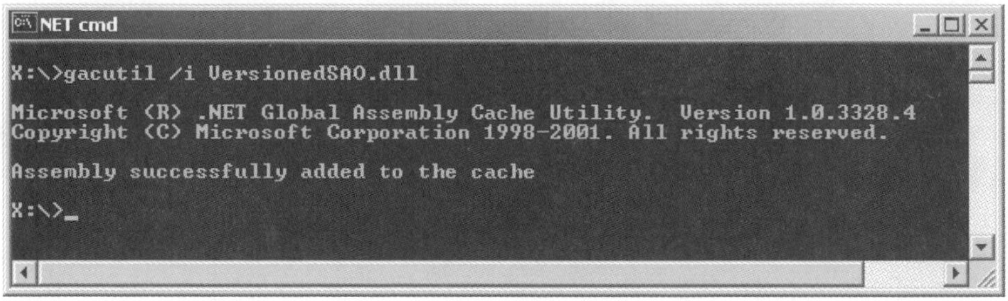

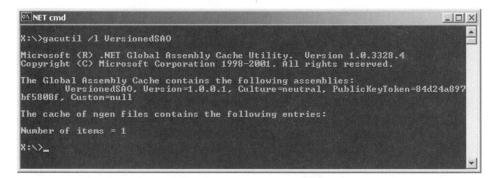

Figure 6-10. Registering the first version in the GAC

This DLL does not have to be placed in the bin/ subdirectory of the IIS virtual directory but is instead loaded directly from the GAC. You therefore have to put the complete strong name in web.config.

You can use gacutil.exe /l <assemblyname> to get the strong name for the given assembly as is shown in Figure 6-11.

Figure 6-11. Displaying the strong name for an assembly

When editing web.config, you have to put the assembly's strong name in the type attribute of the <wellknown> entry:

```
<configuration>
  <system.runtime.remoting>
    <application>
      <service>
        <wellknown mode="Singleton"
            type="VersionedSAO.SomeSAO,
    VersionedSAO, Version=1.0.0.1,Culture=neutral,PublicKeyToken=84d24a897bf5808f"
            objectUri="MySAO.soap" />
```

```
        </service>
      </application>
    </system.runtime.remoting>
</configuration>
```

> **NOTE** *The type entry may only be line-wrapped between the class name and the assembly's strong name—no breaks are allowed* within *the name!*

Building the First Client

For the implementation of the client, you can extract the metadata using SoapSuds:

```
soapsuds-ia:VersionedSAO -nowp -oa:generated_meta_V1_0_0_1.dll
```

In the following example, I show you the implementation of a basic client that contacts the SAO and requests version information using the getSAOVersion() method. After setting a reference to generated_meta_V1_0_0_1.dll, you can compile the source code shown in Listing 6-8.

Listing 6-8. Version 1.0.0.1 of the Client Application

```
using System;
using System.Runtime.Remoting;
using System.Runtime.Remoting.Lifetime;
using System.Threading;
using VersionedSAO; // from generated_meta_xxx.dll

namespace Client
{
    class Client
    {
        static void Main(string[] args)
        {
            String filename = "client.exe.config";
            RemotingConfiguration.Configure(filename);

            SomeSAO obj = new SomeSAO();
            String result = obj.getSAOVersion();

            Console.WriteLine("Result: {0}",result);
```

```
                  Console.WriteLine("Finished ... press <return> to exit");
                  Console.ReadLine();
               }
           }
}
```

As the metadata assembly (generated_meta_V1_0_0_1.dll) does not have to be accessed using its strong name, the configuration file for the client looks quite similar to the previous examples:

```
<configuration>
  <system.runtime.remoting>
    <application>

        <client>
           <wellknown
               type="VersionedSAO.SomeSAO, generated_meta_V1_0_0_1"
               url="http://localhost/VersionedSAO/MySAO.soap" />
        </client>

    </application>
  </system.runtime.remoting>
</configuration>
```

When this client is started, you will see the output shown in Figure 6-12.

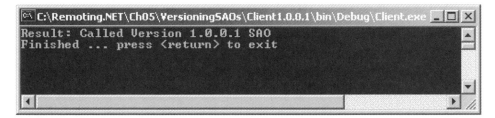

Figure 6-12. Output of the client using the v1.0.0.1 SAO

Enhancing the Server

Assume you now want to improve the server with the implementation of additional application requirements that might break your existing clients. To allow them to continue working correctly, you will have to let the clients choose which version of the SAO they want to access.

In the new server's implementation, shown in Listing 6-9, you first have to change the `AssemblyVersion` attribute to reflect the new version number, and you will also want to change the server's only method to return a different result than that of the v1.0.0.1 server.

> **NOTE** *When compiling the project, you will use the exactly same keyfile (mykey.key) for generating the assembly's strong name!*

Listing 6-9. The New Version 2.0.0.1 of the Server
```
using System;
using System.Runtime.Remoting.Lifetime;
using System.Runtime.Remoting;
using System.Reflection;
using System.Runtime.CompilerServices;

[assembly: AssemblyCulture("")] // default
[assembly: AssemblyVersion("2.0.0.1")]
[assembly: AssemblyDelaySign(false)]
[assembly: AssemblyKeyFile("mykey.key")]

namespace VersionedSAO
{
    public class SomeSAO: MarshalByRefObject
    {
        public String getSAOVersion()
        {
            return "Called Version 2.0.0.1 SAO";
        }
    }
}
```

After compiling and installing the assembly in the GAC using GacUtil, you can list the contents of the assembly cache as shown in Figure 6-13.

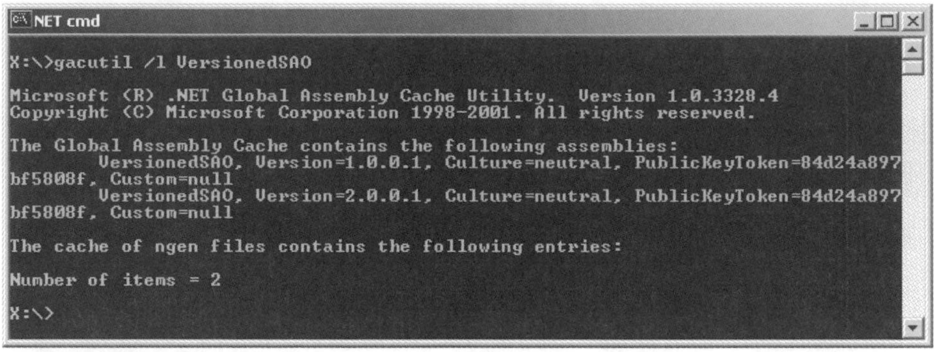

Figure 6-13. GAC contents after installing the second assembly

To allow a client to connect to either the old or the new assembly, you have to include a new <wellknown> entry in web.config that also points to the newly created SAO and uses a different URL:

```
<configuration>
  <system.runtime.remoting>
    <application>
      <service>

        <wellknown mode="Singleton"
            type="VersionedSAO.SomeSAO,
  VersionedSAO, Version=1.0.0.1,Culture=neutral,PublicKeyToken=84d24a897bf5808f"
            objectUri="MySAO.soap" />

        <wellknown mode="Singleton"
            type="VersionedSAO.SomeSAO,
  VersionedSAO, Version=2.0.0.1,Culture=neutral,PublicKeyToken=84d24a897bf5808f"
            objectUri="MySAO_V2.soap" />

      </service>
    </application>
  </system.runtime.remoting>
</configuration>
```

Developing the New Client

To allow a client application to access the second version of the SAO, you again have to generate the necessary metadata using SoapSuds:

```
soapsuds -ia:VersionedSAO -nowp -oa:generated_meta_V2_0_0_1.dll
```

After adding the reference to the newly generated metadata assembly, you also have to change to the client-side configuration file to point to the new URL:

```
<configuration>
  <system.runtime.remoting>
    <application>
      <client>
        <wellknown
                  type="VersionedSAO.SomeSAO, generated_meta_V2_0_0_1"
                  url="http://localhost/VersionedSAO/MySAO_V2.soap" />
      </client>

    </application>
  </system.runtime.remoting>
</configuration>
```

You can now start both the new and the old client to get the outputs shown in Figure 6-14 for the first version and in Figure 6-15 for the second.

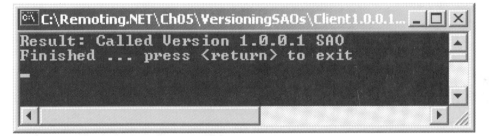

Figure 6-14. Version 1 client running

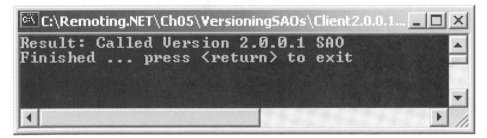

Figure 6-15. Version 2 client running

Both clients are running side by side at the same time, accessing the same physical server. You can also see that there was no change needed to the first client, which is the primary requisite for consistent lifecycle management.

Versioning of Client-Activated Objects

Now that you know about the lifecycle management issues with SAOs, I have to tell you that versioning of CAOs is completely different. But first, let's start with a more general look at the creation of Client Activated Objects.

When CAOs are instantiated by the client (using the new operator or Activator.CreateInstance), a ConstructionCallMessage is sent to the server. In this message, the client passes the name of the object it wants to be created to the server-side process. It also includes the strong name (if available) of the assembly in which the server-side object is located. This version information is stored in the [SoapType()] attribute of the SoapSuds-generated assembly. SoapSuds does this automatically whenever the assembly, passed to it with the -ia parameter, is strong named.

Let's have a look at the C# source shown in Listing 6-10, which is generated by soapsuds -ia -nowp -gc from a simplistic CAO. I've inserted several line breaks to enhance its readability:

Listing 6-10. The SoapSuds-Generated Nonwrapped Proxy's Source

```
using System;
using System.Runtime.Remoting.Messaging;
using System.Runtime.Remoting.Metadata;
using System.Runtime.Remoting.Metadata.W3cXsd2001;
namespace Server {

[Serializable,
SoapType(SoapOptions=SoapOption.Option1|
SoapOption.AlwaysIncludeTypes|SoapOption.XsdString|
SoapOption.EmbedAll,

XmlNamespace="http://schemas.microsoft.com/clr/nsassem/Server/Server%2C%20
Version%3D2.0.0.1%2C%20Culture%3Dneutral%2C%20PublicKeyToken%3D84d24a897bf
5808f",
XmlTypeNamespace="http://schemas.microsoft.com/clr/nsassem/Server/Server%2
C%20Version%3D2.0.0.1%2C%20Culture%3Dneutral%2C%20PublicKeyToken%3D84d24a8
97bf5808f")]

    public class SomeCAO : System.MarshalByRefObject
    {
```

```
[SoapMethod(SoapAction=
"http://schemas.microsoft.com/clr/nsassem/Server.SomeCAO/Server#doSomething")]
    public void doSomething()
    {
        return;
    }


}
}
```

The strings in the XmlNamespace and XmlTypeNamespace attributes are
URLEncoded variants of the standard version information. In plain text, they
read as follows (omitting the base namespace):

Server, Version=2.0.0.1, Culture=neutral, PublicKeyToken= 84d24a897bf5808f

Doesn't look that scary anymore? In fact, this is the common .NET representation of a strong name as seen before.

What you can see now is that this proxy assembly will reference a server-side
object called Server.SomeCAO, which is located in the assembly Server with the
strong name shown previously. Whenever a client creates a remote instance of
this CAO, the server will try to instantiate the exact version of this Type.

What the server does when the requested version is not available is to take
the *highest* version of the specified assembly. When versions 1.0.1.0 and 2.0.0.1
are available in the GAC, and Version 1.0.0.1 is requested, the server will choose
2.0.0.1 to instantiate the requested object—*even though they differ in the major
version number.*

> **NOTE** *This behavior differs from the standard .NET versioning approach,
> in which the highest version with the same major and minor version
> is chosen.*

To emulate the standard behavior for resolving assembly versions, or to redi-
rect to a completely different version, you can use the assemblyBinding entry in
the application's configuration file:

```
<configuration>
  <system.runtime.remoting>
    <application name="SomeServer">

      <channels>
        <channel ref="http" port="5555" />
      </channels>
```

```
      <service>
        <activated type="Server.SomeCAO, Server" />
      </service>

    </application>
  </system.runtime.remoting>
  <runtime>
   <assemblyBinding xmlns="urn:schemas-microsoft-com:asm.v1">
      <dependentAssembly>
        <assemblyIdentity name="server"
                publicKeyToken="84d24a897bf5808f"
                culture="neutral" />
        <bindingRedirect oldVersion="1.0.0.1"
                newVersion="1.0.1.1" />
      </dependentAssembly>
   </assemblyBinding>
  </runtime>
</configuration>
```

In this case, the server will take any requests for Version 1.0.0.1 and use Version 1.0.1.1 instead. Remember that this only works when the assembly is registered in the GAC and that you have to use `soapsuds -ia:<assembly> -nowp -oa:<meta.dll>` for each server-side version, as the `[SoapType()]` attribute defines this behavior.

Versioning of [Serializable] Objects

Because a [Serializable] object is marshaled by value and its data is passed as a copy, versioning behavior is once more different from SAOs or CAOs. First let's again have a look at the transfer format of the Customer object (and not the complete message) from a server similar to the one in the first example in Chapter 1:

```
<a1:Customer id="ref-4" xmlns:a1="http://schemas.microsoft.com/clr/nsassem/   ⤸
VersionedSerializableObjects/VersionedSerializableObjects%2C%20Version%3D1.   ⤸
0.0.1%2C%20Culture%3Dneutral%2C%20PublicKeyToken%3D84d24a897bf5808f">
<FirstName id="ref-5">John</FirstName>
<LastName id="ref-6">Doe</LastName>
<DateOfBirth>1950-12-12T00:00:00.0000000+01:00</DateOfBirth>
</a1:Customer>
```

As you can see here, the complete namespace information, including the assembly's strong name, is sent over the wire.

When the client that fetched this Customer object using a statement like `Customer cust = CustomerManager.getCustomer(42)` does not have access to this *exact* version, a SerializationException ("Parse Error, no assembly associated with Xml key") will be thrown.

To enable a "one-way relaxed" versioning schema, you can include the attribute `includeVersions = "false"` in the formatter's configuration entry as shown here:

```
<configuration>
  <system.runtime.remoting>
    <application name="SomeServer">
      <channels>
        <channel ref="http" port="5555">
          <serverProviders>
              <formatter ref="soap" includeVersions="false"/>
          </serverProviders>
        </channel>
      </channels>
    </application>
  </system.runtime.remoting>
</configuration>
```

After this change, the server will return a different serialized form of the object, which does not contain the assembly's strong name.

The newly returned Customer object's data will look like this:

```
<a1:Customer id="ref-4"
xmlns:a1="http://schemas.microsoft.com/clr/nsassem/VersionedSerializable
Objects/VersionedSerializableObjects">
<FirstName id="ref-5">John</FirstName>
<LastName id="ref-6">Doe</LastName>
<DateOfBirth>1950-12-12T00:00:00.0000000+01:00</DateOfBirth>
</a1:Customer>
```

This last step, however, has not yet solved all issues with versioned [Serializable] objects. Let's get back to the original need for versioning in the first place: functionality is added to an application, and you want the currently available clients to keep working. This leads to the question of what will happen, when you add another property to either the client or the server side's shared assembly (in the example, I'll use public String Title for the property). The Customer class now looks like this:

```
[Serializable]
public class Customer
{
    public String FirstName;
    public String LastName;
    public DateTime DateOfBirth;
    public String Title; // new!
}
```

When the new Customer object (let's call it Version 2.0.0.1 or just Version 2 for short) is available at the client, and the old object (Version 1, without the Title property) at the server, the client is able to complete the call to Customer cust = CustomerManager.getCustomer(42). The client simply ignores the fact that the server did not send a value for the Customer object's Title property.

It won't work the other way though. When the server has Version 2 of the Customer object and the client only has Version 1, a SerializationException ("Member name 'VersionedSerializableObjects.Customer Title' not found") will be thrown when the client tries to interpret the server's response. This is exactly what you wanted to avoid. To work around these limitations, you have to have a look at the ISerializable interface, which allows you to specify custom serialization methods:

```
public interface ISerializable
{
    void GetObjectData(SerializationInfo info, StreamingContext context);
}
```

When implementing ISerializable, you simply have to call the SerializationInfo object's AddValue() method for each field you want to include in the serialized form of the current object.

To serialize the Customer object's properties from Version 1 of the preceding example (without the Title property), you can do the following:

```
public void GetObjectData(SerializationInfo info, StreamingContext context) {
    info.AddValue("FirstName",FirstName);
    info.AddValue("LastName",LastName);
    info.AddValue("DateOfBirth",DateOfBirth);
}
```

In addition to this implementation of GetObjectData(), you have to provide a special constructor for your object that takes a SerializationInfo and a StreamingContext object as parameters:

```
public Customer (SerializationInfo info, StreamingContext context) {
    FirstName = info.GetString("FirstName");
    LastName = info.GetString("LastName");
    DateOfBirth = info.GetDateTime("DateOfBirth");
}
```

This constructor is called whenever a stream that contains a Customer object is about to be deserialized.

> **NOTE** *It's also possible to include nested objects when using ISerializable. In this case, you have to call* info.GetValue(String name, Type type) *and cast the result to the correct type. All of those additional objects have to be [Serializable], implement ISerializable, or be MarshalByRefObjects as well.*

You can see Version 1 of the Customer object, which is now implemented using the ISerializable interface in Listing 6-11.

Listing 6-11. The First Version of the Serializable Object

```
using System;
using System.Runtime.Serialization;

namespace VersionedSerializableObjects
{
    [Serializable]
    public class Customer: ISerializable
    {
        public String FirstName;
        public String LastName;
        public DateTime DateOfBirth;

        public Customer (SerializationInfo info, StreamingContext context)
        {
            FirstName = info.GetString("FirstName");
            LastName = info.GetString("LastName");
            DateOfBirth = info.GetDateTime("DateOfBirth");
        }
```

```
        public void GetObjectData(SerializationInfo info,
                        StreamingContext context)
        {
            info.AddValue("FirstName",FirstName);
            info.AddValue("LastName",LastName);
            info.AddValue("DateOfBirth",DateOfBirth);
        }
    }
}
```

When the fields of this object have to be extended to include a Title property, as in the preceding example, you have to adopt GetObjectData() and the special constructor.

In the constructor, you have to enclose the access to the newly added property in a try/catch block. This enables you to react to a missing value, which might occur when the remote application is still working with Version 1 of the object.

In Listing 6-12 the value of the Customer object's Title property is set to "n/a" when the SerializationInfo object does not contain this property in serialized form.

Listing 6-12. Manual Serialization Allows More Sophisticated Versioning

```
using System;
using System.Runtime.Serialization;

namespace VersionedSerializableObjects {
    [Serializable]
    public class Customer: ISerializable {
        public String FirstName;
        public String LastName;
        public DateTime DateOfBirth;
        public String Title;

        public Customer (SerializationInfo info, StreamingContext context) {
            FirstName = info.GetString("FirstName");
            LastName = info.GetString("LastName");
            DateOfBirth = info.GetDateTime("DateOfBirth");
            try {
                Title = info.GetString("Title");
            } catch (Exception e) {
                Title = "n/a";
            }
        }
```

```
    public void GetObjectData(SerializationInfo info,
                    StreamingContext context)
    {
        info.AddValue("FirstName",FirstName);
        info.AddValue("LastName",LastName);
        info.AddValue("DateOfBirth",DateOfBirth);
        info.AddValue("Title",Title);
    }

  }
}
```

Using this serialization technique will ensure that you can match server and client versions without breaking any existing applications.

Using Asynchronous Calls

In the .NET Framework, there are generally two ways of executing methods and processing their responses asynchronously:

- Using a delegate's combination of `BeginInvoke()` and `EndInvoke()`

- Using events (which implicitly use delegates)

For the most part, both are possible in .NET Remoting as well. Due to implementation differences, you nevertheless have to be careful when using asychronous method execution.

Using Delegates

Using a delegate's `BeginInvoke()`/`EndInvoke()` combination just simulates an asynchronous call, as the underlying connection will still be synchronous (when using one of the default HTTP or binary channels). This means that separate HTTP connections are made for each concurrently running asynchronous call.

> **NOTE**   *According to the documentation, the clientConnectionLimit attribute, which can be set in the configuration file's <channel> entry for HTTP channel, should limit the number of simultaneous connections to a single server. This is not true in this case.*

The Problem with Implementing Delegates

If you attempt to use delegates with objects from SoapSuds-generated DLLs, you will end up with TypeLoadExceptions, due to the way types are resolved in the remoting framework. Specifically, the .NET Framework tries to load the Type according to the SoapType attribute's XmlTypeNamespace property. This attribute is embedded by SoapSuds to allow for a correct server-side versioning of activation calls to CAOs, as seen previously.

You can observe this problem with the code shown in Listing 6-13, which will give the output shown in Figure 6-16 when used with a SoapSuds-generated DLL.

Listing 6-13. Trying to Use a Delegate with a SoapSuds-Generated Proxy

```
using System;
using System.Collections;
using System.Runtime.Remoting;
using Server;

namespace Client
{
    class Client
    {
        delegate void DoSomethingDelegate ();

        static void Main(string[] args)
        {
            String filename = "client.exe.config";
            RemotingConfiguration.Configure(filename);

            SomeSAO sao = new SomeSAO();

            // calling it synchronously to prove that
            // everything's alright

            Console.WriteLine("Will call synchronously");
            sao.DoSomething();
            Console.WriteLine("Synchronous call is ok");

            DoSomethingDelegate del = new DoSomethingDelegate(sao.DoSomething);

            try {
                Console.WriteLine("BeginInvoke will be called");
                IAsyncResult ar = del.BeginInvoke(null,null);
```

```
            Console.WriteLine("EndInvoke will be called");
            del.EndInvoke(ar);

            Console.WriteLine("Invocation done");
        } catch (Exception e) {
            Console.WriteLine("EXCEPTION \n{0}",e.Message);
        }

        Console.ReadLine();
    }
  }
}
```

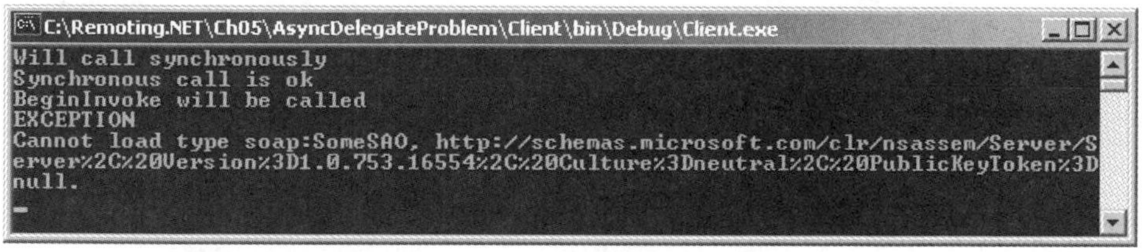

Figure 6-16. Using a delegate with a SoapSuds-generated DLL

Implementing a SoapSuds -gc Workaround

Several possible workarounds exist for this problem. When using only SAOs, for example, the SoapType attribute is not needed. You can therefore run soapsuds -ia:<assembly> -nowp -gc to generate C# code and manually remove this attribute, which will solve the delegate problem. Nevertheless, this doesn't work with CAOs!

You can see the output of soapsuds -ia:server -nowp -gc for a very simple SAO in Listing 6-14 (I inserted some line breaks to enhance the readability).

Listing 6-14. SoapSuds -gc Output for a Simple SAO
```
using System;
using System.Runtime.Remoting.Messaging;
using System.Runtime.Remoting.Metadata;
using System.Runtime.Remoting.Metadata.W3cXsd2001;
namespace Server {

    [Serializable,
      SoapType(SoapOptions=SoapOption.Option1|SoapOption.AlwaysIncludeTypes|
      SoapOption.XsdString|SoapOption.EmbedAll,
```

```
      XmlNamespace=@"http://schemas.microsoft.com/clr/nsassem/Server/Server%2C  ⤶
%20Version%3D1.0.753.26188%2C%20Culture%3Dneutral%2C%20PublicKeyToken%3Dnull",

      XmlTypeNamespace=@"http://schemas.microsoft.com/clr/nsassem/Server/Serve  ⤶
r%2C%20Version%3D1.0.753.26188%2C%20Culture%3Dneutral%2C%20PublicKeyToken%3Dn  ⤶
ull")]

    public class SomeSAO : System.MarshalByRefObject
    {
        [SoapMethod(SoapAction=@"http://schemas.microsoft.com/clr/nsassem/Server.
SomeSAO/Server#DoSomething")]
        public void DoSomething()
        {
            return;
        }


    }
}
```

You can then simply add this source file to your Visual Studio .NET project and remove the complete SoapType attribute.

> **NOTE** *Don't forget to change the configuration file! The* type *property for the <wellknown> entry on the client side has to be changed from pointing to your generated_meta.dll (as in* <wellknown type="Server.SomeSAO, **generated_meta**" /> *) to include the name of the client-side exe (as in* <wellknown type="Server.SomeSAO, **client**" />*).*

The resulting source file without this attribute is shown in Listing 6-15:

Listing 6-15: The SoapSuds-Generated server.cs After Removing the Attribute

```csharp
using System;
using System.Runtime.Remoting.Messaging;
using System.Runtime.Remoting.Metadata;
using System.Runtime.Remoting.Metadata.W3cXsd2001;
namespace Server {

    [Serializable]
    public class SomeSAO : System.MarshalByRefObject
    {
        [SoapMethod(SoapAction=@"http://schemas.microsoft.com/clr/nsassem/Server.
SomeSAO/Server#DoSomething")]
        public void DoSomething()
        {
            return;
        }

    }
}
```

You can see the output of the previous client with the addition of this generated and changed proxy source in Figure 6-17.

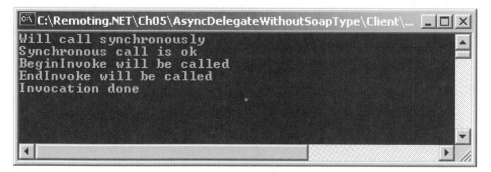

Figure 6-17. SAOs work asynchronously when removing the SoapType attribute.

Using Delegates with Wrapper Methods

Another possibility, which also works for CAOs, is to leave the XmlTypeAttribute intact, but to use a wrapper method in the client application that forwards the call to your remote object. This wrapper method is called asynchronously from the client application and renders the remoting call itself synchronous in regard to the wrapper method.

In this case, you can go back to using the SoapSuds-generated DLL from the first example, and you will only have to adopt the client to add another method that forwards the call, as shown in Listing 6-16.

Listing 6-16: The Client Using a Wrapper Function

```
using System;
using System.Collections;
using System.Runtime.Remoting;
using Server;

namespace Client
{
    class Client
    {
        delegate void DoSomethingDelegate (SomeSAO sao);

        static void WrappedDoSomething(SomeSAO sao) {
            // this method will just forward the call to the SAO
            sao.DoSomething();
        }

        static void Main(string[] args)
        {
            String filename = "client.exe.config";
            RemotingConfiguration.Configure(filename);

            SomeSAO sao = new SomeSAO();

            DoSomethingDelegate del = new DoSomethingDelegate(WrappedDoSomething);
            try {
                Console.WriteLine("BeginInvoke will be called");
                IAsyncResult ar = del.BeginInvoke(sao, null,null);

                Console.WriteLine("EndInvoke will be called");
                del.EndInvoke(ar);
```

```
        Console.WriteLine("Invocation done");
      } catch (Exception e) {
        Console.WriteLine("EXCEPTION \n{0}",e.Message);
      }

      Console.ReadLine();
    }
  }
}
```

I have to admit that this is quite an unattractive workaround, as it turns the call into a synchronous remoting call. (Synchronous to the `WrappedDoSomething()` method, but still asynchronous in regard to `void Main()`!) Nevertheless, if you just want to call a single method asynchronously, this might be the right way to go without having to change too much of your SoapSuds-generated proxy code.

Remoting Events

As you might have already guessed from the previous topics, you're already reaching an area of .NET Remoting where the intuitive way of solving the problem might not be the correct one. The remoting of events is another such topic.

First and foremost, as you've seen before, asynchronous calls don't go very well with SoapSuds-generated metadata. Because of this, I'll go back to using interfaces defined in a shared DLL. The reason why I hadn't been following this approach is that you'd miss the opportunity to use the new operator to transparently create references to remote objects. Instead, you would have to use `Activator.GetObject()` for SAOs and a factory design pattern for CAOs.

To avoid hard coding the URLs in the client application and to provide consistency with the standard .NET Remoting configuration file, you can use the helper class shown in Listing 6-17, which allows you to create a remote object even if it's been designed using an interface or an abstract base.

Listing 6-17. The RemotingHelper Called with typeof(ISomeInterface)

```
using System;
using System.Collections;
using System.Runtime.Remoting;

namespace RemotingTools
{
  public class RemotingHelper {
    private static bool _isInit;
    private static IDictionary _wellKnownTypes;
```

```
    public static Object GetObject(Type type) {
        if (! _isInit) InitTypeCache();
        WellKnownClientTypeEntry entr =
            (WellKnownClientTypeEntry) _wellKnownTypes[type];

        if (entr == null) {
            throw new RemotingException("Type not found!");
        }

        return Activator.GetObject(entr.ObjectType,entr.ObjectUrl);
    }

    public static void InitTypeCache() {
        _wellKnownTypes= new Hashtable();
        foreach (WellKnownClientTypeEntry entr in
            RemotingConfiguration.GetRegisteredWellKnownClientTypes()) {
            _wellKnownTypes.Add (entr.ObjectType,entr);
        }
    }
  }
}
```

When you want to instantiate a remote object that implements the interface IMyInterface (which is defined in a shared DLL called General.dll), you can use the following configuration file to register the interface as a remote object:

```
<configuration>
  <system.runtime.remoting>
    <application>

      <channels>
        <channel ref="http"/>
      </channels>

      <client>
        <wellknown type="General.IMyInterface, General"
                   url="http://localhost:5555/MySAO.soap" />
      </client>

    </application>
  </system.runtime.remoting>
</configuration>
```

After doing this and reading the configuration file with
RemotingConfiguration.Configure(), you'll be able to create a reference to the
remote SAO using the following statement:

```
IMyInterface sao = (IMyInterface) RemotingHelper.GetObject(typeof(IMyInterface);
```

without hard coding the URL. Remember, though, that this approach only works
when you want to register *exactly one* server-side object for each interface.

The Problem with Events

Let's say you have to implement a type of broadcast application in which a number of clients register themselves at the servers as *listeners* and other clients can
send messages that will be broadcast to all listening clients.

You need to take into account two key facts when using this kind of application. The first one is by design: when the event occurs, client and server will
change roles. This means that the client in reality becomes the server (for the
callback method), and the server will act as a client and try to contact the "real"
client. This is shown in Figure 6-18.

> **CAUTION** *This implies that clients located behind firewalls are not able to
> receive events using any of the included channels!*

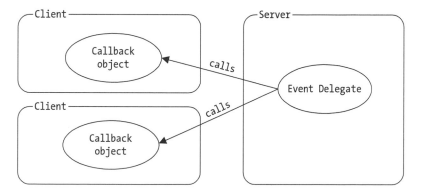

Figure 6-18. The clients will be contacted by the server.

The second issue can be seen when you are "intuitively" developing this application. In this case, you'd probably start with the interface definition shown in Listing 6-18, which would be compiled to General.dll and shared between the clients and the server.

Listing 6-18. The IBroadcaster Interface (Nonworking Sample)

```
using System;
using System.Runtime.Remoting.Messaging;

namespace General {

    public delegate void MessageArrivedHandler(String msg);

    public interface IBroadcaster {
        void BroadcastMessage(String msg);
        event MessageArrivedHandler MessageArrived;
    }
}
```

This interface allows clients to register themselves to receive a notification by using the `MessageArrived` event. When another client calls `BroadcastMessage()`, this event will be invoked and the listening clients called back. The server-side implementation of this interface is shown in Listing 6-19.

Listing 6-19. The Server-Side Implementation of IBroadcaster

```
using System;
using System.Runtime.Remoting;
using System.Threading;
using General;

namespace Server
{

    public class Broadcaster: MarshalByRefObject, IBroadcaster
    {

        public event General.MessageArrivedHandler MessageArrived;

        public void BroadcastMessage(string msg) {
            // call the delegate to notify all listeners
            Console.WriteLine("Will broadcast message: {0}", msg);
            MessageArrived(msg);
        }
```

```
    public override object InitializeLifetimeService() {
        // this object has to live "forever"
        return null;
    }
}

class ServerStartup
{
    static void Main(string[] args)
    {
        String filename = "server.exe.config";
        RemotingConfiguration.Configure(filename);

        Console.WriteLine ("Server started, press <return> to exit.");
        Console.ReadLine();
    }
}
}
```

The listening client's implementation would be quite straightforward in this case. The only thing you'd have to take care of is that the object that is going to be called back to handle the event has to be a MarshalByRefObject as well. This is shown in Listing 6-20.

Listing 6-20. The First Client's Implementation, That Won't Work

```
using System;
using System.Runtime.Remoting;
using General;
using RemotingTools; // RemotingHelper

namespace EventListener
{
    class EventListener
    {
        static void Main(string[] args)
        {
            String filename = "eventlistener.exe.config";
            RemotingConfiguration.Configure(filename);

            IBroadcaster bcaster =
                (IBroadcaster) RemotingHelper.GetObject(typeof(IBroadcaster));

            Console.WriteLine("Registering event at server");
```

```
            // callbacks can only work on MarshalByRefObjects, so
            // I created a different class for this as well
            EventHandler eh = new EventHandler();
            bcaster.MessageArrived +=
               new MessageArrivedHandler(eh.HandleMessage);

            Console.WriteLine("Event registered. Waiting for messages.");
            Console.ReadLine();
         }
      }

   public class EventHandler: MarshalByRefObject {
      public void HandleMessage(String msg) {
         Console.WriteLine("Received: {0}",msg);
      }

      public override object InitializeLifetimeService() {
         // this object has to live "forever"
         return null;
      }
   }
}
```

When implementing this so-called intuitive solution, you'll be presented with the error message shown in Figure 6-19.

Figure 6-19. An exception occurs when combining the delegate with the remote event.

This exception occurs while the request is deserialized at the server. At this point, the delegate is restored from the serialized message and it tries to validate the target method's signature. For this validation, the delegate attempts to load the assembly containing the destination method. In the case presented previously, this will be the client-side assembly EventListener.exe, which is not available at the server.

You're probably thinking, "Great, but how can I use events nevertheless?" I show you how in the next section.

Refactoring the Event Handling

As always, there's the relatively easy solution of shipping the delegate's destination assembly to the caller. This would nevertheless mean that the client-side application has to be referenced at the server—doesn't sound that nice, does it?

Instead, you can introduce an intermediate MarshalByRefObject (including the implementation, not only the interface) that will be located in General.dll and will therefore be accessible by both client and server:

```
public class BroadcastEventWrapper: MarshalByRefObject {
    public event MessageArrivedHandler MessageArrivedLocally;

    [OneWay]
    public void LocallyHandleMessageArrived (String msg) {
        // forward the message to the client
        MessageArrivedLocally(msg);
    }

    public override object InitializeLifetimeService() {
        // this object has to live "forever"
        return null;
    }
}
```

> **NOTE** *This is still not the final solution, as there are some problems with using [OneWay] events in real-world applications as well. I cover this shortly after the current example!*

This wrapper is created in the client's context and provides an event that can be used to call back the "real" client. The server in turn receives a delegate to the BroadcastEventWrapper's `LocallyHandleMessageArrived()` method. This method activates the BroadcastEventWrapper's `MessageArrivedLocally` event, which will be handled by the client. You can see the sequence in Figure 6-20.

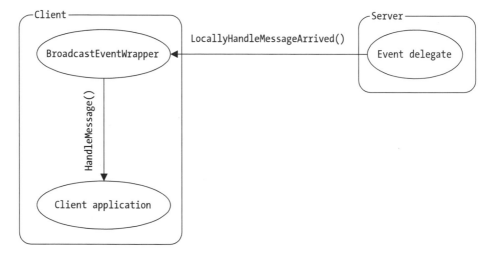

Figure 6-20. Event handling with an intermediate wrapper

The server's event will therefore be handled by a MarshalByRefObject that is known to it (as it's contained in general.dll) so that the delegate can resolve the method's signature. As the BroadcastEventWrapper runs in the client context, its own delegate has access to the real client-side event handler's signature.

The complete source code to General.dll is shown in Listing 6-21.

Listing 6-21. The Shared Assembly Now Contains the BroadcastEventWrapper

```
using System;
using System.Runtime.Remoting.Messaging;

namespace General {

    public delegate void MessageArrivedHandler(String msg);

    public interface IBroadcaster {
        void BroadcastMessage(String msg);
        event MessageArrivedHandler MessageArrived;
    }
```

```
public class BroadcastEventWrapper: MarshalByRefObject {
    public event MessageArrivedHandler MessageArrivedLocally;

    [OneWay]
    public void LocallyHandleMessageArrived (String msg) {
        // forward the message to the client
        MessageArrivedLocally(msg);
    }

    public override object InitializeLifetimeService() {
        // this object has to live "forever"
        return null;
    }


    }
}
```

The listening client's source code has to be changed accordingly. Instead of passing the server a delegate to its own HandleMessage() method, it has to create a BroadcastEventWrapper and pass the server a delegate to this object's LocallyHandleMessageArrived() method. The client also has to pass a delegate to its own HandleMessage() method (the "real" one) to the event wrapper's MessageArrivedLocally event.

The changed listening client's source code is shown in Listing 6-22.

Listing 6-22. The New Listening Client's Source Code

```
using System;
using System.Runtime.Remoting;
using General;
using RemotingTools; // RemotingHelper

namespace EventListener
{
    class EventListener
    {
        static void Main(string[] args)
        {
            String filename = "eventlistener.exe.config";
            RemotingConfiguration.Configure(filename);

            IBroadcaster bcaster =
                (IBroadcaster) RemotingHelper.GetObject(typeof(IBroadcaster));
```

```
            // this one will be created in the client's context and a
            // reference will be passed to the server
            BroadcastEventWrapper eventWrapper =
               new BroadcastEventWrapper();

            // register the local handler with the "remote" handler
            eventWrapper.MessageArrivedLocally +=
               new MessageArrivedHandler(HandleMessage);

            Console.WriteLine("Registering event at server");
            bcaster.MessageArrived +=
               new MessageArrivedHandler(eventWrapper.LocallyHandleMessageArrived);

            Console.WriteLine("Event registered. Waiting for messages.");
            Console.ReadLine();
        }

        public static void HandleMessage(String msg) {
            Console.WriteLine("Received: {0}",msg);
        }
    }
}
```

When this client is started, you will see the output in Figure 6-21, which shows you that the client is currently waiting for remote events. You can, of course, start an arbitrary number of clients, because the server-side event is implicitly based on a MulticastDelegate.

Figure 6-21. The client is waiting for messages.

To start broadcasting messages to all listening clients, you'll have to implement another client. I'm going to call this one EventInitiator in the following examples. The EventInitiator will simply connect to the server-side SAO and invoke its BroadcastMessage() method. You can see the complete source code for EventInitiator in Listing 6-23.

Listing 6-23. EventInitiator Simply Calls BroadcastMessage()

```
using System;
using System.Runtime.Remoting;
using System.Runtime.Remoting.Activation;
using General;
using RemotingTools; // RemotingHelper


namespace Client
{
   class Client
   {

      static void Main(string[] args)
      {
          String filename = "EventInitiator.exe.config";
          RemotingConfiguration.Configure(filename);

          IBroadcaster bcast =
             (IBroadcaster) RemotingHelper.GetObject(typeof(IBroadcaster));

          bcast.BroadcastMessage("Hello World! Events work fine now ... ");

          Console.WriteLine("Message sent");
          Console.ReadLine();
      }
   }
}
```

When EventInitiator is started, the output shown in Figure 6-22 will be displayed at each listening client, indicating that the remote events now work as expected.

Figure 6-22. Remote events now work successfully!

Why [OneWay] Events Are a Bad Idea

You might have read in some documents and articles that remoting event handlers should be defined as [OneWay] methods. The reason is that *without* defining remote event handlers this way, an exception will occur whenever a client is unreachable or has been disconnected without first unregistering the event handler.

When just forwarding the call to your event's delegate, as shown in the previous server-side example, two things will happen: the event will not reach all listeners, and the client that initiated the event in the first place will receive an exception. This is certainly not what you want to happen.

When using [OneWay] event handlers instead, the server will try to contact each listener but won't throw an exception if it's unreachable. This seems to be a good thing at first glance. Imagine, however, that your application will run for several months without restarting. As a result, a lot of "unreachable" event handlers will end up registered, and the server will try to contact each of them every time. Not only will this take up network bandwidth, but your performance will suffer as well, as each "nonworking" call might take up some seconds, adding up to minutes of processing time for each event. This, again, is something you wouldn't want in your broadcast application.

Instead of using the default event invocation mechanism (which is fine for local applications), you will have to develop a server-side wrapper that calls all event handlers in a try/catch block and removes all nonworking handlers afterwards. This implies that you define the event handlers *without* the [OneWay] attribute! To make this work, you first have to remove this attribute from the shared assembly:

```
public class BroadcastEventWrapper: MarshalByRefObject {
    public event MessageArrivedHandler MessageArrivedLocally;

    // don't use OneWay here!
    public void LocallyHandleMessageArrived (String msg) {
        // forward the message to the client
        MessageArrivedLocally(msg);
    }

    public override object InitializeLifetimeService() {
        // this object has to live "forever"
        return null;
    }
}
```

In the server-side code, you remove the call to `MessageArrived()` and instead implement the logic shown in Listing 6-23, which iterates over the list of registered delegates and calls each one. When an exception is thrown by the framework because the destination object is unreachable, the delegate will be removed from the event.

Listing 6-23. Invoking Each Delegate on Your Own

```
using System;
using System.Runtime.Remoting;
using System.Threading;
using General;

namespace Server
{

    public class Broadcaster: MarshalByRefObject, IBroadcaster
    {

        public event General.MessageArrivedHandler MessageArrived;

        public void BroadcastMessage(string msg) {
            Console.WriteLine("Will broadcast message: {0}", msg);
            SafeInvokeEvent(msg);
        }

        private void SafeInvokeEvent(String msg) {
            // call the delegates manually to remove them if they aren't
            // active anymore.
```

```
        if (MessageArrived == null) {
            Console.WriteLine("No listeners");
        } else {

            Console.WriteLine("Number of Listeners: {0}",
                             MessageArrived.GetInvocationList().Length);


            MessageArrivedHandler mah=null;

            foreach (Delegate del in MessageArrived.GetInvocationList()) {
                try {
                    mah = (MessageArrivedHandler) del;
                    mah(msg);
                } catch (Exception e) {
                    Console.WriteLine("Exception occured, will remove Delegate");
                    MessageArrived -= mah;
                }
            }
        }
    }

    public override object InitializeLifetimeService() {
        // this object has to live "forever"
        return null;
    }
}


class ServerStartup
{
    static void Main(string[] args)
    {
        String filename = "server.exe.config";
        RemotingConfiguration.Configure(filename);

        Console.WriteLine ("Server started, press <return> to exit.");
        Console.ReadLine();
    }
}
}
```

When using events in this way, you ensure the best possible performance, no matter how long your server application keeps running.

Summary

In this chapter you learned about the details of .NET Remoting–based application. You now know how lifetime is managed and how you can dynamically configure an object's time to live. If this doesn't suffice, implementing client- or server-side sponsors gives you the opportunity to manage an object's lifetime independently of any TTLs.

You also read about versioning, and you can now look at the whole application's lifecycle over various versions and know what to watch out for in regard to SAOs and CAOs and know how the ISerializable interface can help you when using [Serializable] objects.

On the last pages of this chapter, you read about the various internals of asynchronous calls, how to use delegates and events, and what to take care of when designing an application that relies on these features. In particular, you learned that using [OneWay] event handlers the intuitive way certainly isn't the best practice.

This chapter is the last one of the first part of the book. You should now be able to solve most challenges that might confront you during design and development of a .NET Remoting application. The second part of this book first shows you the inner workings of the architecture. In Chapter 7, you will read about how the various layers can be extended to match the framework's features with your applications' demands, and I provide a lot of source code to demonstrate these concepts in the following chapters.

CHAPTER 7

Inside the Framework

As I STATED IN THE INTRODUCTION to this book, .NET provides an unprecedented
extensibility for the remoting framework. The layered architecture of the .NET
Remoting Framework can be customized by either completely replacing the
existing functionality of a given tier or chaining new implementation with
the baseline .NET features.

Before working on the framework and its extensibility, I really encourage you
to get a thorough understanding of the existing layers and their inner workings in
this architecture. This chapter will give you that information. **But be forewarned:
This chapter contains some heavy stuff.** It shows you how .NET Remoting really
works. Some of the underlying concepts are quite abstract, but you don't necessarily need to know them if you just want to *use* .NET Remoting. If you want to
understand or *extend* it, however, the information contained in this chapter
is vital.

If you're only interested in the use of additional sinks, you'll find information
pertaining to that topic in Chapter 8.

Looking at the Five Elements of Remoting

The .Net Remoting architecture, as you can see in Figure 7-1, is based on five core
types of objects:

- *Proxies:* These objects masquerade as remote objects and forward calls.

- *Messages:* Message objects contain the necessary data to execute a remote
  method call.

- *Message sinks:* These objects allow custom processing of messages during
  a remote invocation.

- *Formatters:* These objects are message sinks as well and will serialize
  a message to a transfer format like SOAP.

- *Transport channels:* Message sinks yet again, these objects will transfer the
  serialized message to a remote process, for example, via HTTP.

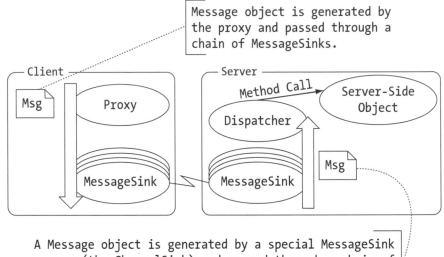

Message object is generated by the proxy and passed through a chain of MessageSinks.

A Message object is generated by a special MessageSink (the ChannelSink) and passed through a chain of MessageSinks. When received by the Dispatcher, it will be translated into a method call on the server-side object.

Figure 7-1. Simplified version of the .NET Remoting architecture

A Bit About Proxies

Instead of dealing with "real" object references (memory references, pointers, and so on), when using remote objects, the client application can only perform methods on object *proxies*. These proxies masquerade, and therefore provide the same interface, as the target object. Instead of executing any method on their own, the proxies forward each method call to the .NET Remoting Framework as a Message object.

This message then passes through the sinks shown previously, until it is finally handled by the server, where it passes though another set of message sinks until the call is placed on the "real" destination object. The server then creates a return message that will be passed back to the proxy. The proxy handles the return message and converts it to the eventual out/ref parameters and the method's return value, which will be passed back to the client application.

Creating Proxies

When using the new operator or calling Activator.GetObject() to acquire a reference to a remote object, the .NET Remoting framework generates two proxy objects. The first is an instance of the generic TransparentProxy (from

System.Runtime.Remoting.Proxies). This is the object that will be returned from the new operator for a remote object.

Whenever you call a method on the reference to a remote object, you will in reality call it on this TransparentProxy. This proxy holds a reference to a RemotingProxy, which is a descendent of the abstract RealProxy class.

During the creation stage, references to the client-side message sink chains are acquired using the sink providers passed during channel creation (or the default, if no custom providers have been specified). These references are stored in the Identity object contained in the RealProxy.

After using the new operator or calling GetObject(), as shown in the following example, the variable obj will point to the TransparentProxy (see Figure 7-2).

```
HttpChannel channel = new HttpChannel();
ChannelServices.RegisterChannel(channel);
SomeClass obj = (SomeClass) Activator.GetObject(
        typeof(SomeClass),
        "http://localhost:1234/SomeSAO.soap");
```

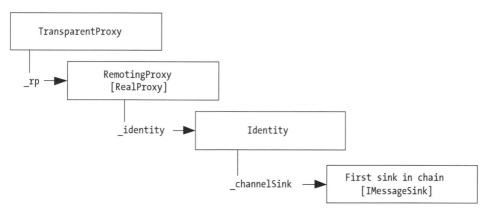

Figure 7-2. Proxies with identity

Creating Messages

When a call is placed on a remote object reference, the TransparentProxy creates a MessageData object and passes this to the RealProxy's PrivateInvoke() method. The RealProxy in turn generates a new Message object and calls InitFields(), passing the MessageData as a parameter. The Message object will now populate its properties by resolving the pointers inside the MessageData object.

For synchronous calls, the RealProxy places a chain of calls on itself, including Invoke(), InternalInvoke(), and CallProcessMessage(). The last one will look up the contained Identity object's sink chain and call SyncProcessMessage() on the first IMessageSink.

When the processing (including server-side handling) has completed, the call to the this method will return an IMessage object containing the response message. The RealProxy will call its own `HandleReturnMessage()` method, which checks for out/ref parameters and will call `PropagateOutParameters()` on the Message object.

You can see a part of this client-side process when using the default HTTP channel, shown in Figure 7-3. If the client would use the TCP channel instead, the channel would consist of a BinaryClientFormatterSink and a TcpClientTransport sink.

Returning Values

After this handling of the response, the RealProxy will return from its `PrivateInvoke()` method, and the IMessage is passed back to the TransparentProxy. Now a lot of "magic" happens behind the scenes: the TransparentProxy will take the return values and out parameters from the Message object and return them to the calling application in the conventional, stack-based method return fashion of the CLR. From the perspective of the client application, it will look as if a normal method call has just returned.

A Bit About the ObjRef Object

When working with CAOs, the client needs the possibility to identify distinct object instances. When passing references to CAOs from one process to another, this identity information has to "travel" with the call. This information is stored in the serializable ObjRef object.

When instantiating a CAO (either by using a custom factory SAO as shown in Chapter 3 or by using the default `RemoteActivation.rem` SAO that is provided by the framework when the CAO is registered at the server side), a serialized ObjRef will be returned by the server.

This ObjRef is taken as a base to initialize the Identity object, and a reference to it will also be kept by the Identity. The ObjRef stores the unique URL to the CAO. This URL is based on a GUID and looks like the following:

```
/b8c0c989_68be_40d6_97b2_0c3fda5bb7ad/1014675796_1.rem
```

Additionally, the ObjRef object stores the server's base URL, which has also been returned by the server.

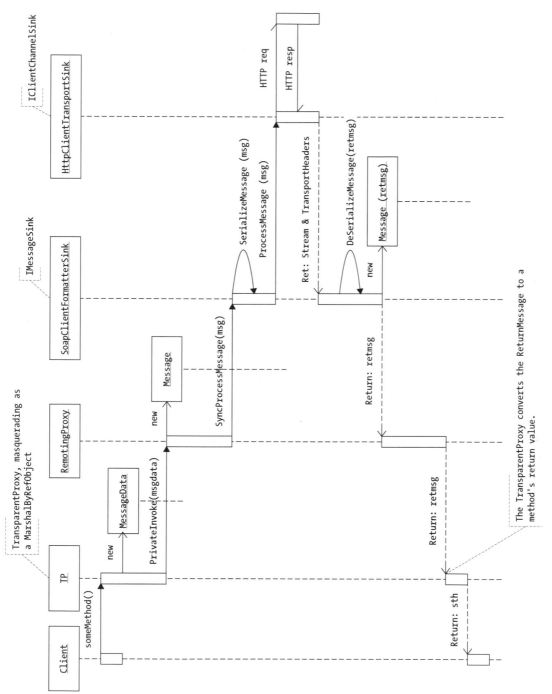

Figure 7-3. *Client-side synchronous message handling (partial)*

> **CAUTION** *This behavior is very different from that of SAOs, where the URL to the server is specified at the client. With CAOs, only the URL needed for the creation of the CAO is known to the client. The real connection end-point URL for the CAO will be returned when creating the object. This can also mean that a host that's behind a firewall might return its private IP address and will therefore render the CAO unusable. To prevent this behavior, make sure to use either the machineName or bindTo attribute in the channel's configuration section as shown in Chapter 4.*

You can check the ObjRef (or any other properties of the proxies) in a sample project simply by setting a breakpoint after the line where you acquire the remote reference of a CAO (for example, `SomeObj obj1 = new SomeObj()` when using configuration files). You can then open the Locals window and browse to the obj1's properties as show in Figure 7-4.

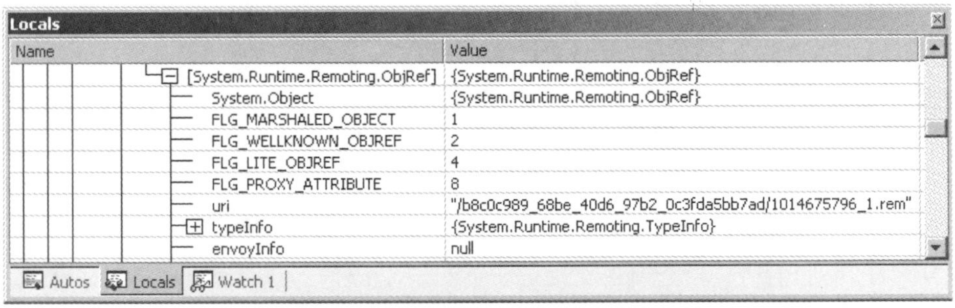

Figure 7-4. Browsing to the ObjRef's properties in the Locals window

You'll find the ObjRef shown in Figure 7-5 at obj1/_TransparentProxy/_rp/_identity/_objRef.

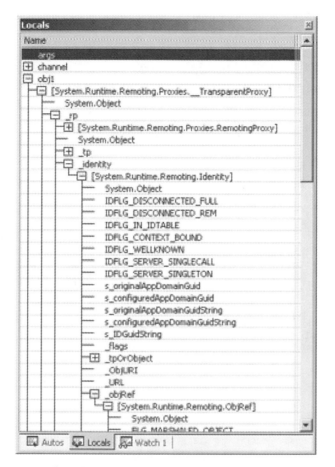

Figure 7-5. Locating the ObjRef in the Locals window

Understanding the Role of Messages

A *message* is basically just a dictionary object hidden behind the IMessage interface. Even though every message is based on this interface, the .NET Framework defines several special types thereof. You'll come across ConstructionCall and MethodCall messages (plus their respective return messages). The main difference between these message types is a predefinition of several entries in the internal dictionary.

While traveling through the chain of sinks, the message passes at least two important points: a formatter and a transport channel. The formatter is a special kind of sink that encodes the internal dictionary into some sort of wire protocol such as SOAP or a binary representation.

The transport channel will transfer a serialized message from one process to another. At the destination, the message's dictionary is restored from the wire protocol by a server-side formatter. After this, it passes through several server-side MessageSinks until it reaches the dispatcher. The dispatcher converts the message into a "real" stack-based method call that will be executed upon the target object. After execution, a return message is generated for most call types (excluding one-way calls) and passed back through the various sinks and channels until it reaches the client-side proxy, where it will be converted to the respective return value or exception.

What's in a Message?

There are several kinds of messages, and each of them is represented by a distinct class, depending on what kind of call it stands for. This object implements the IDictionary interface to provide key/value-based access to its properties.

A partial definition of MethodCall is shown here:

```
public class System.Runtime.Remoting.Messaging.MethodCall:
{
    // only properties are shown

    public int ArgCount { virtual get; }
    public object[] Args { virtual get; }
    public bool HasVarArgs { virtual get; }
    public int InArgCount { virtual get; }
    public object[] InArgs { virtual get; }
    public LogicalCallContext LogicalCallContext { virtual get; }
    public MethodBase MethodBase { virtual get; }
    public string MethodName { virtual get; }
    public object MethodSignature { virtual get; }
    public IDictionary Properties { virtual get; }
    public string TypeName { virtual get; }
    public string Uri { virtual get; set; }
}
```

These values can be accessed in two ways. The first is by directly referencing the properties from the message object, as in methodname = msg.MethodName. The second way is to access the properties using the IDictionary interface with one of the predefined keys shown in the table that follows.

When doing this, a wrapper object (for example a MCMDictionary for MethodCallMessages) will be generated. This wrapper has a reference to the original message so that it can resolve a call to its dictionary values by providing the data from the underlying Message object's properties. Here you will see the dictionary keys and corresponding properties for a sample method call message:

DICTIONARY KEY	MESSAGE'S PROPERTY	DATA TYPE	SAMPLE VALUE
__Uri	Uri	String	/MyRemoteObject.soap
__MethodName	MethodName	String	setValue
__MethodSignature	MethodSignature	Object	*null*
__TypeName	TypeName	String	General.BaseRemoteObject, General
__Args	Args	Object[]	{42}
__CallContext	LogicalCallContext	Object	*null*

The second kind of message, used during the instantiation of CAOs, is the ConstructionCall. This object extends MethodCall and provides the following additional properties:

```
public class System.Runtime.Remoting.Messaging.ConstructionCall :
{
    // only properties are shown
    public Type ActivationType { virtual get; }
    public string ActivationTypeName { virtual get; }
    public IActivator Activator { virtual get; virtual set; }
    public object[] CallSiteActivationAttributes { virtual get; }
    public IList ContextProperties { virtual get; }
}
```

Examining Message Sinks

The transfer of a message from a client application to a server-side object is done by so-called *message sinks*. A sink will basically receive a message from another object, apply its own processing, and delegate any additional work to the next sink in a chain.

There are three basic interfaces for message sinks: IMessageSink, IClientChannelSink, and IServerChannelSink. As you can see in the following interface description, IMessageSink defines two methods for processing a message and a property getter for acquiring the reference for the next sink in the chain.

```
public interface IMessageSink
{

    IMessageSink NextSink { get; }

    IMessageCtrl AsyncProcessMessage(IMessage msg,
                                        IMessageSink replySink);

    IMessage SyncProcessMessage(IMessage msg);
}
```

Whenever an IMessageSink receives a message using either
SyncProcessMessage() or AsyncProcessMessage(), it may first check whether it
can handle this message. If it's able to do so, it will apply its own processing
and afterwards pass the message on to the IMessageSink referenced in its
NextSink property.

At some point in the chain, the message will reach a formatter (which is also
an IMessageSink) that will serialize the message to a defined format and pass it
on to a secondary chain of IClientChannelSink objects.

> **NOTE** *Formatters implement IClientFormatterSink by convention. This
> interface is a combination of IMessageSink and IClientChannelSink.*

```
public interface IClientChannelSink
{

    // Properties
    IClientChannelSink NextChannelSink { get; }

    // Methods
    void AsyncProcessRequest(IClientChannelSinkStack sinkStack,
                                IMessage msg,
                                ITransportHeaders headers,
                                Stream stream);

    void AsyncProcessResponse(IClientResponseChannelSinkStack sinkStack,
                                object state,
                                ITransportHeaders headers,
                                Stream stream);
```

```
Stream GetRequestStream(IMessage msg,
                        ITransportHeaders headers);

void ProcessMessage(IMessage msg,
                    ITransportHeaders requestHeaders,
                    Stream requestStream,
                    ref ITransportHeaders responseHeaders,
                    ref Stream responseStream);
}
```

The main difference between IMessageSink and IClientChannelSink is that the former can access and change the original dictionary, independent of any serialization format, whereas the latter has access to the serialized message as a stream.

After processing the message, the IClientChannelSink also passes it on to the next sink in its chain until it reaches a transport channel like HttpClientTransportSink (which also implements IClientChannelSink) for the default HTTP channel.

Serialization through Formatters

A Message object needs to be serialized into a stream before it can be transferred to a remote process, a task which is performed by a *formatter*. The .NET Remoting Framework provides you with two default formatters, the SoapFormatter and the BinaryFormatter, which can both be used via HTTP or TCP connections.

> **NOTE** *In the samples that follow, you get a chance to take a look at the SoapFormatter, but the same information applies to BinaryFormatter (or any custom formatter) as well.*

After the message completes the preprocessing stage by passing through the chain of IMessageSink objects, it will reach the formatter via the SyncProcessMessage() method.

On the client side, the SoapClientFormatterSink passes the IMessage on to its SerializeMessage() method. This function sets up the TransportHeaders and asks its NextSink (which will be the respective IClientChannelSink—that is, the HttpClientTransportSink) for the request stream onto which it should write the serialized data. If the request stream is not yet available, it will create a new ChunkedMemoryStream that will later be passed to the channel sink.

The real serialization is started from `CoreChannel.SerializeSoapMessage()`, which creates a SoapFormatter (from the System.Runtime.Serialization.Formatters.Soap namespace) and calls its `Serialize()` method.

You can see the SOAP output of the formatter for a sample call to `obj.setValue(42)` in the following excerpt. Remember that this is only the serialized form of the request—it is not yet transfer dependent (it does not contain any HTTP headers, for example).

```
<SOAP-ENV:Envelope
 xmlns:xsi="http://www.w3.org/2001/XMLSchema-instance"
 xmlns:xsd="http://www.w3.org/2001/XMLSchema"
 xmlns:SOAP-ENC="http://schemas.xmlsoap.org/soap/encoding/"
 xmlns:SOAP-ENV="http://schemas.xmlsoap.org/soap/envelope/"
 SOAP-ENV:encodingStyle="http://schemas.xmlsoap.org/soap/encoding/"
 xmlns:i2="http://schemas.microsoft.com/clr/nsassem/General.BaseRemoteObj  ↵
ect/General">
    <SOAP-ENV:Body>
      <i2:setValue id="ref-1">
          <newval>42</newval>
      </i2:setValue>
    </SOAP-ENV:Body>
</SOAP-ENV:Envelope>
```

Moving Messages through Transport Channels

After the last IClientChannelSink (which can be either the formatter or custom channel sink) has been called, it forwards the message, stream, and headers to the `ProcessMessage()` method of the associated *transfer channel*. In addition to the stream generated by the formatter, this function needs an ITransportHeaders object, which has been populated by the formatter as well, as a parameter.

The transport sink's responsibility is to convert these headers into a protocol-dependent format—for example, into HTTP headers. It will then open a connection to the server (or check if it's is already open, for TCP channels or HTTP 1.1 keepalive connections) and send the headers and the stream's content over this connection.

Following the previous example, the HTTP headers for the SOAP remoting call will look like this:

```
POST /MyRemoteObject.soap HTTP/1.1
User-Agent: Mozilla/4.0+(compatible; MSIE 6.0; Windows 5.0.2195.0; MS .NET
Remoting;
MS .NET CLR 1.0.2914.16 )
SOAPAction:
"http://schemas.microsoft.com/clr/nsassem/General.BaseRemoteObject/General#
setValue"
Content-Type: text/xml; charset="utf-8"
Content-Length: 510
Expect: 100-continue
Connection: Keep-Alive
Host: localhost
```

This leads to the following complete HTTP request for the setValue(int) method of a sample remote object:

```
POST /MyRemoteObject.soap HTTP/1.1
User-Agent: Mozilla/4.0+(compatible; MSIE 6.0; Windows 5.0.2195.0; MS .NET
Remoting;
MS .NET CLR 1.0.2914.16 )
SOAPAction:
"http://schemas.microsoft.com/clr/nsassem/General.BaseRemoteObject/General#
setValue"
Content-Type: text/xml; charset="utf-8"
Content-Length: 510
Expect: 100-continue
Connection: Keep-Alive
Host: localhost

<SOAP-ENV:Envelope
    xmlns:xsi="http://www.w3.org/2001/XMLSchema-instance"
    xmlns:xsd="http://www.w3.org/2001/XMLSchema"
    xmlns:SOAP-ENC="http://schemas.xmlsoap.org/soap/encoding/"
    xmlns:SOAP-ENV="http://schemas.xmlsoap.org/soap/envelope/"
    SOAP-ENV:encodingStyle="http://schemas.xmlsoap.org/soap/encoding/"
    xmlns:i2=
      "http://schemas.microsoft.com/clr/nsassem/General.BaseRemoteObject/General">
  <SOAP-ENV:Body>
    <i2:setValue id="ref-1">
      <newval>42</newval>
    </i2:setValue>
  </SOAP-ENV:Body>
</SOAP-ENV:Envelope>
```

I highlighted the important parts in this request so that you can see the values that have been taken from the message object's dictionary.

Client-Side Messaging

As you know by now, the message is created by the combination of the TransparentProxy and RemotingProxy, which send it to the first entry of the message sink chain. After this creation, the message will pass four to six stages, depending on the channel's configuration. You can see this in Figure 7-6.

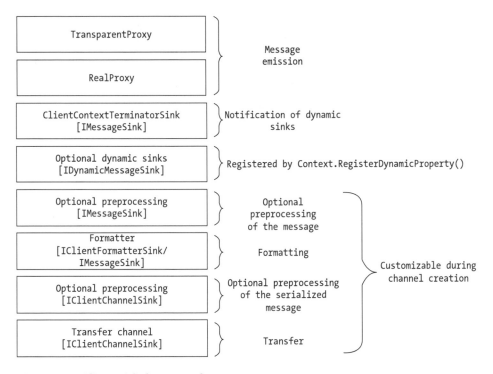

Figure 7-6. Client-side layers and message stages

The contents of the preprocessing, formatting, and transfer layers are customizable during the creation of the channel. When creating a default HTTP channel, for example, only a SoapClientFormatterSink (as the formatting layer) and an HttpClientTransportSink (as the transport layer) will be created; by default neither a preprocessing layer nor any dynamic context sinks are registered.

ClientContextTerminatorSink and Dynamic Sinks

The ClientContextTerminatorSink is automatically registered for all channels. It is the first sink that gets called and in turn notifies any dynamic context sinks associated with the current remoting context. These dynamic sinks will receive the message via the IDynamicMessageSink interface:

```
public interface IDynamicMessageSink
{
    void ProcessMessageStart(IMessage reqMsg, bool bCliSide, bool bAsync);
    void ProcessMessageFinish(IMessage replyMsg, bool bCliSide, bool bAsync);
}
```

These sinks don't need to pass the information to any other sink in a chain. Instead, this is done automatically by the context terminator sink, which will call the relevant methods on a list of registered dynamic sinks before passing the message on to the next IMessageSink.

You'll find more on the creation and implementation of dynamic sinks in Chapter 8.

SoapClientFormatterSink

After passing through optional custom IMessageSink objects, the message reaches the formatter. As shown previously, the formatter's task is to take the message's internal dictionary and serialize it to a defined wire format. The output of the serialization is an object implementing ITransferHeaders and a stream from which the channel sink will be able to read the serialized data.

After generating these objects, the formatter calls ProcessMessage() on its assigned IClientChannelSink and as a result starts to pass the message to the secondary chain—the channel sink chain.

HttpClientChannel

At the end of the chain of client channel sinks, the message ultimately reaches the transfer channel, which also implements the IClientChannelSink interface. When the ProcessMessage() method of this channel sink is called, it opens a connection to the server (or uses an existing connection) and passes the data using the defined transfer protocol. The server now processes the request message and returns a ReturnMessage in serialized form. The client-side channel sink will take this data and split it into an ITransferHeader object, which contains the headers, and into a stream containing the serialized payload. These two objects are then returned as out parameters of the ProcessMessage() method.

After this splitting, the response message travels back through the chain of IClientChannelSinks until reaching the formatter, where it is deserialized and an IMessage object created. This object is then returned back through the chain of IMessageSinks until it reaches the two proxies. The TransparentProxy decodes the message, generates the method return value, and fills the respective out or ref parameters.

The original method call—which has been placed by the client application—then returns and the client now has access to the method's responses.

Server-Side Messaging

During the creation of the server-side channel (I use the HttpServerChannel in the following description, but the same applies to the TCPServerChannel as well), the server-side sink chain is created and a TcpListener is spawned in a new thread. This object starts to listen on the specified port and notifies the HttpServerSocketHandler when a connection is made.

The message then passes through the layers shown in Figure 7-7.

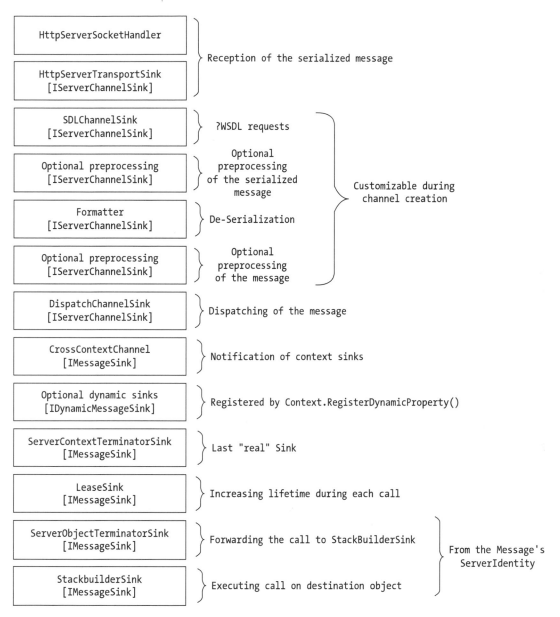

Figure 7-7. Server-side messaging layers

One of the main differences between client-side and server-side message processing is that on the server side, each sink's ProcessMessage() method takes a parameter of type ServerChannelSinkStack. Every sink that is participating in a call pushes itself onto this stack before forwarding the call to the next sink in the chain. The reason for this is that the sinks do not know up front if the call will be handled synchronously or asynchronously. Every sink that's been pushed onto the stack will get the chance to handle the asynchronous reply later.

You can see the IServerChannelSink interface here:

```
public interface IServerChannelSink {

    IServerChannelSink NextChannelSink { get; }

    ServerProcessing ProcessMessage(IServerChannelSinkStack sinkStack,
                                    IMessage requestMsg,
                                    ITransportHeaders requestHeaders,
                                    Stream requestStream,
                                    ref IMessage responseMsg,
                                    ref ITransportHeaders responseHeaders,
                                    ref Stream responseStream);

    void AsyncProcessResponse(IServerResponseChannelSinkStack sinkStack,
                              object state,
                              IMessage msg,
                              ITransportHeaders headers,
                              Stream stream);

    Stream GetResponseStream(IServerResponseChannelSinkStack sinkStack,
                             object state,
                             IMessage msg,
                             ITransportHeaders headers);

}
```

HttpServerChannel and HttpServerTransportSink

When a connection to the server-side channel is opened, an instance of HttpServerSocketHandler is created and supplied with a delegate that points to the HttpServerTransportSink's ServiceRequest() method. This method will be called after the background thread finishes reading the request stream.

The HttpServerTransportSink sets up the ServerChannelSinkStack and pushes itself onto this stack before forwarding the call to the next sink.

After the chain has finished processing the message (that is, after the method call has been executed), it generates the HTTP response headers. These will be either "200 OK" for synchronous calls or "202 Accepted" for one way messages.

SDLChannelSink

The SDLChannelSink is a very special kind of sink that really shows the power of the .NET Remoting Framework's extensibility. Contrary to most other sinks, it does not forward any requests to the destination object, but instead generates the WSDL information needed for the creation of proxies.

It does this whenever it encounters either of the strings "?WSDL" or "?SDL" at the end of an HTTP GET request. In this case, the WSDL will be generated by calling the ConvertTypesToSchemaToStream() method from System.Runtime.Remoting.MetadataServices.MetaData.

> **NOTE**   *MetaData is the same class SoapSuds uses when generating proxies.*

When the HTTP request is of type POST *or* when it is a GET request that does not end with the string "?WSDL" or "?SDL", the message will be passed to the next sink.

SoapServerFormatterSink and BinaryServerFormatterSink

The default server-side HTTP channel uses both formatters in a chained fashion. The first formatter that's used is the SoapServerFormatterSink. This sink first checks whether the serialized message contained in the request stream is a SOAP message. If this is the case, it is deserialized, and the resulting IMessage object is passed to the next sink (which is BinaryServerFormatterSink). In this case, the stream (which is needed as an input parameter to the next sink) will be passed as null.

If the stream does not contain a SOAP-encoded message, it will be copied to a MemoryStream and passed to the BinaryServerFormatterSink.

The binary formatter employs the same logic and passes either the deserialized message (which it might have already gotten from the SOAP formatter, *or* which it can deserialize on its own) or the stream (if it cannot decode the message) to the next sink.

Both BinaryServerFormatterSink and SoapServerFormatterSink only push themselves onto the SinkStack (before calling ProcessMessage() on the subsequent sink) when they can handle the message. If neither BinaryServerFormatterSink nor SoapServerFormatterSink could deserialize the message *and* the next sink is not another formatter, an exception is thrown.

DispatchChannelSink

After passing through an optional layer of IMessageSink objects, the message reaches the dispatcher. The DispatchChannelSink takes the decoded IMessage and forwards it to ChannelServices.DispatchMessage(). This method checks for disconnected or timed-out objects and dynamically instantiates SAOs (Singleton or SingleCall) if they do not exist at the server.

After the possible creation of the necessary destination object, it promotes this call to CrossContextChannel.SyncProcessMessage() or CrossContextChannel.AsyncProcessMessage() if the call's target is a one-way method.

CrossContextChannel

The CrossContextChannel notifies dynamic context sinks and passes the IMessage on to ServerContextTerminatorSink. A dynamic sink does not implement IMessageSink, but rather the interface IDynamicMessageSink which is shown here:

```
public interface IDynamicMessageSink
{
    void ProcessMessageStart(IMessage reqMsg, bool bCliSide, bool bAsync);
    void ProcessMessageFinish(IMessage replyMsg, bool bCliSide, bool bAsync);
}
```

The same logic is applied as with client-side dynamic sinks: these sinks do not have to call any additional sinks in the chain, as this will be taken care of by the framework.

The ProcessMessageStart() method is called *before* passing the message on to ServerContextTerminatorSink and ProcessMesssageFinish() is called after the call to the context terminator sink returns. Both methods may change the IMessage object's properties.

You can read more about dynamic sinks later in Chapter 8.

ServerContextTerminatorSink

This sink's behavior is probably the most complex one. It is the last "hardwired" sink, and therefore has no *direct* references to other sinks in the chain. So how can the method call specified in the message be executed?

The ServerContextTerminatorSink looks at the IMessage's ServerIdentity object, using InternalSink.GetServerIdentity(), and requests this object's message sink chain using ServerIdentity.GetServerObjectChain().

The ServerIdentity's object chain is populated by a call to the static method CreateServerObjectChain() of the Context class. This call creates a ServerObjectTerminatorSink at the absolute end of the chain and puts other sinks before it. These other sinks are obtained from the DomainSpecificRemotingData object, which is held in the RemotingData property of AppDomain.

DomainSpecificRemotingData by default contains a reference to LeaseSink that will be placed in the chain *before* the terminator sink. The resulting sink chain, which is obtained from the ServerIdentity object, is shown in Figure 7-8.

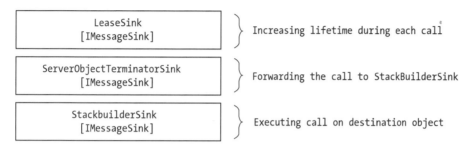

Figure 7-8. Sinks from the ServerIdentity object

LeaseSink

The lease sink will have a reference to the destination MarshalByRefObject's lease. It simply calls the RenewOnCall() method of this lease and passes the call on to the next sink. The RenewOnCall() method looks at the RenewOnCallTime configuration setting (default of two minutes) and sets the object's time to live to this value.

ServerObjectTerminatorSink and StackbuilderSink

The object terminator sink will forward the call to the StackBuilderSink. This final message sink is a kind of "magic" sink. First it checks if it's okay to remotely call the method specified in the IMessage object. It does this by checking whether the destination object matches the request, meaning that there is a "direct match," or the object implements the requested interfaces or is derived from the requested base class.

After verifying the message, the sink uses several external functions to create a stack frame (that is, it makes the transition between message-based execution and stack-based execution) and calls the destination method. It then generates a return message that contains the result and, if available, the values from any ref or out parameters. This ReturnMessage object is then returned from the call to SyncProcessMessage().

All About Asynchronous Messaging

The previous part of this chapter only covers synchronous processing due to one reason: it's a lot easier and consistent between client and server than other types of processing.

As you know from the examples and figures earlier in this chapter, several methods are available for message handling: on the client side, there are the IMessageSink and the IClientChannelSink interfaces. Both sink types approach the handling of asynchronous messages in a substantially different manner, as described in the next sections.

Asynchronous IMessageSink Processing

When handling the messages in a synchronous manner in an IMessageSink chain, the response message will simply be the return value of the method call. You can see this in the following snippet, which shows a sample IMessageSink (I've omitted parts of the interface and only display the SyncProcessMessage() method here):

```
Class MySink1: IMessageSink {
    IMessageSink _nextSink;
    IMessage SyncProcessMessage(IMessage msg) {

        // here you can do something with the msg

        IMessage retMsg = _nextSink.SyncProcessMessage(msg);

        // here you can do something with the retMsg

        // and then, simply return the retMsg to the previous sink
        return retMsg;
    }
}
```

When implementing asynchronous processing that is triggered whenever you use a Delegate's BeginInvoke() method, the call to NextSink.AsyncProcessMessage() is returned immediately. The response message is sent to a secondary chain, which is passed in the replySink parameter of the call to AsyncProcessMessage().

First, I show you how to do asynchronous processing when you *don't* want to be notified of the call's return:

```
public class MySink1: IMessageSink {
    IMessageSink _nextSink;
    IMessageCtrl AsyncProcessMessage(IMessage msg,
                                     IMessageSink replySink);


        // here you can do something with the msg


        return _nextSink.AsyncProcessMessage(msg, replySink);
    }
}
```

In replySink, you'll receive the first entry to a chain of IMessageSink objects that want to be notified upon completion of the asynchronous call.

If you want to handle the reply message in a sink of your own, you have to instantiate a new IMessageSink object and "chain" it to the existing list of reply sinks. You can see this in the following snippet (again, parts of the interface have been omitted):

```
public class MyReplySink: IMessageSink {
    IMessageSink _nextSink;

    MyReplySink(IMessageSink next) {
        // .ctor used to connect this sink to the chain
        _nextSink = next;
    }

    IMessage SyncProcessMessage(IMessage msg) {
        // the msg will be the reply message!

        // here you can do something with the msg

        // and then, pass it onto the next reply sink in the chain
        IMessage retMsg = _nextSink.SyncProcessMessage(msg);

        return retMsg;
    }
}

public class MySink1: IMessageSink {
    IMessageSink _nextSink;
    IMessageCtrl AsyncProcessMessage(IMessage msg,
                                     IMessageSink replySink);


        // here you can do something with the msg
```

```
        // create a new reply sink which is chained to the existing replySink
        IMessageSink myReplyChain = new MyReplySink(replySink);

        // call the next sink's async processing
        return _nextSink.AsyncProcessMessage(msg, myReplyChain);
    }
}
```

When the async call is completed in this example, you'll have the option to
change the reply message in the MyReplySink.SyncProcessMessage() method.

> **NOTE** *The reply message is processed synchronously; only the generation*
> *of the message happens asynchronously at the server.*

Asynchronous IClientChannelSink Processing

As you can see in the following partial definition of the IClientChannelSink interface, there are, in contrast to the IMessageSink interface, distinct methods for
handling the asynchronous request and reply.

```
public interface IClientChannelSink
{
    void AsyncProcessRequest(IClientChannelSinkStack sinkStack,
                             IMessage msg,
                             ITransportHeaders headers,
                             Stream stream);

    void AsyncProcessResponse(IClientResponseChannelSinkStack sinkStack,
                              object state,
                              ITransportHeaders headers,
                              Stream stream);
}
```

When the AsyncProcessRequest() method is called while an IMessage
travels through a sink chain, it will receive an IClientChannelSinkStack as
a parameter. This sink stack contains all sinks that want to be notified when
the asynchronous processing returns. If your sink wants to be included in this
notification, it has to push itself onto this stack before calling the next sink's
AsyncProcessRequest() method.

You can see this in the following snippet (only parts are shown):

```
public class SomeSink: IClientChannelSink
{

    IClientChannelSink _nextChnlSink;

    public void AsyncProcessRequest(IClientChannelSinkStack sinkStack,
                                    IMessage msg,
                                    ITransportHeaders headers,
                                    Stream stream)
    {

        // here you can work with the message

        // pushing this sink onto the stack
        sinkStack.Push (this,null);

        // calling the next sink
        _nextChnlSink.AsyncProcessRequest(sinkStack,msg,headers,stream);
    }
}
```

The sinkStack object that is passed to AsyncProcessRequest() is of type ClientChannelSinkStack and implements the following IClientChannelSinkStack interface, which allows a sink to push itself onto the stack:

```
public interface IClientChannelSinkStack : IClientResponseChannelSinkStack
{
    object Pop(IClientChannelSink sink);
    void Push(IClientChannelSink sink, object state);
}
```

Whatever is being passed as the state parameter of Push() will be received by sink's AsyncProcessResponse() method upon completion of the call. It can contain any information the sink might need while processing the response. For built-in sinks, this will be the original message that triggered the request.

As the previous interface extends the IClientReponseChannelSinkStack interface, I'll show you this one here as well:

```
public interface IClientResponseChannelSinkStack
{
    void AsyncProcessResponse(ITransportHeaders headers, Stream stream);
    void DispatchException(Exception e);
    void DispatchReplyMessage(IMessage msg);
}
```

The `AsyncProcessResponse()` method of the ClientChannelSinkStack pops one sink from stack and calls this sink's `AsyncProcessResponse()` method. Therefore, the "reverse" chaining that uses the sink stack works simply by recursively calling the stack's `AsyncProcessResponse()` method from each sink. This is shown in the following piece of code:

```
public class SomeSink: IClientChannelSink
{
       public void AsyncProcessResponse(
                     IClientResponseChannelSinkStack sinkStack,
                     object state,
                     ITransportHeaders headers,
                     Stream stream);
       {

          // here you can work with the stream or headers

          // calling the next sink via the sink stack
          sinkStack.AsyncProcessResponse(headers,stream);
       }
}
```

Generating the Request

In the following text, I show you how an asynchronous request is generated and how the response is handled. The example I'll use is based on the following custom sinks:

- *MyMessageSink:* A custom IMessageSink

- *MyResponseSink:* A sink created by MyMessageSink as a handler for the asynchronous response

- *MyChannelSink:* A custom IClientChannelSink implementation

Regardless of whether the request is synchronous or asynchronous, the IMessageSink chain is handled *before* any calls to a IClientChannelSink. Immediately before the first call to `IClientChannelSink.AsyncProcessRequest()`, a ClientSinkStack object is instantiated and gets a reference to the IMessageSink reply chain. You can see the beginning of an asynchronous call in Figure 7-9.

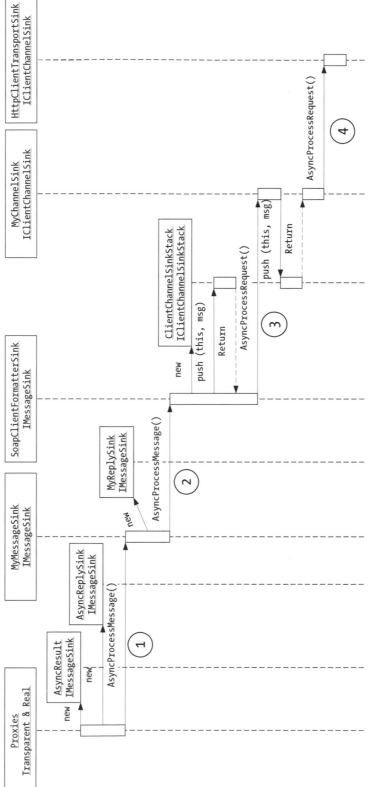

Figure 7-9. First phase of an asynchronous call

In Figures 7-10 through 7-14, you'll see the contents of the replySink and the SinkStack that are passed as parameters at the points marked (1) through (4) in Figure 7-9. In Figure 7-10 you can see the predefined reply chain that is established for each asynchronous call *before* reaching the first IMessageSink. The purpose of these sinks is to handle the asynchronous response in a form that's compatible with the "conventional" delegate mechanism.

The final sink for the asynchronous reply will be the AsyncResult object that is returned from the delegate's BeginInvoke() method.

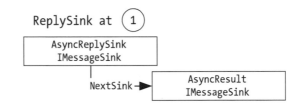

Figure 7-10. SinkStack before call to first custom IMessageSink

When MyMessageSink's AsyncProcessResponse() method is called, it generates a new reply sink, named MyReplySink, that is linked to the existing reply chain. You can see the ReplySink parameter that is passed to the next sink in Figure 7-11.

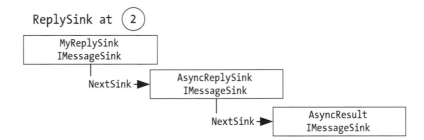

Figure 7-11. SinkStack before call to SoapClientFormatterSink

Figure 7-12 shows you the contents of the ClientChannelSinkStack after SoapClientFormatterSink has finished its processing. The stack contains a reference to the previous IMessageSink stack, shown in Figure 7-11, and points to the first entry in the stack of IClientFormatterSinks. This is quite interesting insofar as the SOAP formatter has been called as an IMessageSink but pushes itself onto the stack of IClientChannelSinks.

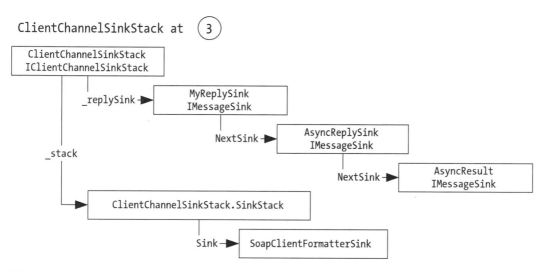

Figure 7-12. SinkStack before call to first custom IClientChannelSink

When the secondary custom IClientChannelSink object, MyChannelSink, is called, it pushes itself onto the stack and calls the `AsyncProcessRequest()` method of HttpClientTransportSink. In Figure 7-13 you can see the resulting channel sink stack before the HTTP request is sent.

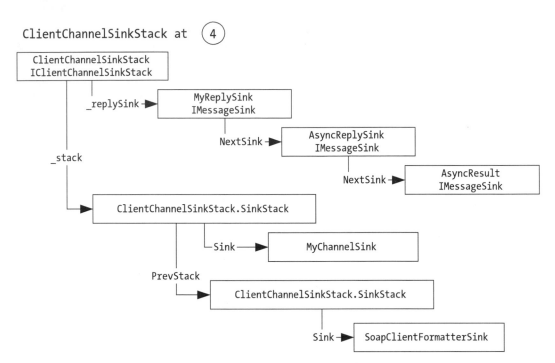

Figure 7-13. SinkStack before call to HttpClientTransportSink

Handling the Response

On receiving the HTTP response, HttpClientTransportSink calls AsyncProcessResponse() on the ClientChannelSinkStack. The sink stack then pops the first entry from the stack (using a different implementation, as with its public Pop() method) and calls AsyncProcessResponse() on the IClientChannelSink that is at the top of the stack. You can see the sequence of calls that follow in Figure 7-14.

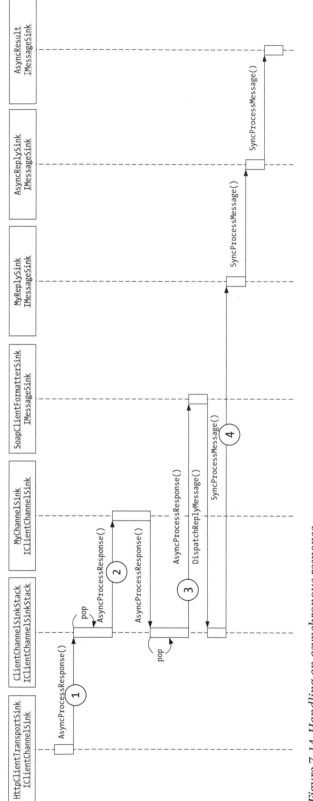

Figure 7-14. Handling an asynchronous response

Before this call—the point marked with (1) in the diagram—the ClientChannelSinkStack will look the same as in Figure 7-13. You can see the state of this stack after the "pop" operation in Figure 7-15.

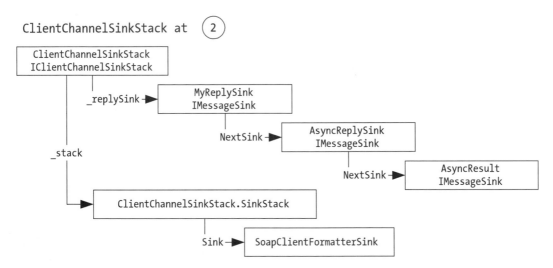

Figure 7-15. The ClientChannelSinkStack before the first sink is called

In the following step, the sink stack places a call to the custom MyChannelSink object. This sink will handle the call as shown in the following source code fragment and will therefore just proceed with invoking AsyncProcessResponse() on the sink stack again.

```
public void AsyncProcessResponse(IClientResponseChannelSinkStack sinkStack,
                                 object state,
                                 ITransportHeaders headers,
                                 Stream stream);
{
        sinkStack.AsyncProcessResponse(headers,stream);
}
```

The ClientChannelSinkStack now pops the next sink from the internal stack and forwards the call on to this SoapClientFormatterSink. You can see the state of the stack at Figure 7-16.

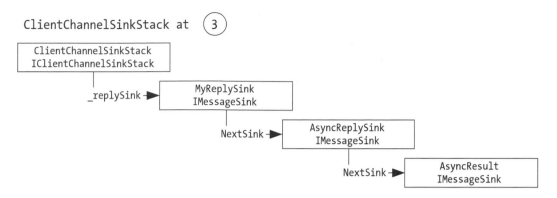

ClientChannelSinkStack at (3)

Figure 7-16. The stack before the call to the SOAP formatter

The SOAP formatter deserializes the HTTP response and creates a new IMessage object. This object is then passed as a parameter to the channel sink stack's DispatchReplyMessage() method.

The sink stack now calls SyncProcessMessage() on the first entry of its reply sink chain, which is shown as (4) in the sequence diagram. After this call, the IMessage travels through the sinks until it reaches the AsyncResult object.

This final sink will examine the response message and prepare the return values for the call to the Delegate's EndInvoke() method.

Exception Handling

When an exception occurs during an IClientChannelSink's processing, it has to call DispatchException() on the sink stack. The stack in this case generates a new ReturnMessage object, passing the original exception as a parameter to its constructor. This newly created return message travels through the chain of IMessageSinks, and the exception will be "unwrapped" by the AsyncResult sink.

Server-Side Asynchronous Processing

On the server side, there are also two kinds of interfaces: IServerChannelSink and IMessageSink. The asynchronous processing for objects implementing IMessageSink is handled in the same way as on the client: the sink has to create another reply sink and pass this to the next sink's AsyncProcessMessage() method.

The handling of asynchronous messages for IServerChannelSink objects is a little bit different. You'll see the relevant parts of this interface below:

```
public interface IServerChannelSink {
    ServerProcessing ProcessMessage(IServerChannelSinkStack sinkStack,
                                    IMessage requestMsg,
                                    ITransportHeaders requestHeaders,
                                    Stream requestStream,
                                    ref IMessage responseMsg,
                                    ref ITransportHeaders responseHeaders,
                                    ref Stream responseStream);

    void AsyncProcessResponse(IServerResponseChannelSinkStack sinkStack,
                              object state,
                              IMessage msg,
                              ITransportHeaders headers,
                              Stream stream);
}
```

When a serialized message is received by an object implementing this interface, it is not yet determined whether it will be handled synchronously or asynchronously. This can only be defined after the message later reaches the formatter.

In the meantime, the sink has to assume that the response *might* be received asynchronously, and therefore will have to push itself (and a possible state object) onto a stack before calling the next sink.

The call to the next sink returns a ServerProcessing value that can be Completed, Async, or OneWay. The sink has to check if this value is Completed and only in such a case might do any post-processing work in ProcessMessage(). If this returned value is OneWay, the sink will not receive any further information when the processing has been finished.

When the next sink's return value is ServerProcessing.Async, the current sink will be notified via the sink stack when the processing has been completed. The sink stack will call AsyncProcessResponse() in this case. After the sink has completed the processing of the response, it has to call sinkStack.AsyncProcessResponse() to forward the call to further sinks.

A sample implementation of ProcessMessage() and AsyncProcessResponse() might look like this:

```csharp
public ServerProcessing ProcessMessage(IServerChannelSinkStack sinkStack,
    IMessage requestMsg,
    ITransportHeaders requestHeaders,
    Stream requestStream,
    out IMessage responseMsg,
    out ITransportHeaders responseHeaders,
    out Stream responseStream)
{

    // Handling of the request will be implemented here

    // pushing onto stack and forwarding the call
    sinkStack.Push(this,null);

     ServerProcessing srvProc = _nextSink.ProcessMessage(sinkStack,
        requestMsg,
        requestHeaders,
        requestStream,
        out responseMsg,
        out responseHeaders,
        out responseStream);

    if (srvProc == ServerProcessing.Complete) {
        // Handling of the response will be implemented here
    }

    // returning status information
    return srvProc;
}

public void AsyncProcessResponse(IServerResponseChannelSinkStack sinkStack,
    object state,
    IMessage msg,
    ITransportHeaders headers,
    Stream stream)
{

    // Handling of the response will be implemented here

    // forwarding to the stack for further processing
    sinkStack.AsyncProcessResponse(msg,headers,stream);
}
```

Summary

In this chapter you learned about the details and inner workings of .NET Remoting. You read about the various processing stages of a message, and you now know the difference between IMessageSink, IClientChannelSink, and IServerChannelSink. You also know how asynchronous requests are processed, and that the inner workings of the asynchronous message handling is different for message sinks and channel sinks.

In the next chapter, I'll show you how those sinks are created using sink providers.

CHAPTER 8

Creation of Sinks

THE PREVIOUS CHAPTER SHOWED YOU the various kinds of sinks and their synchronous and asynchronous processing of requests. What I have omitted until now is one of the most important steps: the instantiation of sinks and sink chains. Sinks are normally not created directly in either your code or with the definition in configuration files. Instead, a chain of sink providers is set up, which will in turn return the sink chains on demand. This chapter shows you the foundation on which to build your own sinks. The implementation of those custom sinks is presented in Chapter 9.

Understanding Sink Providers

As you've seen in Chapter 4, you can define a chain of sinks in a .NET configuration file as shown in the following code. (This example is for a client-side configuration file; for server-side chains, you have to replace clientProviders with serverProviders.)

```
<configuration>
  <system.runtime.remoting>
    <application>
      <channels>
        <channel ref="http">
          <clientProviders>
            <provider type="MySinks.SomeMessageSinkProvider, Client" />
            <formatter ref="soap" />
            <provider type="MySinks.SomeClientChannelSinkProvider, Client" />
          </clientProviders>
        </channel>
      </channels>
    </application>
  </system.runtime.remoting>
</configuration>
```

To cover this example more thoroughly, I'll expand the
`<formatter ref="soap" />` setting using the "real" value from machine.config
(including the necessary strong name here):

```
<formatter id="soap",
  type="System.Runtime.Remoting.Channels.SoapClientFormatterSinkProvider,
  System.Runtime.Remoting, Version=1.0.3300.0, Culture=neutral,
  PublicKeyToken=b77a5c561934e089"/>
```

The complete chain now looks like this:

```
<provider type="MySinks.SomeMessageSinkProvider, Client" />
<formatter id="soap",
  type="System.Runtime.Remoting.Channels.SoapClientFormatterSinkProvider,
  System.Runtime.Remoting, Version=1.0.3300.0, Culture=neutral,
  PublicKeyToken=b77a5c561934e089"/>

<provider type="MySinks.SomeClientChannelSinkProvider, Client" />
```

As you can see in these examples, the chain is *not* defined using the sinks'
names/types (which would be, for example, SoapClientFormatterSink). Instead,
a chain of *providers* is set up. A provider can be either client or server side and
has to implement at least one of these interfaces:

```
public interface IClientChannelSinkProvider
{
    IClientChannelSinkProvider Next { get; set; }

    IClientChannelSink CreateSink(IChannelSender channel,
                                  string url,
                                  object remoteChannelData);
}

public interface IServerChannelSinkProvider
{
    IServerChannelSinkProvider Next { get; set; }

    IServerChannelSink CreateSink(IChannelReceiver channel);
    void GetChannelData(IChannelDataStore channelData);
}
```

You can see in this interface declaration that there is indeed a chain set up
using the Next property of each provider.

Creating Client-Side Sinks

After loading the configuration file shown previously, this provider chain will consist of the objects shown in Figure 8-1. The first three providers are loaded from the configuration, whereas the last one (HttpClientTransportSinkProvider) is by default instantiated by the HTTP channel.

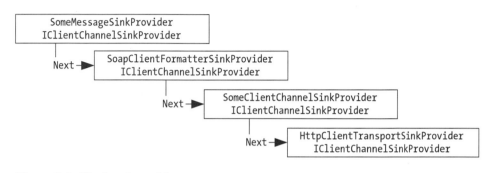

Figure 8-1. Chain of providers

On the client side, these sink providers are associated with the client-side channel. You can access the channel object using the following line of code:

```
IChannel chnl = ChannelServices.GetChannel("http");
```

> **NOTE** *The "http" in this code line refers to the channel's unique name. For HTTP and binary channels, these names are set in machine.config.*

The channel object's contents relevant for creation of the sinks are shown in Figure 8-2.

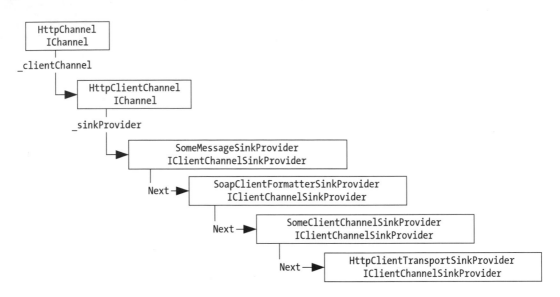

Figure 8-2. IChannel with populated sink providers

When a reference to a remote SAO object is created (for CAOs, an additional ConstructionCall message is sent to the server and the proxy's identity object populated), a lot of things happen behind the scenes. At some time during the use of the new operator or the call to `Activator.GetObject()`, the method `RemotingServices.Connect()` is called. What happens after this call is shown (in part) in Figure 8-3.

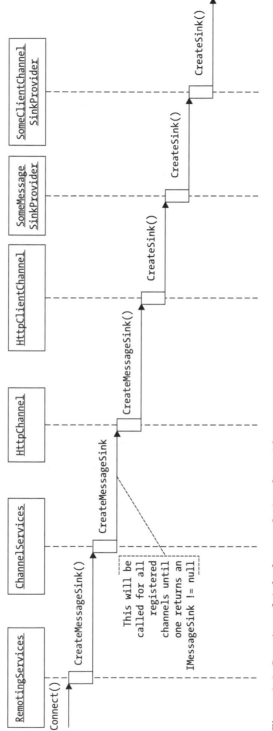

Figure 8-3. Creation of sinks from a chain of providers

241

After being invoked from RemotingServices, ChannelServices calls CreateMessageSink() on each registered channel until one of them accepts the URL that is passed as a parameter. The HTTP channel, for example, will work on any URLs that start with http: or https:, whereas the TCP channel will only accept those with a tcp: protocol designator.

When the channel recognizes the given URL, it calls CreateMessageSink() on its client-side channel.

> **NOTE** *HTTP channel internally consists of both the client-side and the server-side transport channel.*

HttpClientChannel, in turn, invokes CreateSink() on the first sink provider (as shown in Figure 8-3). What the different sink providers do now corresponds to the following code (shown for a sample SomeClientChannelSinkProvider):

```
public class SomeClientChannelSinkProvider: IClientChannelSinkProvider
{
    private IClientChannelSinkProvider next = null;

    public IClientChannelSink CreateSink(IChannelSender channel,
                                         string url,
                                         object remoteChannelData)
    {
        IClientChannelSink nextSink = null;

          // checking for additional sink providers
        if (next != null)
        {
            nextSink = next.CreateSink(channel,url,remoteChannelData);
        }

        // returning first entry of a sink chain
        return new SomeClientChannelSink(nextSink);
    }
}
```

Each sink provider first calls CreateSink() on the next entry in the provider chain and then returns its own sink on top of the sink chain returned from this call. The exact syntax for placing a new sink at the beginning of the chain is not specified, but in this case the SomeClientSink provides a constructor that takes an IClientChannelSink object as a parameter and sets its _nextChnlSink instance variable as shown in the following snippet (again, only parts of the class are shown here):

```
public class SomeClientChannelSink: IClientChannelSink
{
    private IClientChannelSink _nextChnlSink;

    public SomeClientChannelSink (IClientChannelSink next)
    {
      _nextChnlSink = next as IClientChannelSink;
    }
}
```

The complete sink chain that is returned from the call to ChannelServices.CreateMessageSink() is then connected to a new TransparentProxy/RealProxy pair's identity object, as shown in Figure 8-4.

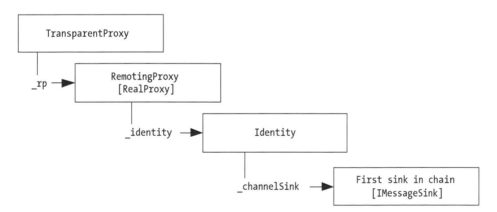

Figure 8-4. The first IMessageSink is connected to the TransparentProxy.

Creating Server-Side Sinks

The creation of server-side sinks works a little differently than the creation of the client-side sinks. As you've seen previously, on the client side the necessary sinks are created when a reference to a remote object is acquired. Contrary to this, server-side sinks are created as soon as a channel is registered.

When the server-side channel is created from a definition in a configuration file, the following constructor will be used:

```
public HttpServerChannel(IDictionary properties,
                         IServerChannelSinkProvider sinkProvider)
```

The IDictionary is taken from the attributes of the <channel> section. When your configuration file, for example, contains this line:

```
<channel ref="http" port="1234" />
```

then the properties dictionary will contain one entry with the key "port" and value 1234.

In the sinkProvider parameter to the constructor, the first entry to the chain of sink providers will be passed to the channel. This chain is constructed from the entries of the <serverProviders> setting in the configuration file.

During the channel setup, which is started from the HTTP channel's constructor, one of two things will happen now. If the <serverProviders> setting is missing, the default sink chain, which is shown in Figure 8-5, will be created.

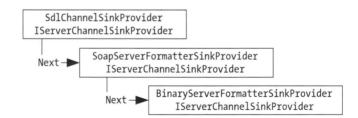

Figure 8-5. The HttpServerChannel's default sink chain

When <serverProviders> has been specified in the configuration file, the sink chain will be created from those values, and none of those default sink providers will be used.

NOTE *This is quite interesting, because in this case, you will not be able to use the "?WSDL" parameter to the URL of your SAO to generate WSDL without explicitly specifying SdlChannelSinkProvider in the <serverProviders> section.*

After this chain of providers has been created, ChannelServices.CreateServerChannelSinkChain() is called. This method takes the sink provider chain as a parameter. It then walks the chain and adds a DispatchChannelSinkProvider object at the end of the chain before calling its CreateSink() method. Finally, it returns the generated sink chain. After receiving this object from ChannelServices, HttpServerChannel will add an HttpServerTransportSink as the first element. The resulting server-side channel object is shown in Figure 8-6.

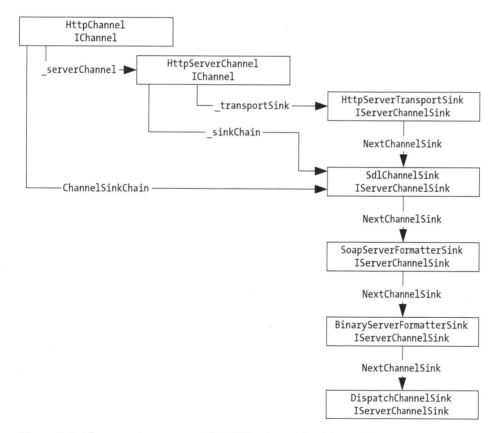

Figure 8-6. The complete server-side HTTP channel's sink stack

Using Dynamic Sinks

As you've seen in the previous chapter, both the client-side and the server-side sink chain can call dynamic sinks. On the server side this is done by the CrossContextChannel and on the client side by the ClientContextTerminatorSink.

Dynamic sinks are associated with a specific *context* (you can read more about contexts in Chapter 11) and therefore will be called for *all* calls passing a context boundary. They cannot be assigned to a specific channel and will even be called for local cross-context or cross-AppDomain calls. The sinks are created by dynamic context properties, which are classes implementing IDynamicProperty and IContributeDynamicSink.

> **NOTE** *IContributeDynamicSink can be compared to a sink provider for dynamic sinks.*

The corresponding interfaces are shown here:

```
public interface IDynamicProperty
{
    string Name { get; }
}


public interface IContributeDynamicSink
{
    IDynamicMessageSink GetDynamicSink();
}
```

The dynamic sink itself, (which has to be returned from GetDynamicSink(), implements the following IDynamicMessageSink interface:

```
public interface IDynamicMessageSink
{
    void ProcessMessageStart(IMessage reqMsg, bool bCliSide, bool bAsync);
    void ProcessMessageFinish(IMessage replyMsg, bool bCliSide, bool bAsync);
}
```

As the names imply, the ProcessMessageStart() method is called *before* the message travels further through the chain, and ProcessMessageFinish() is called when the call has been handled by the sink.

The following dynamic sink will simply write a line to the console, whenever a message passes a remoting boundary.

```
public class MyDynamicSinkProvider: IDynamicProperty, IContributeDynamicSink
{
    public string Name
    {
        get { return "MyDynamicSinkProvider"; }
    }

    public IDynamicMessageSink GetDynamicSink()
    {
        return new MyDynamicSink();
    }

}


public class MyDynamicSink: IDynamicMessageSink
{
    public void ProcessMessageStart(IMessage reqMsg, bool bCliSide,
                                    bool bAsync)
    {
        Console.WriteLine("--> MyDynamicSink: ProcessMessageStart");
    }

    public void ProcessMessageFinish(IMessage replyMsg, bool bCliSide,
                                     bool bAsync)
    {
        Console.WriteLine("--> MyDynamicSink: ProcessMessageFinish");
    }
}
```

To register an IDynamicProperty with the current context, you can use the following code:

```
Context ctx = Context.DefaultContext;
IDynamicProperty prp = new MyDynamicSinkProvider();
Context.RegisterDynamicProperty(prp, null, ctx);
```

Summary

In this chapter you read about the creation of the various kinds of sinks. Together with the previous chapter, you're now fully equipped to implement your own sinks to enhance the feature set of .NET Remoting. You also made first contact with dynamic context sinks, a topic that is covered in more detail in Chapter 11.

I admit that the last two chapters have been quite heavy in content, but in the next chapter I reward your patience by showing some real-world sinks that employ all the techniques presented here.

CHAPTER 9

Extending .NET Remoting

IN CHAPTERS 7 AND 8, I told you a lot about the various places that can be extended by custom sinks and providers. What I didn't tell you is *why* you'd want to change the default remoting behavior. There are a lot of reasons for doing so:

- Compression or encryption of the message's contents

- Passing additional information from the client to the server. For example, you could pass the client-side thread's priority to the server so that the remote execution is performed using the same priority.

- Extending the look and feel of .NET Remoting. You could, for example, switch to a per-host authentication model instead of the default per-object model.

- Debugging your applications by dumping the message's contents to the console or to a log file.

- And last but not least, custom sinks and providers enable you to use other transport mediums such as MSMQ or even SMTP/POP3

You might ask why Microsoft didn't already implement these features itself. The only answer I can give you is that most programmers, including myself, really *prefer* being able to change the framework and add the necessary features themselves in a clean and documented way. You can look forward to getting message sinks from various third-party providers, including Web sites from which you can download sinks with included source code.

Creating a Compression Sink

The first thing to ask yourself before starting to implement a new feature for
.NET Remoting is whether you'll want to work on the original message (that is,
the underlying dictionary) or on the serialized message that you'll get from the
stream. In the case of compression, you won't really care about the message's
contents and instead just want to compress the resulting stream at the client side
and decompress it on the server side *before* reaching the server's SoapFormatter.

You can see the planned client-side sink chain in Figure 9-1 and the server-
side chain in Figure 9-2.

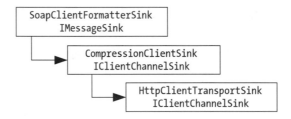

Figure 9-1. Client-side sink chain with the compression sink

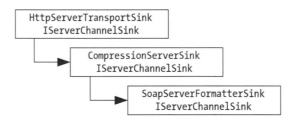

Figure 9-2. Server-side sink chain with the compression sink

After having decided upon the two new sinks, you can identify all classes that
need to be written:

- *CompressionClientSink:* Implements IClientChannelSink, compresses the
  request stream, and decompresses the response stream

- *CompressionClientSinkProvider:* Implements IClientChannelSinkProvider
  and is responsible for the creation of the sink

- *CompressionServerSink:* Implements IServerChannelSink, decompresses
  the request, and compresses the response before it is sent back to
  the client

• *CompressionServerSinkProvider:* Implements IServerChannelSinkProvider and creates the server-side sink

Unfortunately, the .NET Framework does not come with classes that natively support compression, so you have to use a third-party compression library. I hereby recommend using Mike Krueger's NZipLib (available from `http://www.icsharpcode.net/OpenSource/NZipLib/default.asp`). This is an open source C# library that is covered by a liberated GPL license. To quote the Web page: *"In plain English, this means you can use this library in commercial closed-source applications."*

Implementing the Client-Side Sink

The client-side sink extends BaseChannelSinkWithProperties and implements IClientChannelSink. In Listing 9-1, you can see a skeleton client channel sink. The positions at which you'll have to implement the preprocessing and post-processing logic have been marked "TODO." This is a fully working sink—it simply doesn't do anything useful yet.

Listing 9-1. A Skeleton IClientChannelSink

```
using System;
using System.Runtime.Remoting.Channels;
using System.Runtime.Remoting.Messaging;
using System.IO;

namespace CompressionSink
{
    public class CompressionClientSink: BaseChannelSinkWithProperties,
                                    IClientChannelSink
    {
        private IClientChannelSink _nextSink;

        public CompressionClientSink(IClientChannelSink next)
        {
            _nextSink = next;
        }
```

```
public IClientChannelSink NextChannelSink
{
   get {
      return _nextSink;
   }
}


public void AsyncProcessRequest(IClientChannelSinkStack sinkStack,
                                IMessage msg,
                                ITransportHeaders headers,
                                Stream stream)
{
   // TODO: Implement the pre-processing

   sinkStack.Push(this,null);
   _nextSink.AsyncProcessRequest(sinkStack,msg,headers,stream);
}


public void AsyncProcessResponse(IClientResponseChannelSinkStack sinkStack,
                                 object state,
                                 ITransportHeaders headers,
                                 Stream stream)
{

   // TODO: Implement the post-processing

   sinkStack.AsyncProcessResponse(headers,stream);
}


public Stream GetRequestStream(IMessage msg,
                               ITransportHeaders headers)
{
   return _nextSink.GetRequestStream(msg, headers);
}


public void ProcessMessage(IMessage msg,
                           ITransportHeaders requestHeaders,
                           Stream requestStream,
                           out ITransportHeaders responseHeaders,
                           out Stream responseStream)
```

```
    {
        // TODO: Implement the pre-processing

        _nextSink.ProcessMessage(msg,
                                    requestHeaders,
                                    requestStream,
                                    out responseHeaders,
                                    out responseStream);

        // TODO: Implement the post-processing

    }
  }
}
```

Before filling this sink with functionality, you create a helper class that communicates with the compression library and returns a compressed or uncompressed copy of a given stream. You can see this class in Listing 9-2.

Listing 9-2. Class Returning Compressed or Uncompressed Streams

```
using System;
using System.IO;
using NZlib.Compression;
using NZlib.Streams;

namespace CompressionSink
{

    public class CompressionHelper
    {

        public static Stream GetCompressedStreamCopy(Stream inStream)
        {
            Stream outStream = new System.IO.MemoryStream();

            DeflaterOutputStream compressStream = new  DeflaterOutputStream(
                    outStream, new Deflater(Deflater.BEST_COMPRESSION));

            byte[] buf = new Byte[1000];
            int cnt = inStream.Read(buf,0,1000);
            while (cnt>0)
            {
                compressStream.Write(buf,0,cnt);
                cnt = inStream.Read(buf,0,1000);
            }
```

```
            compressStream.Finish();
            compressStream.Flush();
            return outStream;
        }

        public static Stream GetUncompressedStreamCopy(Stream inStream)
        {
            return new InflaterInputStream(inStream);
        }
    }
}
```

When implementing the compression functionality in the client-side sink, you have to deal with both synchronous and asynchronous processing. The synchronous implementation is quite straightforward. Before passing control further down the chain, the sink simply compresses the stream. When it has finished processing (that is, when the server has sent its response), the message sink will decompress the stream and return it to the calling function as an out parameter:

```
public void ProcessMessage(IMessage msg,
                           ITransportHeaders requestHeaders,
                           Stream requestStream,
                           out ITransportHeaders responseHeaders,
                           out Stream responseStream)
{
    // generate a compressed stream using NZipLib

    requestStream  =  CompressionHelper.GetCompressedStreamCopy(requestStream);

    // forward the call to the next sink
    _nextSink.ProcessMessage(msg, requestHeaders, requestStream,
                         out responseHeaders, out responseStream);

    // uncompress  the response
    responseStream = CompressionHelper.GetUncompressedStreamCopy(responseStream);
}
```

As you've seen in the previous chapter, asynchronous handling is split between two methods. In the current example, you add the compression to AsyncProcessRequest() and the decompression to AsyncProcessResponse(), as shown in the following piece of code:

```
public void AsyncProcessRequest(IClientChannelSinkStack sinkStack,
                                IMessage msg,
                                ITransportHeaders headers,
                                Stream stream)
{


    // generate a compressed stream using NZipLib
    stream = CompressionHelper.GetCompressedStreamCopy(stream);

    // push onto stack and forward the request
    sinkStack.Push(this,null);
    _nextSink.AsyncProcessRequest(sinkStack,msg,headers,stream);
}


public void AsyncProcessResponse(IClientResponseChannelSinkStack sinkStack,
                                 object state,
                                 ITransportHeaders headers,
                                 Stream stream)
{

    // uncompress the response
    stream = CompressionHelper.GetUncompressedStreamCopy(stream);

    // forward the request
    sinkStack.AsyncProcessResponse(headers,stream);
}
```

Implementing the Server-Side Sink

The server-side sink's task is to decompress the incoming stream before passing it on to the formatter. In Listing 9-3, you can see a skeleton IServerChannelSink.

Listing 9-3. A Basic IServerChannelSink

```
using System;
using System.Runtime.Remoting.Channels;
using System.Runtime.Remoting.Messaging;
using System.IO;

namespace CompressionSink
{
```

```
public class CompressionServerSink: BaseChannelSinkWithProperties,
                                    IServerChannelSink
{

    private IServerChannelSink _nextSink;

    public CompressionServerSink(IServerChannelSink next)
    {
        _nextSink = next;
    }

    public IServerChannelSink NextChannelSink
    {
        get
        {
            return _nextSink;
        }
    }

    public void AsyncProcessResponse(IServerResponseChannelSinkStack sinkStack,
        object state,
        IMessage msg,
        ITransportHeaders headers,
        Stream stream)
    {
        // TODO: Implement the post-processing

        // forwarding to the stack for further processing
        sinkStack.AsyncProcessResponse(msg,headers,stream);
    }

    public Stream GetResponseStream(IServerResponseChannelSinkStack sinkStack,
        object state,
        IMessage msg,
        ITransportHeaders headers)
    {
        return null;
    }

    public ServerProcessing ProcessMessage(IServerChannelSinkStack sinkStack,
        IMessage requestMsg,
        ITransportHeaders requestHeaders,
        Stream requestStream,
```

```
            out IMessage responseMsg,
            out ITransportHeaders responseHeaders,
            out Stream responseStream)
    {
        // TODO: Implement the pre-processing

        // pushing onto stack and forwarding the call
        sinkStack.Push(this,null);

        ServerProcessing srvProc = _nextSink.ProcessMessage(sinkStack,
            requestMsg,
            requestHeaders,
            requestStream,
            out responseMsg,
            out responseHeaders,
            out responseStream);

        // TODO: Implement the post-processing

        // returning status information
        return srvProc;
    }
  }
}
```

An interesting difference between client-side and server-side sinks is that the server-side sink does not distinguish between synchronous and asynchronous calls during the request stage. Only later in the sink stack will this decision be made and the call possibly returned asynchronously—therefore you always have to push the current sink onto the sinkStack whenever you want the response to be post-processed. To follow the preceding example, you implement ProcessMessage() and AsyncProcessResponse() to decompress the request and compress the response.

```
public ServerProcessing ProcessMessage(IServerChannelSinkStack sinkStack,
    IMessage requestMsg,
    ITransportHeaders requestHeaders,
    Stream requestStream,
    out IMessage responseMsg,
    out ITransportHeaders responseHeaders,
    out Stream responseStream)
{
    // uncompressing the request
    requestStream = CompressionHelper.GetUncompressedStreamCopy(requestStream);
```

```
        // pushing onto stack and forwarding the call
        sinkStack.Push(this,null);

        ServerProcessing srvProc = _nextSink.ProcessMessage(sinkStack,
            requestMsg, requestHeaders, requestStream,
            out responseMsg, out responseHeaders, out responseStream);

        // compressing the response
        responseStream = CompressionHelper.GetCompressedStreamCopy(responseStream);

        // returning status information
        return srvProc;
    }

    public void AsyncProcessResponse(IServerResponseChannelSinkStack sinkStack,
        object state,
        IMessage msg,
        ITransportHeaders headers,
        Stream stream)
    {
        // compressing the response
        stream = CompressionHelper.GetCompressedStreamCopy(stream);

        // forwarding to the stack for further processing
        sinkStack.AsyncProcessResponse(msg,headers,stream);
    }
```

Congratulations! If you've been following along with the examples, you have now finished your first channel sinks. To start using them, you only have to implement two providers that take care of the sink's initialization.

Creating the Sink Providers

Before you can use your sinks in a .NET Remoting application, you have to create a server-side and a client-side sink provider. These classes look nearly identical for most sinks you're going to implement.

In the CreateSink() method, you first create the next provider's sinks and then put the compression sink on top of the chain before returning it, as shown in Listing 9-4.

Listing 9-4. The Client-Side Sink Provider

```csharp
using System;
using System.Runtime.Remoting.Channels;
using System.Collections;

namespace CompressionSink
{
    public class CompressionClientSinkProvider: IClientChannelSinkProvider
    {
        private IClientChannelSinkProvider _nextProvider;

        public CompressionClientSinkProvider(IDictionary properties,
                ICollection providerData)
        {
            // not yet needed
        }

        public IClientChannelSinkProvider Next
        {
            get {return _nextProvider; }
            set {_nextProvider = value;}
        }

        public IClientChannelSink CreateSink(IChannelSender channel,
            string url,
            object remoteChannelData)
        {
            // create other sinks in the chain
            IClientChannelSink next = _nextProvider.CreateSink(channel,
                url,
                remoteChannelData);

            // put our sink on top of the chain and return it
            return new CompressionClientSink(next);
        }
    }
}
```

The server-side sink provider that is shown in Listing 9-5 looks nearly identical, but returns IServerChannelSink instead of IClientChannelSink.

Listing 9-5. The Server-Side Sink Provider

```csharp
using System;
using System.Runtime.Remoting.Channels;
using System.Collections;

namespace CompressionSink
{
    public class CompressionServerSinkProvider: IServerChannelSinkProvider
    {
        private IServerChannelSinkProvider _nextProvider;

        public CompressionServerSinkProvider(IDictionary properties,
                ICollection providerData)
        {
            // not yet needed
        }

        public IServerChannelSinkProvider Next
        {
            get {return _nextProvider; }
            set {_nextProvider = value;}
        }

        public IServerChannelSink CreateSink(IChannelReceiver channel)
        {
            // create other sinks in the chain
            IServerChannelSink next = _nextProvider.CreateSink(channel);

            // put our sink on top of the chain and return it
            return new CompressionServerSink(next);
        }

        public void GetChannelData(IChannelDataStore channelData)
        {
            // not yet needed
        }

    }
}
```

Using the Sinks

To use the sinks on the client and server side of a channel, you simply have to include them in your configuration files. In the client-side configuration file, you have to incorporate the information shown in the following code. If you place the CompressionSink assembly in the GAC, mind that you have to specify the complete strong name in the type attribute!

```
<configuration>
 <system.runtime.remoting>
  <application>
   <channels>
    <channel ref="http">

       <clientProviders>
          <formatter ref="soap" />
          <provider
          type="CompressionSink.CompressionClientSinkProvider, CompressionSink" />
       </clientProviders>

    </channel>
   </channels>
  </application>
 </system.runtime.remoting>
</configuration>
```

The server-side configuration file will look similar to the following:

```
<configuration>
 <system.runtime.remoting>
  <application>
   <channels>
    <channel ref="http" port="1234">

      <serverProviders>
         <provider
         type="CompressionSink.CompressionServerSinkProvider, CompressionSink" />
         <formatter ref="soap"/>
      </serverProviders>
```

```
        </channel>
      </channels>
    </application>
  </system.runtime.remoting>
</configuration>
```

Figure 9-3 shows a TCP trace from a client/server connection that isn't using this sink, whereas Figure 9-4 shows the improvement when compression is used.

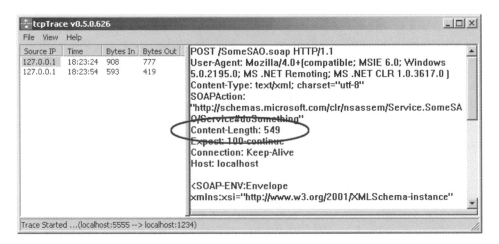

Figure 9-3. TCP trace of an HTTP/SOAP connection[1]

In the circled area, you can see that the HTTP Content-Length header goes down from 549 bytes to 234 bytes when using the compression sink.

> **NOTE** *This is a* proof-of-concept *example. Instead of using compression in this scenario, you could easily switch to binary encoding to save even more bytes to transfer. But keep in mind that the compression sink also works with the binary formatter!*

---

[1] You can get this tcpTrace tool at http://www.pocketsoap.com.

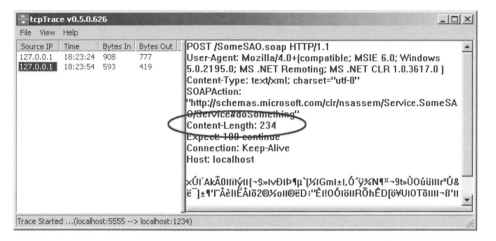

Figure 9-4. TCP trace of an HTTP connection with compressed content

Extending the Compression Sink

The server-side sink as presented in the previous section has at least one serious problem when used in real-world applications: it doesn't yet detect if the stream is compressed or not and will always try to decompress it. This will lead to an inevitable exception when the request stream has not been compressed before.

In an average remoting scenario, you have two types of users. On the one hand, there are local (LAN) users who connect to the server via high-speed links. If these users compress their requests, it's quite possible that the stream compression would take up more time (in regard to client- and server-side CPU time plus transfer time) than the network transfer of the uncompressed stream would. On the other hand, you might have several remote users who connect via lines ranging from speedy T1s down to 9600 bps wireless devices. *These* users will quite certainly profit from sending requests in a compressed way.

The first step to take when implementing these additional capabilities in a channel sink is to determine how the server will know that the request stream is compressed. Generally this can be done by adding additional fields to the ITransportHeader object that is passed as a parameter to ProcessMessage() and AsyncProcessRequest().

These headers are then transferred to the server and can be obtained by the server-side sink by using the ITransportHeaders that it receives as a parameter to its ProcessMessage() method. By convention, these additional headers should start with the prefix X-, so that you can simply add a statement like the following in the client-side sink's ProcessMessage() method to indicate that the content will be compressed:

```
requestHeaders["X-Compress"]="yes";
```

The complete AsyncProcessRequest() method now looks like this:

```
public void AsyncProcessRequest(IClientChannelSinkStack sinkStack,
                                IMessage msg,
                                ITransportHeaders headers,
                                Stream stream)
{
    headers["X-Compress"]="yes";

    stream = CompressionHelper.GetCompressedStreamCopy(stream);

    // push onto stack and forward the request
    sinkStack.Push(this,null);
    _nextSink.AsyncProcessRequest(sinkStack,msg,headers,stream);
}
```

When the server receives this request, it processes the message and replies with a compressed stream as well. The server also indicates this compression by setting the X-Compress header. The complete client-side code for AsyncProcessResponse() and ProcessMessage() will therefore look at the response headers and decompress the message if necessary:

```
public void ProcessMessage(IMessage msg,
                           ITransportHeaders requestHeaders,
                           Stream requestStream,
                           out ITransportHeaders responseHeaders,
                           out Stream responseStream)
{

    requestStream = CompressionHelper.GetCompressedStreamCopy(requestStream);
    requestHeaders["X-Compress"] = "yes";

    // forward the call to the next sink
    _nextSink.ProcessMessage(msg,
                             requestHeaders,
                             requestStream,
                             out responseHeaders,
                             out responseStream);

    // deflate the response if necessary
    String xcompress = (String) responseHeaders["X-Compress"];
```

```
    if (xcompress != null && xcompress == "yes")
    {
        responseStream =
                CompressionHelper.GetUncompressedStreamCopy(responseStream);
    }
}

public void AsyncProcessResponse(IClientResponseChannelSinkStack sinkStack,
                                 object state,
                                 ITransportHeaders headers,
                                 Stream stream)
{

    // decompress the stream if necessary
    String xcompress = (String) headers["X-Compress"];

    if (xcompress != null && xcompress == "yes")
    {
        stream = CompressionHelper.GetUncompressedStreamCopy(stream);
    }


    // forward the request
    sinkStack.AsyncProcessResponse(headers,stream);
}
```

The server-side channel sink's `ProcessMessage()` method works a little bit differently. As you've seen in Chapter 7, when the message reaches this method, it's not yet determined if the call will be executed synchronously or asynchronously. Therefore the sink has to push itself onto a sink stack that will be used when replying asynchronously.

As the `AsyncProcessResponse()` method for the channel sink has to know whether the original request has been compressed or not, you'll need to use the second parameter of the `sinkStack.Push()` method, which is called during `ProcessMessage()`. In this parameter you can put any object that enables you to later determine the state of the request. This state object will be passed as a parameter to `AsyncProcessResponse()`. The complete server-side implementation of `ProcessMessage()` and `AsyncProcessResponse()` therefore looks like this:

```
public ServerProcessing ProcessMessage(IServerChannelSinkStack sinkStack,
    IMessage requestMsg,
    ITransportHeaders requestHeaders,
    Stream requestStream,
    out IMessage responseMsg,
    out ITransportHeaders responseHeaders,
    out Stream responseStream)
{

    bool isCompressed=false;


    // decompress the stream if necessary
    String xcompress = (String) requestHeaders["X-Compress"];
    if (xcompress != null && xcompress == "yes")
    {
        requestStream = CompressionHelper.GetUncompressedStreamCopy(requestStream);
        isCompressed = true;
    }


    // Pushing onto stack and forwarding the call.
    // The state object contains true if the request has been compressed,
    // else false.
    sinkStack.Push(this,isCompressed);

    ServerProcessing srvProc = _nextSink.ProcessMessage(sinkStack,
        requestMsg,
        requestHeaders,
        requestStream,
        out responseMsg,
        out responseHeaders,
        out responseStream);

    if (srvProc == ServerProcessing.Complete ) {
        // compressing the response if necessary
        if (isCompressed)
        {
            responseStream=
                    CompressionHelper.GetCompressedStreamCopy(responseStream);
            responseHeaders["X-Compress"] = "yes";
        }
    }
```

```
    // returning status information
    return srvProc;
}


public void AsyncProcessResponse(IServerResponseChannelSinkStack sinkStack,
    object state,
    IMessage msg,
    ITransportHeaders headers,
    Stream stream)
{
    // fetching the flag from the async-state
    bool hasBeenCompressed = (bool) state;

    // compressing the response if necessary
    if (hasBeenCompressed)
    {
        stream=CompressionHelper.GetCompressedStreamCopy(stream);
        headers["X-Compress"] = "yes";
    }



    // forwarding to the stack for further processing
    sinkStack.AsyncProcessResponse(msg,headers,stream);
}
```

As you can see in Figures 9-5, which shows the HTTP request, and Figure 9-6, which shows the corresponding response, the complete transfer is compressed and the custom HTTP header X-Compress is populated.

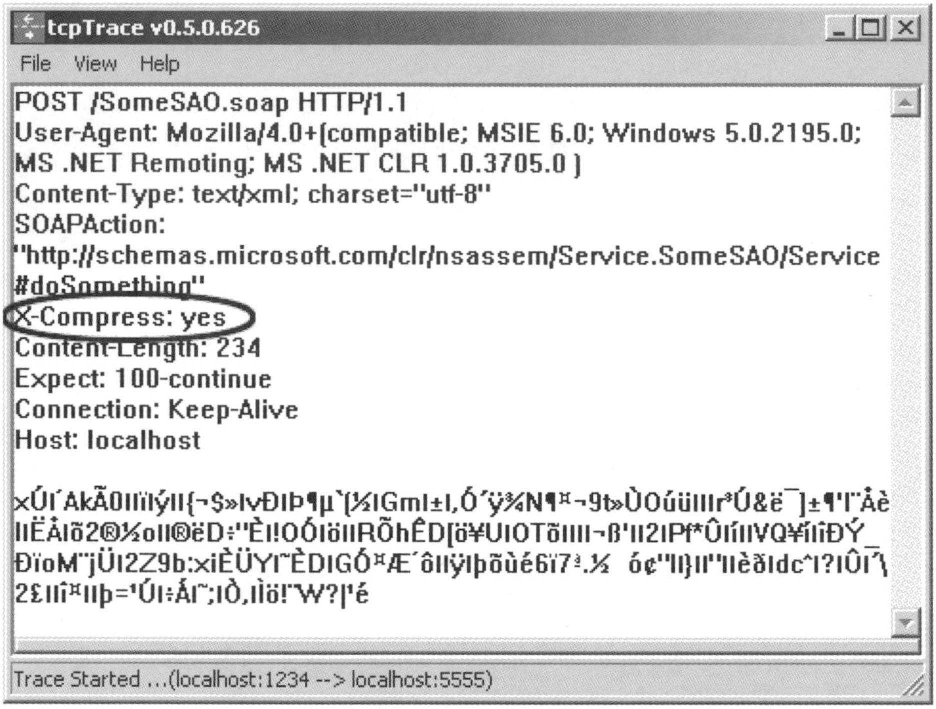

Figure 9-5. The compressed HTTP request

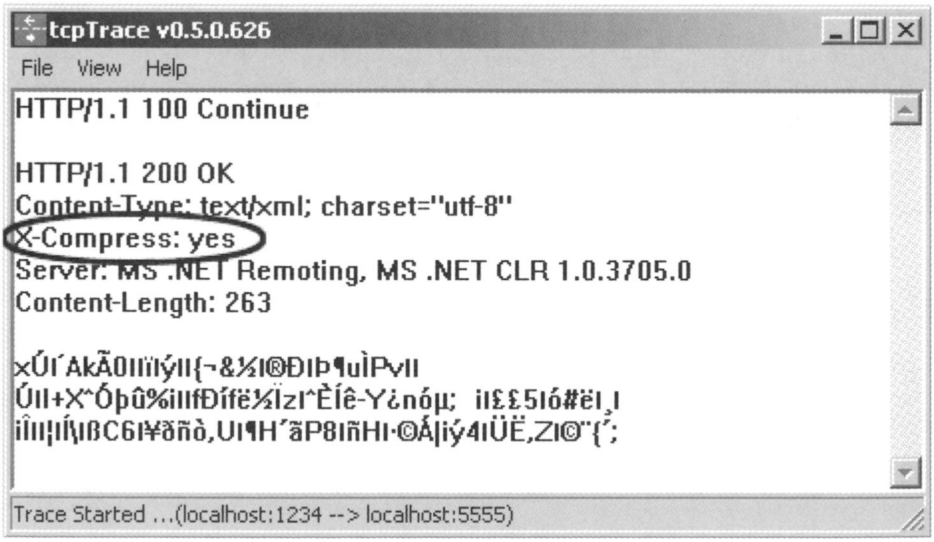

Figure 9-6. The compressed HTTP response

Encrypting the Transfer

Even though using an asymmetric/symmetric combination such as HTTPS/SSL for the encryption of the network traffic provides the only real security, in some situations HTTPS isn't quite helpful.

First, .NET Remoting by default only supports encryption when using an HTTP channel and when hosting the server-side components in IIS. If you want to use a TCP channel or host your objects in a Windows service, there's no default means of secure communication.

Second, even if you use IIS to host your components, callbacks that are employed with event notification will *not* be secured. This is because your client (which is the server for the callback object) does not publish its objects using HTTPS, but only HTTP.

Essential Symmetric Encryption

Symmetric encryption is based on one key fact: client and server will have access to the *same* encryption key. This key is not a password as you might know it, but instead is a binary array in common sizes from 40 to 192 bits. Additionally, you have to choose from among a range of encryption algorithms supplied with the .NET Framework: DES, TripleDES, RC2, or Rijndael.

To generate a random key for a specified algorithm, you can use the following code snippet. You will find the key in the byte[] variable mykey afterwards.

```
String algorithmName = "TripleDES";
SymmetricAlgorithm alg = SymmetricAlgorithm.Create(algorithmName);

int keylen = 128;
alg.KeySize = keylen;
alg.GenerateKey();

byte[] mykey = alg.Key;
```

Because each algorithm has a limited choice of valid key lengths, and because you might want to save this key to a file, you can run the separate KeyGenerator console application, which is shown in Listing 9-6.

Listing 9-6. A Complete Keyfile Generator
```
using System;
using System.IO;
using System.Security.Cryptography;
```

```
class KeyGen
{
    static void Main(string[] args)
    {
        if (args.Length != 1 && args.Length != 3)
        {
            Console.WriteLine("Usage:");
            Console.WriteLine("KeyGenerator <Algorithm> [<KeySize> <Outputfile>]");
            Console.WriteLine("Algorithm can be: DES, TripleDES, RC2 or Rijndael");
            Console.WriteLine();
            Console.WriteLine("When only <Algorithm> is specified, the program");
            Console.WriteLine("will print a list of valid key sizes.");
            return;
        }

        String algorithmname = args[0];

        SymmetricAlgorithm alg = SymmetricAlgorithm.Create(algorithmname);

        if (alg == null)
        {
            Console.WriteLine("Invalid algorithm specified.");
            return;
        }

        if (args.Length == 1)
        {
            // just list the possible key sizes
            Console.WriteLine("Legal key sizes for algorithm {0}:",algorithmname);
            foreach (KeySizes size in alg.LegalKeySizes)
            {
                if (size.SkipSize != 0)
                {
                    for (int i = size.MinSize;i<=size.MaxSize;i=i+size.SkipSize)
                    {
                        Console.WriteLine("{0} bit", i);
                    }
                }
                else
                {
                    if (size.MinSize != size.MaxSize)
                    {
                        Console.WriteLine("{0} bit", size.MinSize);
                        Console.WriteLine("{0} bit", size.MaxSize);
                    }
```

```
            else
            {
                Console.WriteLine("{0} bit", size.MinSize);
            }
        }
    }
    return;
}


// user wants to generate a key
int keylen = Convert.ToInt32(args[1]);
String outfile = args[2];
try
{
    alg.KeySize = keylen;
    alg.GenerateKey();
    FileStream fs = new FileStream(outfile,FileMode.CreateNew);
    fs.Write(alg.Key,0,alg.Key.Length);
    fs.Close();
    Console.WriteLine("{0} bit key written to {1}.",
                alg.Key.Length * 8,
                outfile);

}
catch (Exception e)
{
    Console.WriteLine("Exception: {0}" ,e.Message);
    return;
}



    }
}
```

When this key generator is invoked with KeyGenerator.exe (without any parameters), it will print a list of possible algorithms. You can then run KeyGenerator.exe <AlgorithmName> to get a list of possible key sizes for the chosen algorithm. To finally generate the key, you have to start KeyGenerator.exe <AlgorithmName> <KeySize> <OutputFile>. To generate a 128-bit key for a TripleDES algorithm and save it in c:\testfile.key, run KeyGenerator.exe TripleDES 128 c:\testfile.key.

The Initialization Vector

Another basic of symmetric encryption is the use of a random *initialization vector* (IV). This is again a byte array, but it's not statically computed during the application's development. Instead, a new one is generated for each encryption taking place.

To successfully decrypt the message, both the key and the initialization vector have to be known to the second party. The key is determined during the application's deployment (at least in the following example) and the IV has to be sent via remoting boundaries with the original message. The IV is therefore not secret on its own.

Creating the Encryption Helper

Next I show you how to build this sink in the same manner as the previous CompressionSink, which means that the sink's core logic will be extracted to a helper class. I call this class EncryptionHelper. The encryption helper will implement two methods, ProcessOutboundStream() and ProcessInboundStream(). The methods' signatures look like this:

```
public static Stream ProcessOutboundStream(
        Stream inStream,
        String algorithm,
        byte[] encryptionkey,
        out byte[] encryptionIV)

public static Stream ProcessInboundStream(
        Stream inStream,
        String algorithm,
        byte[] encryptionkey,
        byte[] encryptionIV)
```

As you can see in the signature, both methods take a stream, the name of a valid cryptoalgorithm, and a byte array that contains the encryption key as parameters. The first method is used to encrypt the stream. It also internally generates the IV and returns it as an out parameter. This IV then has to be serialized by the sink and passed to the other party in the remoting call. ProcessInboundStream(), on the other hand, expects the IV to be passed to it, so this value has to be obtained by the sink before calling this method. The implementation of these helper methods can be seen in Listing 9-7.

*Listing 9-7. The EncryptionHelper Encapsulates the Details of the
Cryptographic Process*

```
using System;
using System.IO;
using System.Security.Cryptography;

namespace EncryptionSink
{

    public class EncryptionHelper
    {

        public static Stream ProcessOutboundStream(
            Stream inStream,
            String algorithm,
            byte[] encryptionkey,
            out byte[] encryptionIV)
        {
            Stream outStream = new System.IO.MemoryStream();

            // setup the encryption properties
            SymmetricAlgorithm alg = SymmetricAlgorithm.Create(algorithm);
            alg.Key = encryptionkey;
            alg.GenerateIV();
            encryptionIV = alg.IV;

            CryptoStream encryptStream = new CryptoStream(
                outStream,
                alg.CreateEncryptor(),
                CryptoStreamMode.Write);

            // write the whole contents through the new streams
            byte[] buf = new Byte[1000];
            int cnt = inStream.Read(buf,0,1000);
            while (cnt>0)
            {
                encryptStream.Write(buf,0,cnt);
                cnt = inStream.Read(buf,0,1000);
            }
            encryptStream.FlushFinalBlock();
            outStream.Seek(0,SeekOrigin.Begin);
            return outStream;
        }
```

```
        public static Stream ProcessInboundStream(
            Stream inStream,
            String algorithm,
            byte[] encryptionkey,
            byte[] encryptionIV)
    {
        // setup decryption properties
        SymmetricAlgorithm alg = SymmetricAlgorithm.Create(algorithm);
        alg.Key = encryptionkey;
        alg.IV = encryptionIV;

        // add the decryptor layer to the stream
        Stream outStream = new CryptoStream(inStream,
            alg.CreateDecryptor(),
            CryptoStreamMode.Read);

        return outStream;
    }

    }
}
```

Creating the Sinks

The EncryptionClientSink and EncryptionServerSink look quite similar to the previous compression sinks. The major difference is that they have custom constructors that are called from their sink providers to set the specified encryption algorithm and key. For outgoing requests, the sinks will set the X-Encrypt header to "yes" and store the initialization vector in Base64 coding in the X-EncryptIV header. The complete client-side sink is shown in Listing 9-8.

Listing 9-8. The EncryptionClientSink

```
using System;
using System.Runtime.Remoting.Channels;
using System.Runtime.Remoting.Messaging;
using System.IO;
using System.Text;

namespace EncryptionSink
{
    public class EncryptionClientSink: BaseChannelSinkWithProperties,
                                       IClientChannelSink
```

```
{
    private IClientChannelSink _nextSink;
    private byte[] _encryptionKey;
    private String _encryptionAlgorithm;

    public EncryptionClientSink(IClientChannelSink next,
        byte[] encryptionKey,
        String encryptionAlgorithm)
    {
        _encryptionKey = encryptionKey;
        _encryptionAlgorithm = encryptionAlgorithm;
        _nextSink = next;
    }

    public void ProcessMessage(IMessage msg,
        ITransportHeaders requestHeaders,
        Stream requestStream,
        out ITransportHeaders responseHeaders,
        out Stream responseStream)
    {

        byte[] IV;

        requestStream = EncryptionHelper.ProcessOutboundStream(requestStream,
            _encryptionAlgorithm,_encryptionKey,out IV);

        requestHeaders["X-Encrypt"]="yes";
        requestHeaders["X-EncryptIV"]= Convert.ToBase64String(IV);


        // forward the call to the next sink
        _nextSink.ProcessMessage(msg,
            requestHeaders,
            requestStream,
            out responseHeaders,
            out responseStream);


        if (responseHeaders["X-Encrypt"] != null &&
            responseHeaders["X-Encrypt"].Equals("yes"))
        {

            IV = Convert.FromBase64String(
                    (String) responseHeaders["X-EncryptIV"]);
```

```
                responseStream = EncryptionHelper.ProcessInboundStream(
                    responseStream,
                    _encryptionAlgorithm,
                    _encryptionKey,
                    IV);
            }


    }

    public void AsyncProcessRequest(IClientChannelSinkStack sinkStack,
                            IMessage msg,
                            ITransportHeaders headers,
                            Stream stream)
    {
        byte[] IV;

        stream = EncryptionHelper.ProcessOutboundStream(stream,
            _encryptionAlgorithm,_encryptionKey,out IV);

        headers["X-Encrypt"]="yes";
        headers["X-EncryptIV"]= Convert.ToBase64String(IV);

        // push onto stack and forward the request
        sinkStack.Push(this,null);
        _nextSink.AsyncProcessRequest(sinkStack,msg,headers,stream);
    }


    public void AsyncProcessResponse(IClientResponseChannelSinkStack sinkStack,
                            object state,
                            ITransportHeaders headers,
                            Stream stream)
    {


        if (headers["X-Encrypt"] != null && headers["X-Encrypt"].Equals("yes"))
        {

            byte[] IV =
                Convert.FromBase64String((String) headers["X-EncryptIV"]);
```

```
        stream = EncryptionHelper.ProcessInboundStream(
            stream,
            _encryptionAlgorithm,
            _encryptionKey,
            IV);
    }


    // forward the request
    sinkStack.AsyncProcessResponse(headers,stream);
}



public Stream GetRequestStream(IMessage msg,
                                 ITransportHeaders headers)
{
    return null; // request stream will be manipulated later
}

public IClientChannelSink NextChannelSink {
    get
    {
        return _nextSink;
    }
}


  }
}
```

The EncryptionServerSink shown in Listing 9-9 works basically in the same way as the CompressionServerSink does. It first checks the headers to determine whether the request has been encrypted. If this is the case, it retrieves the encryption initialization vector from the header and calls EncryptionHelper to decrypt the stream.

Listing 9-9. The EncryptionServerSink

```
using System;
using System.Runtime.Remoting.Channels;
using System.Runtime.Remoting;
using System.Runtime.Remoting.Messaging;
using System.IO;

namespace EncryptionSink
{
```

```
public class EncryptionServerSink: BaseChannelSinkWithProperties,
                                IServerChannelSink
{

    private IServerChannelSink _nextSink;
    private byte[] _encryptionKey;
    private String _encryptionAlgorithm;

    public EncryptionServerSink(IServerChannelSink next, byte[] encryptionKey,
            String encryptionAlgorithm)
    {
        _encryptionKey = encryptionKey;
        _encryptionAlgorithm = encryptionAlgorithm;
        _nextSink = next;
    }

    public ServerProcessing ProcessMessage(IServerChannelSinkStack sinkStack,
        IMessage requestMsg,
        ITransportHeaders requestHeaders,
        Stream requestStream,
        out IMessage responseMsg,
        out ITransportHeaders responseHeaders,
        out Stream responseStream) {

        bool isEncrypted=false;

        //checking the headers
        if (requestHeaders["X-Encrypt"] != null &&
            requestHeaders["X-Encrypt"].Equals("yes"))
        {
            isEncrypted = true;

            byte[] IV = Convert.FromBase64String(
                (String) requestHeaders["X-EncryptIV"]);

            // decrypt the request
            requestStream = EncryptionHelper.ProcessInboundStream(
                requestStream,
                _encryptionAlgorithm,
                _encryptionKey,
                IV);
        }
```

```
      // pushing onto stack and forwarding the call,
      // the flag "isEncrypted" will be used as state
      sinkStack.Push(this,isEncrypted);

      ServerProcessing srvProc = _nextSink.ProcessMessage(sinkStack,
          requestMsg,
          requestHeaders,
          requestStream,
          out responseMsg,
          out responseHeaders,
          out responseStream);

      if (isEncrypted)
      {
          // encrypting the response if necessary
          byte[] IV;

          responseStream =
              EncryptionHelper.ProcessOutboundStream(responseStream,
              _encryptionAlgorithm,_encryptionKey,out IV);

          responseHeaders["X-Encrypt"]="yes";
          responseHeaders["X-EncryptIV"]= Convert.ToBase64String(IV);
      }

      // returning status information
      return srvProc;
}

public void AsyncProcessResponse(IServerResponseChannelSinkStack sinkStack,
    object state,
    IMessage msg,
    ITransportHeaders headers,
    Stream stream)
{
    // fetching the flag from the async-state
    bool isEncrypted = (bool) state;


    if (isEncrypted)
    {
        // encrypting the response if necessary
        byte[] IV;
```

```
        stream = EncryptionHelper.ProcessOutboundStream(stream,
            _encryptionAlgorithm,_encryptionKey,out IV);

        headers["X-Encrypt"]="yes";
        headers["X-EncryptIV"]= Convert.ToBase64String(IV);
    }


    // forwarding to the stack for further ProcessIng
    sinkStack.AsyncProcessResponse(msg,headers,stream);
}

public Stream GetResponseStream(IServerResponseChannelSinkStack sinkStack,
    object state,
    IMessage msg,
    ITransportHeaders headers)
{
    return null;
}

public IServerChannelSink NextChannelSink {
    get {
        return _nextSink;
    }
}
```

    }
}

Creating the Providers

Contrary to the previous sink, the EncryptionSink expects certain parameters to be present in the configuration file. The first one is "algorithm", which specifies the cryptographic algorithm that should be used (DES, TripleDES, RC2, or Rijndael). The second parameter, "keyfile", specifies the location of the previously generated symmetric keyfile. The same file has to be available to both the client and the server sink.

The following excerpt from a configuration file shows you how the client-side sink will be configured:

```
<configuration>
 <system.runtime.remoting>
  <application>
   <channels>
    <channel ref="http">

     <clientProviders>
      <formatter ref="soap" />
      <provider type="EncryptionSink.EncryptionClientSinkProvider, EncryptionSink"
                         algorithm="TripleDES" keyfile="testkey.dat" />
     </clientProviders>

    </channel>
   </channels>
  </application>
 </system.runtime.remoting>
</configuration>
```

In the following snippet you see how the server-side sink can be initialized:

```
<configuration>
 <system.runtime.remoting>
  <application>
   <channels>
    <channel ref="http" port="5555">

     <serverProviders>
     <provider type="EncryptionSink.EncryptionServerSinkProvider, EncryptionSink"
                         algorithm="TripleDES" keyfile="testkey.dat" />
      <formatter ref="soap"/>
     </serverProviders>

    </channel>
   </channels>
  </application>
 </system.runtime.remoting>
</configuration>
```

You can access additional parameters in the sink provider's constructor as shown in the following source code fragment:

```
public EncryptionClientSinkProvider(IDictionary properties,
        ICollection providerData)
{
  String encryptionAlgorithm = (String) properties["algorithm"];
}
```

In addition to reading the relevant configuration file parameters, both the client-side sink provider (shown in Listing 9-10) and the server-side sink provider (shown in Listing 9-11) have to read the specified keyfile and store it in a byte array. The encryption algorithm and the encryption key are then passed to the sink's constructor.

Listing 9-10. The EncryptionClientSinkProvider

```
using System;
using System.IO;
using System.Runtime.Remoting.Channels;
using System.Runtime.Remoting;
using System.Collections;

namespace EncryptionSink
{
    public class EncryptionClientSinkProvider: IClientChannelSinkProvider
    {
        private IClientChannelSinkProvider _nextProvider;

        private byte[] _encryptionKey;
        private String _encryptionAlgorithm;

        public EncryptionClientSinkProvider(IDictionary properties,
                ICollection providerData)
        {
            _encryptionAlgorithm = (String) properties["algorithm"];
            String keyfile = (String) properties["keyfile"];

            if (_encryptionAlgorithm == null || keyfile == null)
            {
                throw new RemotingException("'algorithm' and 'keyfile' have to " +
                    "be specified for EncryptionClientSinkProvider");
            }
```

```csharp
            // read the encryption key from the specified fike
            FileInfo fi = new FileInfo(keyfile);

            if (!fi.Exists)
            {
                throw new RemotingException("Specified keyfile does not exist");
            }

            FileStream fs = new FileStream(keyfile,FileMode.Open);
            _encryptionKey = new Byte[fi.Length];
            fs.Read(_encryptionKey,0,_encryptionKey.Length);
        }

        public IClientChannelSinkProvider Next
        {
            get {return _nextProvider; }
            set {_nextProvider = value;}
        }

        public IClientChannelSink CreateSink(IChannelSender channel, string url,
                object remoteChannelData)
        {
            // create other sinks in the chain
            IClientChannelSink next = _nextProvider.CreateSink(channel,
                url, remoteChannelData);

            // put our sink on top of the chain and return it
            return new EncryptionClientSink(next,_encryptionKey,
                _encryptionAlgorithm);
        }
    }
}
```

Listing 9-11. The EncryptionServerSinkProvider

```csharp
using System;
using System.IO;
using System.Runtime.Remoting.Channels;
using System.Runtime.Remoting;
using System.Collections;

namespace EncryptionSink
{
    public class EncryptionServerSinkProvider: IServerChannelSinkProvider
    {
```

```csharp
private byte[] _encryptionKey;
private String _encryptionAlgorithm;

private IServerChannelSinkProvider _nextProvider;

public EncryptionServerSinkProvider(IDictionary properties,
    ICollection providerData)
{
    _encryptionAlgorithm = (String) properties["algorithm"];
    String keyfile = (String) properties["keyfile"];

    if (_encryptionAlgorithm == null || keyfile == null)
    {
        throw new RemotingException("'algorithm' and 'keyfile' have to " +
            "be specified for EncryptionServerSinkProvider");
    }


    // read the encryption key from the specified fike
    FileInfo fi = new FileInfo(keyfile);

    if (!fi.Exists)
    {
        throw new RemotingException("Specified keyfile does not exist");
    }

    FileStream fs = new FileStream(keyfile,FileMode.Open);
    _encryptionKey = new Byte[fi.Length];
    fs.Read(_encryptionKey,0,_encryptionKey.Length);
}

public IServerChannelSinkProvider Next
{
    get {return _nextProvider; }
    set {_nextProvider = value;}
}

public IServerChannelSink CreateSink(IChannelReceiver channel)
{
    // create other sinks in the chain
    IServerChannelSink next = _nextProvider.CreateSink(channel);
```

```
        // put our sink on top of the chain and return it
        return new EncryptionServerSink(next,
            _encryptionKey,_encryptionAlgorithm);
    }


    public void GetChannelData(IChannelDataStore channelData)
    {
        // not yet needed
    }


}
}
```

When including the sink providers in your configuration files as presented previously, the transfer will be encrypted as shown in Figure 9-7.

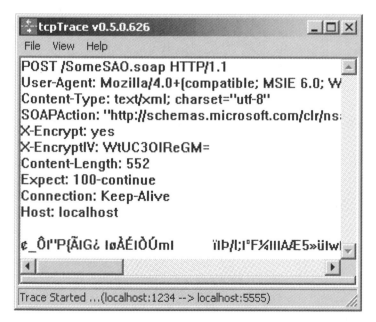

Figure 9-7. A TCP-trace of the encrypted HTTP traffic

You can, of course, also chain the encryption and compression sinks together to receive an encrypted *and* compressed stream.

Passing Runtime Information

The previous sinks were IClientChannelSinks and IServerChannelSinks. This means that they work on the resulting stream *after* the formatter has serialized the IMessage object. IMessageSinks, in contrast, can work directly on the message's contents *before* they are formatted. This means that any changes you make to the IMessage's contents will be serialized and therefore reflected in the resulting stream.

> **CAUTION** *Even though you might be tempted to change the IMessage object's content in an IClientChannelSink, be aware that this change is* not *propagated to the server, because the serialized stream has already been generated from the underlying IMessage!*

Because of this distinction, client-side IMessageSinks can be used to pass runtime information from the client to the server. In the following example, I show you how to send the client-side thread's current priority to the server so that remote method calls will execute with the same priority.

To send arbitrary data from the client to the server, you can put it into the Message object's logical call context. In this way, you can transfer objects that either are serializable or extend MarshalByRefObject. For example, to pass the client-side thread's current context for every method call to the server, you can implement the following SyncProcessMessage() method:

```
public IMessage SyncProcessMessage(IMessage msg)
{
   if (msg as IMethodCallMessage != null)
   {
      LogicalCallContext lcc =
         (LogicalCallContext) msg.Properties["__CallContext"];

      lcc.SetData("priority",Thread.CurrentThread.Priority);
      return _nextMsgSink.SyncProcessMessage(msg);
   }
   else
   {
      return _nextMsgSink.SyncProcessMessage(msg);
   }
}
```

The same has to be done for AsyncProcessMessage() as well:

```
public IMessageCtrl AsyncProcessMessage(IMessage msg, IMessageSink replySink)
{
   if (msg as IMethodCallMessage != null)
   {
      LogicalCallContext lcc =
         (LogicalCallContext) msg.Properties["__CallContext"];

      lcc.SetData("priority",Thread.CurrentThread.Priority);
      return _nextMsgSink.AsyncProcessMessage(msg,replySink);
   }
   else
   {
      return _nextMsgSink.AsyncProcessMessage(msg,replySink);
   }
}
```

On the server side, you have to implement an IServerChannelSink to take the call context from the IMessage object and set Thread.CurrentThread.Priority to the contained value:

```
public ServerProcessing ProcessMessage(IServerChannelSinkStack sinkStack,
   IMessage requestMsg,
   ITransportHeaders requestHeaders,
   Stream requestStream,
   out IMessage responseMsg,
   out ITransportHeaders responseHeaders,
   out Stream responseStream)
{
   LogicalCallContext lcc =
      (LogicalCallContext) requestMsg.Properties["__CallContext"];

   // storing the current priority
   ThreadPriority oldprio = Thread.CurrentThread.Priority;

   // check if the logical call context contains "priority"
   if (lcc != null && lcc.GetData("priority") != null)
   {
      // fetch the priorty from the call context
      ThreadPriority priority =
         (ThreadPriority) lcc.GetData("priority");
```

```
        Console.WriteLine("  -> Pre-execution priority change {0} to {1}",
            oldprio.ToString(),priority.ToString());

        // set the priority
        Thread.CurrentThread.Priority = priority;
    }



    // push on the stack and pass the call to the next sink
    // the old priority will be used as "state" for the response
    sinkStack.Push(this,oldprio);

    ServerProcessing spres =  _next.ProcessMessage (sinkStack,
        requestMsg, requestHeaders, requestStream,
        out responseMsg,out responseHeaders,out responseStream);

    //restore priority if call is not asynchronous

    if (spres != ServerProcessing.Async)
    {
        if (lcc != null && lcc.GetData("priority") != null)
        {
            Console.WriteLine("  -> Post-execution change back to {0}",oldprio);
            Thread.CurrentThread.Priority = oldprio;
        }
    }
    return spres;
}
```

The sink provider for the server-side sink is quite straightforward. It looks
more or less the same as those for the previous IServerChannelSinks.

On the client side, some minor inconveniences stem from this approach.
Remember that you implemented an IMessageSink and not an
IClientChannelSink in this case. Looking for an IMessageSinkProvider will not
give you any results, so you'll have to implement an IClientChannelSink provider
in this case as well—even though the sink is in reality an IMessageSink. The problem with this can be seen when looking at the following part of the
IClientChannelSinkProvider interface:

```
IClientChannelSink CreateSink(IChannelSender channel,
        string url,
        object remoteChannelData);
```

This indicates CreateSink() has to return an IClientChannelSink in any case, even if your sink only needs to implement IMessageSink. You now have to extend your IMessageSink to implement IClientChannelSink as well. You also have to use caution because IClientChannelSink defines more methods that have to be implemented. Those methods are called when the sink is used as a channel sink (that is, after the formatter) and not as a message sink. You might not want to allow your users to position the sink *after* the formatter (because it wouldn't work there because it's changing the IMessage object's content), so you want to throw exceptions in those methods.

The complete client-side PriorityEmitterSink, which throws those exceptions when used in the wrong sequence, is shown in Listing 9-12.

Listing 9-12. The Complete PriorityEmitterSink

```
using System;
using System.Collections;
using System.IO;
using System.Runtime.Remoting;
using System.Runtime.Remoting.Channels;
using System.Runtime.Remoting.Messaging;
using System.Threading;

namespace PrioritySinks
{
 public class PriorityEmitterSink : BaseChannelObjectWithProperties,
                                    IClientChannelSink, IMessageSink
  {
    private IMessageSink _nextMsgSink;

    public IMessageCtrl AsyncProcessMessage(IMessage msg, IMessageSink replySink)
    {
        // only for method calls
        if (msg as IMethodCallMessage != null)
        {
            LogicalCallContext lcc =
                (LogicalCallContext) msg.Properties["__CallContext"];
            lcc.SetData("priority",Thread.CurrentThread.Priority);
            return _nextMsgSink.AsyncProcessMessage(msg,replySink);
        }
        else
        {
            return _nextMsgSink.AsyncProcessMessage(msg,replySink);
        }
    }
```

```csharp
public IMessage SyncProcessMessage(IMessage msg)
{
    // only for method calls
    if (msg as IMethodCallMessage != null)
    {
        LogicalCallContext lcc =
            (LogicalCallContext) msg.Properties["__CallContext"];
        lcc.SetData("priority",Thread.CurrentThread.Priority);
        return _nextMsgSink.SyncProcessMessage(msg);
    }
    else
    {
        return _nextMsgSink.SyncProcessMessage(msg);
    }
}


public PriorityEmitterSink (object next)
{
    if (next as IMessageSink != null)
    {
        _nextMsgSink = (IMessageSink) next;
    }
}



public IMessageSink NextSink
{
    get
    {
        return _nextMsgSink;
    }
}

public IClientChannelSink NextChannelSink
{
    get
    {
        throw new RemotingException("Wrong sequence.");
    }
}
```

```
    public void AsyncProcessRequest(IClientChannelSinkStack sinkStack,
        IMessage msg,
        ITransportHeaders headers,
        Stream stream)
    {
        throw new RemotingException("Wrong sequence.");
    }

    public void AsyncProcessResponse(
        IClientResponseChannelSinkStack sinkStack,
        object state,
        ITransportHeaders headers,
        Stream stream)
    {
        throw new RemotingException("Wrong sequence.");
    }

    public System.IO.Stream GetRequestStream(IMessage msg,
        ITransportHeaders headers)
    {
        throw new RemotingException("Wrong sequence.");
    }

    public void ProcessMessage(IMessage msg,
        ITransportHeaders requestHeaders,
        Stream requestStream,
        out ITransportHeaders responseHeaders,
        out Stream responseStream)
    {
        throw new RemotingException("Wrong sequence.");
    }
  }
}
```

The client-side PriorityEmitterSinkProvider, which is shown in Listing 9-13, is quite straightforward to implement. The only interesting method is CreateSink().

Listing 9-13. The Client-Side PriorityEmitterSinkProvider

```
using System;
using System.Collections;
using System.Runtime.Remoting.Channels;

namespace PrioritySinks
{

    public class PriorityEmitterSinkProvider: IClientChannelSinkProvider
    {

        private IClientChannelSinkProvider next = null;

        public PriorityEmitterSinkProvider(IDictionary properties,
            ICollection providerData)
        {
            // not needed
        }

        public IClientChannelSink CreateSink(IChannelSender channel,
            string url, object remoteChannelData)
        {
            IClientChannelSink nextsink =
                next.CreateSink(channel,url,remoteChannelData);

            return new PriorityEmitterSink(nextsink);
        }

        public IClientChannelSinkProvider Next
        {
            get { return next; }
            set { next = value; }
        }

    }
}
```

Because the server-side sink shown in Listing 9-14 is an IServerChannelSink and not an IMessageSink, as is the client-side sink, the implementation is more consistent. You don't need to implement any additional interface here.

Listing 9-14. The Server-Side PriorityChangerSink

```
using System;
using System.Collections;
using System.IO;
using System.Runtime.Remoting;
using System.Runtime.Remoting.Messaging ;
using System.Runtime.Remoting.Channels;
using System.Threading;

namespace PrioritySinks
{

    public class PriorityChangerSink : BaseChannelObjectWithProperties,
        IServerChannelSink, IChannelSinkBase
    {

        private IServerChannelSink _next;

        public PriorityChangerSink (IServerChannelSink next)
        {
            _next = next;
        }

        public void AsyncProcessResponse (
                    IServerResponseChannelSinkStack sinkStack,
                    Object state,
                    IMessage msg,
                    ITransportHeaders headers,
                    Stream stream)
        {
            // restore the priority
            ThreadPriority priority = (ThreadPriority) state;
            Console.WriteLine(" -> Post-execution change back to {0}",priority);
            Thread.CurrentThread.Priority = priority;
        }

        public Stream GetResponseStream (IServerResponseChannelSinkStack sinkStack,
                    Object state,
                    IMessage msg,
                    ITransportHeaders headers )
        {
            return null;
        }
```

```
public ServerProcessing ProcessMessage(IServerChannelSinkStack sinkStack,
    IMessage requestMsg,
    ITransportHeaders requestHeaders,
    Stream requestStream,
    out IMessage responseMsg,
    out ITransportHeaders responseHeaders,
    out Stream responseStream)
{
    LogicalCallContext lcc =
        (LogicalCallContext) requestMsg.Properties["__CallContext"];

    // storing the current priority
    ThreadPriority oldprio = Thread.CurrentThread.Priority;

    // check if the logical call context contains "priority"
    if (lcc != null && lcc.GetData("priority") != null)
    {
        // fetch the priorty from the call context
        ThreadPriority priority =
            (ThreadPriority) lcc.GetData("priority");

        Console.WriteLine("-> Pre-execution priority change {0} to {1}",
            oldprio.ToString(),priority.ToString());

        // set the priority
        Thread.CurrentThread.Priority = priority;
    }



    // push on the stack and pass the call to the next sink
    // the old priority will be used as "state" for the response
    sinkStack.Push(this,oldprio);

    ServerProcessing spres =  _next.ProcessMessage (sinkStack,
        requestMsg, requestHeaders, requestStream,
        out responseMsg,out responseHeaders,out responseStream);

    //restore priority if call is not asynchronous
```

```
            if (spres != ServerProcessing.Async)
            {
                if (lcc != null && lcc.GetData("priority") != null)
                {
                    Console.WriteLine("-> Post-execution change back to {0}",
                            oldprio);
                    Thread.CurrentThread.Priority = oldprio;
                }
            }

            return spres;

        }


        public IServerChannelSink NextChannelSink
        {
            get {return _next;}
            set {_next = value;}
        }
    }
}
```

The corresponding server-side sink provider, which implements IServerChannelSinkProvider, is shown in Listing 9-15.

Listing 9-15. The Server-Side PriorityChangerSinkProvider

```
using System;
using System.Collections;
using System.Runtime.Remoting.Channels;

namespace PrioritySinks
{
    public class PriorityChangerSinkProvider: IServerChannelSinkProvider
    {
        private IServerChannelSinkProvider next = null;

        public PriorityChangerSinkProvider(IDictionary properties,
            ICollection providerData)
        {
            // not needed
        }
```

```
        public void GetChannelData (IChannelDataStore channelData)
        {
            // not needed
        }

        public IServerChannelSink CreateSink (IChannelReceiver channel)
        {
            IServerChannelSink nextSink = next.CreateSink(channel);
            return new PriorityChangerSink(nextSink);
        }

        public IServerChannelSinkProvider Next
        {
            get { return next; }
            set { next = value; }
        }

    }
}
```

To test this sink combination, use the following SAO, which returns the server-side thread's current priority:

```
public class TestSAO: MarshalByRefObject
{
    public String getPriority()
    {
        return System.Threading.Thread.CurrentThread.Priority.ToString();
    }
}
```

This SAO is called several times with different client-side thread priorities. The configuration file that is used by the server is shown here:

```
<configuration>
  <system.runtime.remoting>
    <application>
      <channels>
        <channel ref="http" port="5555">
```

```xml
          <serverProviders>
            <formatter ref="soap" />
                    <provider
              type="PrioritySinks.PriorityChangerSinkProvider, PrioritySinks" />
          </serverProviders>

        </channel>
      </channels>

      <service>
        <wellknown mode="Singleton"
                type="Server.TestSAO, Server" objectUri="TestSAO.soap" />
      </service>

    </application>
  </system.runtime.remoting>
</configuration>
```

The client-side configuration file will look like this:

```xml
<configuration>
 <system.runtime.remoting>
    <application>
        <channels>
         <channel ref="http">

            <clientProviders>
              <provider
                 type="PrioritySinks.PriorityEmitterSinkProvider, PrioritySinks" />
              <formatter ref="soap" />
            </clientProviders>

         </channel>
      </channels>

      <client>
         <wellknown type="Server.TestSAO, generated_meta"
                    url="http://localhost:5555/TestSAO.soap" />
      </client>

    </application>
  </system.runtime.remoting>
</configuration>
```

For the test client, you can use SoapSuds to extract the metadata. When you run the application in Listing 9-16, you'll see the output shown in Figure 9-8.

Listing 9-16. The Test Client

```
using System;
using System.Runtime.Remoting;
using Server; // from generated_meta.dll
using System.Threading;

namespace Client
{
    delegate String getPrioAsync();

    class Client
    {
        static void Main(string[] args)
        {
            String filename = "client.exe.config";
            RemotingConfiguration.Configure(filename);

            TestSAO obj = new TestSAO();
            test(obj);

            Thread.CurrentThread.Priority = ThreadPriority.Highest;
            test(obj);

            Thread.CurrentThread.Priority = ThreadPriority.Lowest;
            test(obj);

            Thread.CurrentThread.Priority = ThreadPriority.Normal;
            test(obj);


            Console.ReadLine();
        }

        static void test(TestSAO obj)
        {
            Console.WriteLine("---------------- START TEST CASE --------------");
            Console.WriteLine("  Local Priority: {0}",
                                Thread.CurrentThread.Priority.ToString());

            String priority1 = obj.getPriority();
```

```
        Console.WriteLine("   Remote priority: {0}",priority1.ToString());
        Console.WriteLine("---------------- END TEST CASE --------------");
    }
  }
}
```

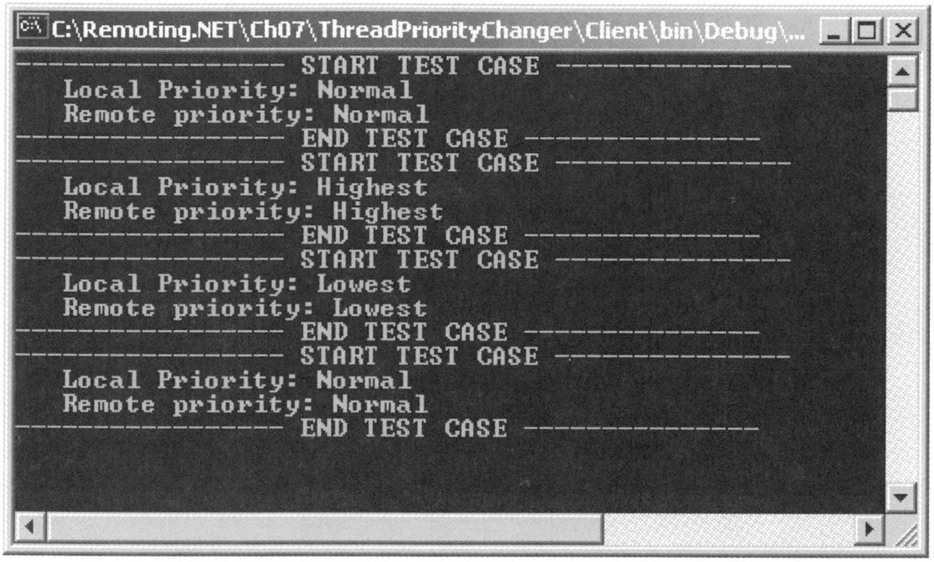

Figure 9-8. The test client's output shows that the sinks work as expected.

Changing the Programming Model

The previous sinks all add functionality to both the client- and the server-side of a .NET Remoting application. The pluggable sink architecture nevertheless also allows the creation of sinks, which change several aspects of the programming model. In Chapter 5, for example, you've seen that passing custom credentials such as username and password involves manual setting of the channel sink's properties for each object:

```
CustomerManager mgr = new CustomerManager();
IDictionary props = ChannelServices.GetChannelSinkProperties(mgr);
props["username"] = "dummyremotinguser";
props["password"] = "12345";
```

In most real-world applications, it is nevertheless preferable to set these properties on a per-host basis, or set them according to the base URL of the destination object. In a perfect world, this would be possible using either configuration files or code, as in the following example:

```xml
<configuration>
  <system.runtime.remoting>
    <application>
     <channels>
      <channel ref="http">
       <clientProviders>

         <formatter ref="soap" />
           <provider type="UrlAuthenticationSink.UrlAuthenticationSinkProvider,
                 UrlAuthenticationSink">

             <url
                 base="http://localhost"
                 username="DummyRemotingUser"
                 password="12345"
             />

             <url
                 base="http://www.somewhere.org"
                 username="MyUser"
                 password="12345"
             />
           </provider>
       </clientProviders>
      </channel>
     </channels>
    </application>
  </system.runtime.remoting>
</configuration>
```

When setting these properties in code, you can simply omit the <url> entries from the configuration file and instead use the following lines to achieve the same behavior:

```
UrlAuthenticator.AddAuthenticationEntry(
    "http://localhost",
    "dummyremotinguser",
    "12345");

UrlAuthenticator.AddAuthenticationEntry(
    "http://www.somewhere.org",
    "MyUser",
    "12345");
```

In fact, this behavior is not supported by default but can be easily implemented using a custom IClientChannelSink.

Before working on the sink itself, you have to write a helper class that provides static methods to store and retrieve authentication entries for given base URLs. All those entries will be stored in an ArrayList and can be retrieved by passing a URL to the GetAuthenticationEntry() method. In addition, default authentication information that will be returned if none of the specified base URLs matches the current object's URL can be set as well. This helper class is shown in Listing 9-17.

Listing 9-17. The UrlAuthenticator Stores Usernames and Passwords

```
using System;
using System.Collections;

namespace UrlAuthenticationSink
{

    internal class UrlAuthenticationEntry
    {
        internal String Username;
        internal String Password;
        internal String UrlBase;

        internal UrlAuthenticationEntry (String urlbase,
            String user,
            String password)
        {
            this.Username = user;
            this.Password = password;
            this.UrlBase = urlbase.ToUpper();
        }
    }

    public class UrlAuthenticator
    {
        private static ArrayList _entries = new ArrayList();
        private static UrlAuthenticationEntry _defaultAuthenticationEntry;

        public static void AddAuthenticationEntry(String urlBase,
            String userName,
            String password)
```

```
        {
            _entries.Add(new UrlAuthenticationEntry(
                urlBase,userName,password));
        }

        public static void SetDefaultAuthenticationEntry(String userName,
            String password)
        {
            _defaultAuthenticationEntry = new UrlAuthenticationEntry(
                null,userName,password);
        }

        internal static UrlAuthenticationEntry GetAuthenticationEntry(String url)
        {
            foreach (UrlAuthenticationEntry entr in _entries)
            {
                // check if a registered entry matches the url-parameter
                if (url.ToUpper().StartsWith(entr.UrlBase))
                {
                    return entr;
                }
            }

            // if none matched, return the default entry (which can be null as well)
            return _defaultAuthenticationEntry;
        }
    }
}
```

The sink itself calls a method that checks if an authentication entry exists for the URL of the current message. It then walks the chain of sinks until reaching the final transport channel sink, on which is set the properties that contain the correct username and password. It finally sets a flag for this object's sink so that this logic will be applied only once per sink chain. The complete source for this sink can be found in Listing 9-18.

Listing 9-18. The UrlAuthenticationSink

```
using System;
using System.Runtime.Remoting.Channels;
using System.Runtime.Remoting.Messaging;
using System.IO;
```

```
namespace UrlAuthenticationSink
{
    public class UrlAuthenticationSink: BaseChannelSinkWithProperties,
                                        IClientChannelSink
    {
        private IClientChannelSink _nextSink;
        private bool _authenticationParamsSet;

        public UrlAuthenticationSink(IClientChannelSink next)
        {
            _nextSink = next;
        }

        public IClientChannelSink NextChannelSink
        {
            get {
                return _nextSink;
            }
        }


        public void AsyncProcessRequest(IClientChannelSinkStack sinkStack,
            IMessage msg,
            ITransportHeaders headers,
            Stream stream)
        {
            SetSinkProperties(msg);
            // don't push on the sinkstack because this sink doesn't need
            // to handle any replies!
            _nextSink.AsyncProcessRequest(sinkStack,msg,headers,stream);
        }

        public void AsyncProcessResponse(
            IClientResponseChannelSinkStack sinkStack,
            object state,
            ITransportHeaders headers,
            Stream stream)
        {
            // not needed
        }
```

```
public Stream GetRequestStream(IMessage msg,
                               ITransportHeaders headers)
{
    return _nextSink.GetRequestStream(msg, headers);
}



public void ProcessMessage(IMessage msg,
                           ITransportHeaders requestHeaders,
                           Stream requestStream,
                           out ITransportHeaders responseHeaders,
                           out Stream responseStream)
{

    SetSinkProperties(msg);

    _nextSink.ProcessMessage(msg,requestHeaders,requestStream,
        out responseHeaders,out responseStream);
}

private void SetSinkProperties(IMessage msg)
{
    if (! _authenticationParamsSet)
    {
        String url = (String) msg.Properties["__Uri"];

        UrlAuthenticationEntry entr =
            UrlAuthenticator.GetAuthorizationEntry(url);

        if (entr != null)
        {
            IClientChannelSink last = this;

            while (last.NextChannelSink != null)
            {
                last = last.NextChannelSink;
            }

            // last now contains the transport channel sink

            last.Properties["username"] = entr.Username;
            last.Properties["password"] = entr.Password;
        }
```

```
            _authenticationParamsSet = true;
        }
    }
  }
}
```

The corresponding sink provider examines the <url> entry, which can be specified in the configuration file *below* the sink provider:

```
<provider type="UrlAuthenticationSink.UrlAuthenticationSinkProvider,
      UrlAuthenticationSink">

    <url
      base="http://localhost"
      username="DummyRemotingUser"
      password="12345"
    />

</provider>
```

The sink provider will receive those entries via the providerData collection, which contains objects of type SinkProviderData. Every instance of SinkProviderData has a reference to a properties dictionary that allows access to the attributes (base, username, and password) of the entry.

When the base URL is set in the configuration file, it simply calls UrlAuthenticator.AddAuthenticationEntry(). If no base URL has been specified, it sets this username/password as the default authentication entry. You can see the complete source code for this provider in Listing 9-19.

Listing 9-19. The UrlAuthenticationSinkProvider

```
using System;
using System.Runtime.Remoting.Channels;
using System.Collections;

namespace UrlAuthenticationSink
{
    public class UrlAuthenticationSinkProvider: IClientChannelSinkProvider
    {
        private IClientChannelSinkProvider _nextProvider;

        public UrlAuthenticationSinkProvider(IDictionary properties,
                ICollection providerData)
```

```
            {
                foreach (SinkProviderData obj in providerData)
                {
                    if (obj.Name == "url")
                    {
                        if (obj.Properties["base"] != null)
                        {
                            UrlAuthenticator.AddAuthenticationEntry(
                                (String) obj.Properties["base"],
                                (String) obj.Properties["username"],
                                (String) obj.Properties["password"]);
                        }
                        else
                        {
                            UrlAuthenticator.SetDefaultAuthenticationEntry(
                                (String) obj.Properties["username"],
                                (String) obj.Properties["password"]);
                        }
                    }

                }
            }

            public IClientChannelSinkProvider Next
            {
                get {return _nextProvider; }
                set {_nextProvider = value;}
            }

            public IClientChannelSink CreateSink(IChannelSender channel,
                    string url,
                    object remoteChannelData)
            {
                // create other sinks in the chain
                IClientChannelSink next = _nextProvider.CreateSink(channel,
                    url,
                    remoteChannelData);

                // put our sink on top of the chain and return it
                return new UrlAuthenticationSink(next);
            }
        }
    }
```

Using This Sink

When using this sink, you can simply add it to your client-side sink chain in the configuration file as shown here:

```
<configuration>
  <system.runtime.remoting>
    <application>
     <channels>
      <channel ref="http">

        <clientProviders>
          <formatter ref="soap" />
          <provider type="UrlAuthenticationSink.UrlAuthenticationSinkProvider,
                 UrlAuthenticationSink" />
        </clientProviders>

      </channel>
     </channels>
    </application>
  </system.runtime.remoting>
</configuration>
```

> **NOTE**   *This sink is an IClientChannelSink, so you have to place it* after *the formatter.*

To specify a username/password combination for a given base URL, you can now add this authentication information to the configuration file by using one or more <url> entries inside the <provider> section:

```
<clientProviders>
   <formatter ref="soap" />
   <provider type="UrlAuthenticationSink.UrlAuthenticationSinkProvider,
                 UrlAuthenticationSink">
       <url
              base="http://localhost"
              username="DummyRemotingUser"
              password="12345"
        />
     </provider>
</clientProviders>
```

If you don't want to hard code this information, you can ask the user of your client program for the username/password and employ the following code to register it with this sink:

```
UrlAuthenticator.AddAuthenticationEntry(<url>, <username>, <password>);
```

To achieve the same behavior as that of the <url> entry in the previous configuration snippet, you use the following command:

```
UrlAuthenticator.AddAuthenticationEntry(
    "http://localhost",
    "dummyremotinguser",
    "12345");
```

Using a Custom Proxy

In the previous parts of this chapter, you read about the possible ways you can extend the .NET Remoting Framework using additional custom message sinks. There is another option for changing the default behavior of the remoting system: custom proxy objects. Figure 9-9 shows you the default proxy configuration.

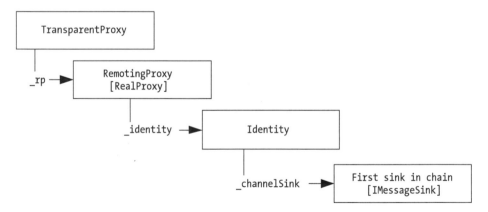

Figure 9-9. The default combination of proxy objects

You can change this by replacing RemotingProxy with a custom proxy that inherits from RealProxy.

> **NOTE** *You'll normally miss the opportunity to use configuration files in this case. To work around this issue, you can use the RemotingHelper class, discussed in Chapter 6.*

To do this, you basically have to implement a class that extends RealProxy, provides a custom constructor, and overrides the Invoke() method to pass the message on to the correct message sink.

As shown in Listing 9-20, the constructor first has to call the base object's constructor and then checks all registered channels to determine whether they accept the given URL by calling their CreateMessageSink() methods. If a channel can service the URL, it returns an IMessageSink object that is the first sink in the remoting chain. Otherwise it returns null. The constructor will throw an exception if no registered channel is able to parse the URL.

Listing 9-20. A Skeleton Custom Remoting Proxy

```
using System;
using System.Collections;
using System.Runtime.Remoting;
using System.Runtime.Remoting.Channels;
using System.Runtime.Remoting.Channels.Http;
using System.Runtime.Remoting.Proxies;
using System.Runtime.Remoting.Messaging;

namespace Client
{
    public class CustomProxy: RealProxy
    {
        String _url;
        String _uri;
        IMessageSink _sinkChain;

        public CustomProxy(Type type, String url) : base(type)
        {
            _url = url;

            // check each registered channel if it accepts the
            // given URL
            IChannel[] registeredChannels = ChannelServices.RegisteredChannels;
            foreach (IChannel channel in registeredChannels )
            {
                if (channel is IChannelSender)
```

```
        {
            IChannelSender channelSender = (IChannelSender)channel;

            // try to create the sink
            _sinkChain = channelSender.CreateMessageSink(_url,
                null, out _uri);

            // if the channel returned a sink chain, exit the loop
            if (_sinkChain != null) break;
        }
    }

    // no registered channel accepted the URL
    if (_sinkChain == null)
    {
        throw new Exception("No channel has been found for " + _url);
    }
}

public override IMessage Invoke(IMessage msg)
{
    msg.Properties["__Uri"] = _url;

    // TODO: process the request message

    IMessage retMsg = _sinkChain.SyncProcessMessage(msg);

    // TODO: process the return message

    return retMsg;
    }
  }
}
```

To employ this proxy, you have to instantiate it using the special constructor by passing the Type of the remote object and its URL. You can then call GetTransparentProxy() on the resulting CustomProxy object and cast the returned TransparentProxy to the remote object's type, as shown in Listing 9-21.

Listing 9-21. Using a Custom Proxy

```
using System;
using System.Runtime.Remoting;
using System.Runtime.Remoting.Channels;
using System.Runtime.Remoting.Channels.Http;
using Service; // from service.dll

namespace Client
{
    class Client
    {
        static void Main(string[] args)
        {
            ChannelServices.RegisterChannel(new HttpChannel());

            CustomProxy prx = new CustomProxy(typeof(Service.SomeSAO),
                "http://localhost:1234/SomeSAO.soap");

            SomeSAO obj = (SomeSAO) prx.GetTransparentProxy();

            String res = obj.doSomething();

            Console.WriteLine("Got result: {0}",res);
            Console.ReadLine();
        }
    }
}
```

To show you an example for a custom proxy, I implement some methods that dump the request and return messages' contents. These methods are called from the proxy's Invoke(), which will be executed whenever your client calls a method on the TransparentProxy object. This is shown in Listing 9-22.

> **NOTE** *You can also call these content dump methods in an IMessageSink!*

Listing 9-22. This Custom Proxy Dumps the Request and Response Messages' Contents

```
using System;
using System.Collections;
using System.Runtime.Remoting;
using System.Runtime.Remoting.Channels;
using System.Runtime.Remoting.Channels.Http;
using System.Runtime.Remoting.Proxies;
using System.Runtime.Remoting.Messaging;

namespace Client
{
    public class CustomProxy: RealProxy
    {
        String _url;
        String _uri;
        IMessageSink _sinkChain;

        public CustomProxy(Type type, String url) : base(type)
        {
            _url = url;

            // check each registered channel if it accepts the
            // given URL
            IChannel[] registeredChannels = ChannelServices.RegisteredChannels;
            foreach (IChannel channel in registeredChannels )
            {
                if (channel is IChannelSender)
                {
                    IChannelSender channelSender = (IChannelSender)channel;

                    // try to create the sink
                    _sinkChain = channelSender.CreateMessageSink(_url,
                        null, out _uri);

                    // if the channel returned a sink chain, exit the loop
                    if (_sinkChain != null) break;
                }
            }

            // no registered channel accepted the URL
            if (_sinkChain == null)
```

```
      {
          throw new Exception("No channel has been found for " + _url);
      }
  }

  public override IMessage Invoke(IMessage msg)
  {
      msg.Properties["__Uri"] = _url;

      DumpMessageContents(msg);

      IMessage retMsg = _sinkChain.SyncProcessMessage(msg);

      DumpMessageContents(retMsg);

      return retMsg;
  }

  private String GetPaddedString(String str)
  {
      String ret = str + "                 ";
      return ret.Substring(0,17);
  }

  private void DumpMessageContents(IMessage msg)
  {
      Console.WriteLine("========================================");
      Console.WriteLine("=========== Message Dump ==============");
      Console.WriteLine("========================================");

      Console.WriteLine("Type: {0}", msg.GetType().ToString());

      Console.WriteLine("--- Properties ---");
      IDictionary dict = msg.Properties;
      IDictionaryEnumerator enm =
              (IDictionaryEnumerator) dict.GetEnumerator();

      while (enm.MoveNext())
      {
          Object key = enm.Key;
          String keyName = key.ToString();
          Object val = enm.Value;
```

```
            Console.WriteLine("{0}: {1}", GetPaddedString(keyName), val);

            // check if it's an object array
            Object[] objval = val as Object[];
            if (objval != null)
            {
                DumpObjectArray(objval);
            }

        }

        Console.WriteLine();
        Console.WriteLine();
    }

    private void DumpObjectArray(object[] data)
    {
        // if empty -> return
        if (data.Length == 0) return;

        Console.WriteLine("\t --- Array Contents ---");
        for (int i = 0; i < data.Length; i++)
        {
            Console.WriteLine("\t{0}: {1}", i, data[i]);
        }
    }
  }
}
```

The output of the preceding client when used with this proxy is shown in
Figure 9-10.

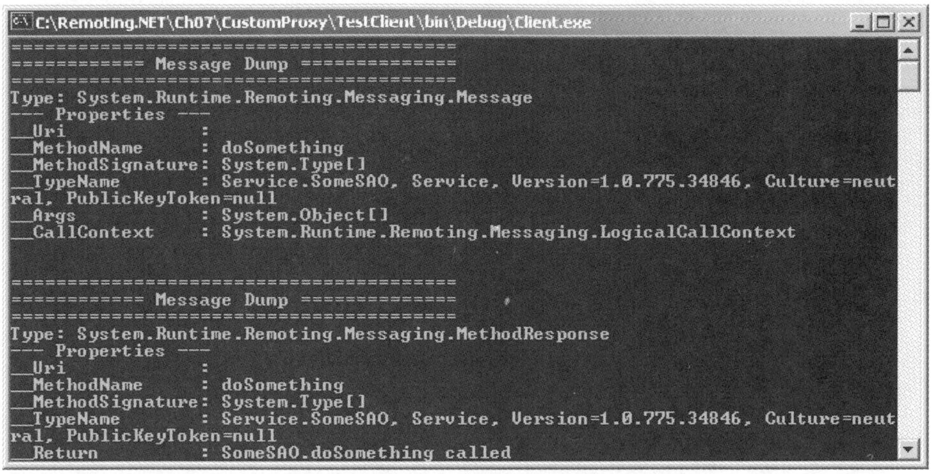

Figure 9-10. Using the custom proxy to dump the messages' contents

Because nearly all the functionality you'll want to implement in a common .NET Remoting scenario can be implemented with IMessageSinks, IClientChannelSinks, or IServerChannelSinks, I suggest you implement functionality by using these instead of custom proxies in .NET Remoting. Sinks provide the additional benefits of being capable of working with configuration files and being chainable. This chaining allows you to develop a set of very focused sinks that can then be combined to solve your application's needs.

Custom proxies are nevertheless interesting because they can also be used for local objects. In this case, you don't have to implement a special constructor, only override Invoke(). You can then pass any MarshalByRefObject to another constructor (which is provided by the parent RealProxy) during creation of the proxy. All method calls to this local object then pass the proxy as an IMessage object and can therefore be processed. You can read more on message-based processing for local applications in Chapter 11.

Summary

In this chapter you have seen how you can leverage the .NET Remoting Framework's extensibility. You should now be able to apply the internals shown in Chapters 7 and 8 to extend and customize the .NET Remoting programming model to suit your needs.

You now know the differences between IMessageSink, which is used before the message reaches the client-side formatter, and IClientChannelSink, which is used after the serialization of the IMessage object. You know that you can add properties to the IMessage object's LogicalCallContext to pass it to the server, where it can be read by an IServerChannelSink, and you can also encrypt or compress a request by using a combination of IClientChannelSinks and IServerChannelSinks.

You also learned how sink providers are developed, and that a client-side IMessageSink has to be created by an IClientChannelSinkProvider as well and therefore has to implement the IClientChannelSink's methods. Finally, you read about custom proxies, which allow you to implement additional functionality before the message reaches the chain of sinks.

In the next chapter, you get a chance to use the knowledge gained here to implement a complete transport channel from scratch.

CHAPTER 10

Developing a Transport Channel

IN THE LAST THREE CHAPTERS you've seen how the .NET Remoting Framework's various layers can be extended. The ultimate example of customization is nevertheless the creation of a specific transport channel.

As you already know by now, the .NET Remoting Framework comes out of the box with two transport channels: HTTP channel and TCP channel. Even though these protocols cover a lot of common scenarios, you might have a special need for other transport channels for some applications. On one hand, protocols like named pipes, for example, could allow for higher performance (with security!) for applications communicating with each other on the same machine. On the other hand, you might have the need for asynchronous communication with MSMQ or even by standard Internet e-mail using SMTP and POP3.

No matter which protocol you choose, you must watch for one thing: most protocols are *either* synchronous *or* asynchronous in their nature. As the remoting framework supports both kinds of calls, you'll need to either map asynchronous .NET Remoting calls onto a synchronous protocol like HTTP or TCP or map synchronous .NET Remoting calls onto an asynchronous protocol like MSMQ or SMTP/POP3.

With the former, you will, for example, have to spawn a secondary thread that waits for the reply and notifies the IAsyncResult (as seen in Chapter 7) whenever a response is returned. The latter demands that you block the calling thread and wake it up as soon as the asynchronous response has been received from the underlying protocol.

Protocol Considerations

First, I have to place a disclaimer here: this chapter will provide you with the necessary ideas and walk you through the process of designing and developing a specialized transport channel. It isn't the objective of this chapter to give you a commercial grade SMTP/POP3 channel. Even though you *could* just use this channel in your application, you'll need to understand it fully before doing so because neither the author nor the publisher will provide any support when you include this channel in your applications.

Okay, now let's start with the implementation of this channel. Before doing this you nevertheless have to *know* the protocol (or at least the relevant parts of it) that you are going to use. Every Internet protocol has its so-called request-for-comment (RFC) documents. The SMTP protocol in its most recent version is shown in RFC2821 and POP3 in RFC1939. You can get them at
`http://www.ietf.org/rfc/rfc2821.txt` and
`http://www.ietf.org/rfc/rfc1939.txt`.

You can generally search for any RFC at
`http://www.faqs.org/rfcs/index.html`, but you should keep in mind that normally RFCs are identified by the full protocol name and not the more common acronym. For example, you'd have to search for "Simple Mail Transfer Protocol", not "SMTP", to find the mentioned RFCs. If you don't know the real protocol name, you can search for the abbreviation on `http://www.webopedia.com/`.

Generally the transfer of e-mails is split between two protocols: SMTP and POP3. SMTP is used to send e-mails from your mail client to a mail server and will then be used for inter–mail-server communication until it reaches a destination mailbox. POP3 is used to receive e-mails from a server's mailbox to your e-mail client.

The Shortcut Route to SMTP . . .

To save you from having to read through the whole RFC2821, I provide here a short summary of the relevant parts needed to implement this channel. First, SMTP uses a request/reply syntax normally sent over a TCP connection to port 25 on the server. The client can send a list of commands, and the server replies to them with a status code and a message. The status code is a three-digit number of which the first digit specifies the class. These are shown in Table 10-1. The message that might be sent after the status code is not standardized and should be ignored or used only for reporting errors back to the user.

Table 10-1. SMTP Response Code Classes

RESPONSE CODE	MEANING
2xx	Positive response. Command accepted and executed.
3xx	Intermediate or transient positive. Command accepted, but more information is needed. In plain English, this means the client can now start to transfer the mail (if received as a reply to the DATA command).
4xx	Transient error. Try again later.
5xx	Permanent error. You quite certainly did something wrong!

A successful SMTP conversion can therefore look like the following code. (The → symbol indicates that the client sends this line and the ← symbol indicates the server's reply.)You can easily try this out yourself by entering **telnet <mailserver> 25**—but be aware that the commands you input might not be echoed back to you.

```
←  220 MyRemotingServer Mercury/32 v3.21c ESMTP server ready.
→  HELO localhost
←  250 MyRemotingServer Hi there, localhost.
→  MAIL FROM: <client_1@localhost>
←  250 Sender OK - send RCPTs.
→  RCPT TO: <server_1@localhost>
←  250 Recipient OK - send RCPT or DATA.
→  DATA
←  354 OK, send data, end with CRLF.CRLF
→  <sending message contents inclusive headers>
→  sending <CR><LF>.<CR><LF> (i.e. a "dot" between two CR/LFs)
←  250 Data received OK.
→  QUIT
←  221 MyRemotingServer Service closing channel.
```

As you can see here, several commands can be sent by the client. At the beginning of the session, after the server announces itself with **220** *servername message*, the client will send **HELO** *hostname*. This starts the SMTP session, and the server responds with **250** *servername message*.

For each e-mail the client wants to send via this server, the following process takes place. First, the client starts with **MAIL FROM:** *<e-mail address>* (note that the e-mail address *has* to be enclosed in angle brackets). The server replies with **250** *message* if it allows e-mails from this sender; otherwise, it replies with a 4xx or 5xx status code. The client then sends one or more **RCPT TO:** *<e-mail address>* commands that designate the recipients of this e-mail and that are also confirmed by **250** *message* replies.

As soon as all recipients have been specified, the client sends **DATA** to notify the server that it's going to send the e-mail's content. The server replies with **354** *message* and expects the client to send the e-mail and finish with "." (dot) on a single new line (that is, the client sends <CR><LF><DOT><CR><LF>). The server then acknowledges the e-mail by replying with **250** *message*.

At this point the client can send further e-mails by issuing **MAIL FROM** or can terminate the session with the **QUIT** command, which will be confirmed by the server via a **221** *message* reply. The server will then also close the TCP connection. Sometime after the message is sent, it will be placed in a user's mailbox from where it can be retrieved by the POP3 protocol.

... And Round-Trip to POP3

Generally POP3 works in quite the same way as SMTP: it's also a request/response protocol. POP3 messages are generally sent over a TCP connection to port 110. Instead of the status codes SMTP relies on, POP3 supports three kinds of replies. The first two are **+OK** *message* to indicate success and **-ERR** *message* to indicate failure. The messages after the status code aren't standardized, and as such should be used only to report errors to your user and not be parsed by a program.

Another type of reply is a *content reply*, which is used whenever you request information from the server that might span multiple lines. In this case the server will indicate the end of the response with the same <CR><LF><DOT><CR><LF> sequence that is used by SMTP to end the transfer of the e-mail text.

A sample POP3 session might look like this. To start it, enter **telnet <mailserver> 110**.

```
←  +OK <1702038211.21388@vienna01>, MercuryP/32 v3.21c ready.
→  USER server_1
←  +OK server_1 is known here.
→  PASS server_1
←  +OK Welcome! 1 messages (231 bytes)
→  LIST
←  +OK 1 messages, 3456 bytes
←  1 231
←  .
→  RETR 1
←  +OK Here it comes...
←  <e-mail text>
←  .
→  DELE 1
←  +OK Message deleted.
→  QUIT
←  +OK vienna01 Server closing down.
```

As you can see in this connection trace, the client authenticates itself at the server by sending the commands **USER** *username* and **PASS** *password*. In this case the password is transported in clear text over the network. Most POP3 servers also support an APOP command based on an MD5 digest that incorporates a server-side timestamp to disable replay attacks. You can read more about this in RFC1939.

The server then replies with a message like **+OK** Welcome! 1 messages (231 bytes). You should never try to parse this reply to receive the message count; instead, either send the command **STAT**, which will be answered by **+OK** *number_of_messages total_bytes* or issue a **LIST** command, which will first return **+OK** *message* and then return this line once for each message: *message_number bytes*. The reply concludes with a <CR><LF><DOT><CR><LF> sequence.

The client can then issue a **RETR** *message_number* command to retrieve the content of a specific message (with a final <CR><LF><DOT><CR><LF> as well) and a **DELE** *message_number* statement to delete it at the server. This deletion is only carried out after sending **QUIT** to the server, which then closes the connection.

Character Encoding Essentials

After reading the last few pages, you are almost fully equipped to start with the design of your channel. The last thing you need to know before you can start to write some code is how the resulting e-mail has to look like.

Because there's no standard for the binding of .NET Remoting to custom transfer protocols, I just elected Simon Fell's recommendation for SOAP binding to SMTP as the target specification for this implementation. You can find the latest version of this document at http://www.pocketsoap.com/specs/smtpbinding/. In essence, it basically says that the content has to be either Base64 or Quoted-Printable encoded and needs to supply a given number of e-mail headers. So, what does this mean? Essentially, the e-mail format we know today has been designed ages ago when memory was expensive, WAN links were slow, and computers liked to deal with 7-bit ASCII characters.

Nowadays we instead use Unicode, which allows us to have *huge* numbers of characters so that even languages like Japanese, Chinese, or Korean can be encoded. This is, of course, far from 7 bit, so you have to find a way to bring such data back to a 7-bit format of "printable characters." Base64 does this for you; it is described in detail in section 5.2 of RFC1521, available at http://www.ietf.org/rfc/rfc1521.txt. To encode a given byte array with the Base64 algorithm, you can use Convert.ToBase64String().

Creating E-mail Headers

An e-mail contains not only the body, but also header information. For a sample
SOAP-via-SMTP request, the complete e-mail might look like this:

```
From: client_1@localhost
To: server_1@localhost
Message-Id: <26fc4f4cd8de4567a66ccea6897dc481@REMOTING>
MIME-Version: 1.0
Content-Type: text/xml; charset=utf-8
Content-Transfer-Encoding: BASE64

...encoded SOAP request here...
```

To match a response message to the correct request, the value of
the Message-Id header will be included in the In-Reply-To header of the
response message:

```
From: server_1@localhost
To: client_1@localhost
Message-Id: <978092785309835523985765458690679@REMOTING>
In-Reply-To: <26fc4f4cd8de4567a66ccea6897dc481@REMOTING>
MIME-Version: 1.0
Content-Type: text/xml; charset=utf-8
Content-Transfer-Encoding: BASE64

...encoded SOAP response here...
```

You also need to include some special headers that are taken from the
ITransportHeaders object of the .NET Remoting request. Those will be preceded by
X-REMOTING- so that a complete Remoting request e-mail might look like this:

```
From: client_1@localhost
To: server_1@localhost
Message-Id: <26fc4f4cd8de4567a66ccea6897dc481@REMOTING>
MIME-Version: 1.0
Content-Type: text/xml; charset=utf-8
Content-Transfer-Encoding: BASE64
X-REMOTING-Content-Type: text/xml; charset="utf-8"
X-REMOTING-SOAPAction: "http://schemas.microsoft.com/clr/ns/System.Runtime
.Remoting.Activation.IActivator#Activate"
X-REMOTING-URI: /RemoteActivationService.rem

...encoded .NET Remoting request here...
```

The encoded .NET Remoting request itself can be based on either the binary formatter or SOAP!

Encapsulating the Protocols

Now that you've got some of the protocol basics down, you're ready for the source code for this channel. Okay, here goes. First you have to encapsulate the SMTP and POP3 protocols that are later used in the client-side and server-side transport channel sinks.

The first part of this is shown in Listing 10-1. This source file encapsulates the lower-level SMTP protocol. It provides a public constructor that needs the hostname of your SMTP-server as a parameter. Its SendMessage() method takes the sender's and recipient's e-mail address and the full e-mail's text (including the headers) as parameters. It then connects to the SMTP server and sends the specified mail.

Listing 10-1. Encapsulating the Lower-Level SMTP Protocol

```
using System;
using System.Net.Sockets;
using System.Net;
using System.IO;
using System.Text;

namespace SMTPChannel
{
    public class SMTPConnection
    {
        private String _hostname;
        private TcpClient _smtpConnection;
        private NetworkStream _smtpStream;
        private StreamReader _smtpResponse;

        public SMTPConnection(String hostname) {
            _hostname = hostname;
        }

        private void Connect() {
            _smtpConnection = new TcpClient(_hostname,25);
            _smtpStream = _smtpConnection.GetStream();
            _smtpResponse = new StreamReader(_smtpStream);
        }
```

```
private void Disconnect() {
    _smtpStream.Close();
    _smtpResponse.Close();
    _smtpConnection.Close();
}

private void SendCommand(String command, int expectedResponseClass) {
    // command: the SMTP command to send
    // expectedResponseClass: first digit of the expected smtp response

    // Throws an exception if the server's responsecode's first
    // digit (resonse class) is > the expectedResponseClass.

    // If expectedResponseClass == 0, it will be ignored

    command = command + "\r\n";
    byte[] cmd = Encoding.ASCII.GetBytes(command);
    _smtpStream.Write(cmd,0,cmd.Length);
    String response = _smtpResponse.ReadLine();

    if (expectedResponseClass != 0) {
        int resp = Convert.ToInt32(response.Substring(0,1));
        if (resp > expectedResponseClass) {
            throw new Exception("SMTP Server returned unexpected " +
                "response:\n'" + response + "'");
        }
    }
}

public void SendMessage(String from, String to, String text) {
    try
    {
        Connect();
        SendCommand("HELO localhost",2);
        SendCommand("MAIL FROM: <" + from + ">",2);
        SendCommand("RCPT TO: <" + to + ">",2);
        SendCommand("DATA",3);
        byte[] bodybytes = Encoding.ASCII.GetBytes(text + "\r\n");
        _smtpStream.Write(bodybytes,0,bodybytes.Length);
        SendCommand(".",3);
        SendCommand("QUIT",0);
    } finally {
        try {
```

```
                Disconnect();
            } catch (Exception e) {/*ignore*/};
        }
    }


    }
}
```

To encapsulate the POP3 protocol, you first have to add a class that will hold the parsed message and its headers. This is shown in Listing 10-2.

Listing 10-2. A Retrieved and Parsed Message

```
using System;
using System.Collections;

namespace SMTPChannel
{
    public class POP3Msg
    {
        public String From;
        public String To;
        public String Body;
        public String Headers;
        public String MessageId;
        public String InReplyTo;
    }
}
```

The helper class POP3Connection encapsulates the lower-level details of the POP3 protocol. After construction, it connects to the server, authenticates the user, and issues a LIST command to retrieve the list of messages waiting.

```
using System;
using System.Net.Sockets;
using System.Net;
using System.IO;
using System.Collections;
using System.Text;

namespace SMTPChannel
{
    public class POP3Connection
    {
```

```csharp
private class MessageIndex
{
    // will be used to store the result of the LIST command
    internal int Number;
    internal int Bytes;

    internal MessageIndex(int num, int msgbytes)
    {
        Number = num;
        Bytes  = msgbytes;
    }
}

private String _hostname;
private String _username;
private String _password;

private TcpClient _pop3Connection;
private NetworkStream _pop3Stream;
private StreamReader _pop3Response;
private IDictionary _msgs;

public POP3Connection(String hostname, String username, String password)
{
    // try to connect to the server with the supplied username
    // and password.

    _hostname = hostname;
    _username = username;
    _password = password;
    try
    {
        Connect();
    }
    catch (Exception e)
    {
        try
        {
            Disconnect();
        }
        catch (Exception ex) {/* ignore */}
```

```
            throw e;
        }
    }


    private void Connect()
    {
        // initialize the list of messages
        _msgs = new Hashtable();

        // open the connection
        _pop3Connection = new TcpClient(_hostname,110);
        _pop3Stream = _pop3Connection.GetStream();
        _pop3Response = new StreamReader(_pop3Stream);

        // ignore first line (server's greeting)
        String response = _pop3Response.ReadLine();

        // authenticate
        SendCommand("USER " + _username,true);
        SendCommand("PASS " + _password,true);

        // retrieve the list of messages
        SendCommand("LIST",true);
        response = _pop3Response.ReadLine();
        while (response != ".")
        {
            // add entries to _msgs dictionary
            int pos = response.IndexOf(" ");
            String msgnumStr = response.Substring(0,pos);
            String bytesStr = response.Substring(pos);

            int msgnum = Convert.ToInt32(msgnumStr);
            int bytes = Convert.ToInt32(bytesStr);

            MessageIndex msgidx = new MessageIndex(msgnum,bytes);
            _msgs.Add (msgidx,msgnum);
            response = _pop3Response.ReadLine();

        }
    }
```

These methods make use of the SendCommand() method, which sends a specified POP3 command to the server and checks the response if indicated:

```
private void SendCommand(String command,bool needOK)
{
    // sends a single command.

    // if needOK is set it will check the response to begin
    // with "+OK" and will throw an exception if it doesn't.

    command = command + "\r\n";
    byte[] cmd = Encoding.ASCII.GetBytes(command);

    // send the command
    _pop3Stream.Write(cmd,0,cmd.Length);
    String response = _pop3Response.ReadLine();

    // check the response
    if (needOK)
    {
        if (!response.Substring(0,3).ToUpper().Equals("+OK"))
        {
            throw new Exception("POP3 Server returned unexpected " +
                "response:\n'" + response + "'");
        }
    }
}
```

The MessageCount property returns the number of messages available at the server:

```
public int MessageCount
{
    get
    {
        // returns the message count after connecting and
        // issuing the LIST command
        return _msgs.Count;
    }
}
```

GetMessage() returns a POP3Msg object, which is filled by retrieving the specified message from the server. It does this by sending the RETR command to the POP3 server and by checking for special e-mail headers. It then populates the POP3Msg object's properties with those headers and the e-mail body:

```
public POP3Msg GetMessage(int msgnum)
{
    // create the resulting object
    POP3Msg tmpmsg = new POP3Msg();

    // retrieve a single message
    SendCommand("RETR " + msgnum,true);
    String response = _pop3Response.ReadLine();

    // read the response line by line and populate the
    // correct properties of the POP3Msg object

    StringBuilder headers = new StringBuilder();
    StringBuilder body = new StringBuilder();
    bool headersDone=false;
    while ((response!= null) && (response != "." ))
    {
        // check if all headers have been read
        if (!headersDone)
        {
            if (response.Length >0)
            {
                // this will only parse the headers which are relevant
                // for .NET Remoting

                if (response.ToUpper().StartsWith("IN-REPLY-TO:"))
                {
                    tmpmsg.InReplyTo = response.Substring(12).Trim();
                }
                else if (response.ToUpper().StartsWith("MESSAGE-ID:"))
                {
                    tmpmsg.MessageId = response.Substring(11).Trim();
                }
                else if (response.ToUpper().StartsWith("FROM:"))
                {
                    tmpmsg.From = response.Substring(5).Trim();
                }
                else if (response.ToUpper().StartsWith("TO:"))
                {
                    tmpmsg.To = response.Substring(3).Trim();
                }
                headers.Append(response).Append("\n");
            }
```

```
        else
        {
            headersDone = true;
        }
    }
    else
    {
        // all headers have been read, add the rest to
        // the body.

        // For .NET Remoting, we need the body in a single
        // line to decode Base64 therefore no <CR><LF>s will
        // be appended!

        body.Append(response);
    }

    // read next line
    response = _pop3Response.ReadLine();
}

// set the complete header and body Strings of POP3Msg
tmpmsg.Body = body.ToString();
tmpmsg.Headers = headers.ToString();
return tmpmsg;
}
```

What's still needed is DeleteMessage(), which flags a message for deletion by sending the DELE command to the server:

```
public void DeleteMessage(int msgnum)
{
    // issue the DELE command to delete the specified message
    SendCommand("DELE " + msgnum,true);
}
```

And finally, you need a method to send the QUIT command and disconnect from the server. This Disconnect() method is shown here:

```
public void Disconnect()
{
    // sends QUIT and disconnects

    try
    {
        // send QUIT to commit the DELEs
        SendCommand("QUIT",false);
    }
    finally
    {
        // close the connection
        _pop3Stream.Close();
        _pop3Response.Close();
        _pop3Connection.Close();
    }
}
```

With those two helper classes presented previously, you'll be able to access SMTP and POP3 servers without having to deal further with the details of those protocols. Nevertheless, what's still missing is a mapping between the .NET Remoting Framework and those e-mail messages.

Checking for New Mail

As POP3 will not notify the client whenever a message has been received, it is necessary to continuously log on to the server to check for new e-mails. This is done by the POP3Polling class. Each instance of this class contacts a given server in regular intervals. If a message is available, it will fetch it and invoke a delegate on another helper class that will then process this message.

The POP3Polling class can be run in two modes: client or server mode. Whenever it's in client mode, it only starts polling after the client has sent a request to the server. As soon as the server's reply is handled, this class stops polling to save network bandwidth. In server mode, it checks the server regularly to handle any remoting requests.

As you can see in the following part of this class, it provides a custom constructor that accepts the server's hostname, username, password, the polling interval, and a flag indicating whether it should run in server or client mode:

```
using System;
using System.Collections;
using System.Threading;
```

```
namespace SMTPChannel
{
    public class POP3Polling
    {
        delegate void HandleMessageDelegate(POP3Msg msg);

        // if it's a remoting server, we will poll forever
        internal bool _isServer;

        // if this is not a server, this property has to be set to
        // start polling
        internal bool _needsPolling;

        // is currently polling
        internal bool _isPolling;

        // polling interval in seconds
        internal int _pollInterval;

        // logon data
        private String _hostname;
        private String _username;
        private String _password;

        internal POP3Polling(String hostname, String username, String password,
                int pollInterval, bool isServer)
        {
            _hostname = hostname;
            _username = username;
            _password = password;
            _pollInterval = pollInterval;
            _isServer = isServer;

            if (!_isServer) { _needsPolling = false; }
        }
```

The following Poll() method does the real work. It is started in a background
thread and checks for new e-mails as long as either _isServer or _needsPolling
(which indicates the need for client-side polling) is true. While it polls the server,
it also sets a flag to prevent reentrancy.

SMTPHelper.MessageReceived() is a static method that is called by using an
asynchronous delegate in a *fire-and-forget* way. This method will handle the
e-mail and forward it to the remoting framework. Have a look at it here:

```
private void Poll()
{
    if (_isPolling) return;
    _isPolling = true;
    do
    {
        Thread.Sleep(_pollInterval * 1000);

        POP3Connection pop = new POP3Connection(_hostname,_username,_password);
        for (int i =1;i<=pop.MessageCount;i++)
        {
            POP3Msg msg =  pop.GetMessage(i);
            HandleMessageDelegate del = new HandleMessageDelegate(
                    SMTPHelper.MessageReceived);
            del.BeginInvoke(msg,null,null);
            pop.DeleteMessage(i);
        }
        pop.Disconnect();
        pop = null;
    } while (_isServer || _needsPolling);
    _isPolling = false;
}
```

The last method of this class, CheckAndStartPolling(), can be called exter-
nally to start the background thread as soon as _needsPolling has been changed.
It does the necessary checks to ensure that only one background thread is running per instance.

```
internal void CheckAndStartPolling()
{
    if (_isPolling) return;

    if (_isServer || _needsPolling)
    {
        Thread thr = new Thread(new ThreadStart(this.Poll));
        thr.Start();
        thr.IsBackground = true;
    }
}
```

Registering a POP3 Server

When creating a custom channel like this, you might want to be able to have one application that can be client and server at the same time. To optimize the polling strategy in this case, you want to have only one instance of the POP3Polling class for a specified e-mail address, and not two separate ones for the client channel and the server channel.

For client-only use of this channel, you also want to have a central point that can be notified as soon as a request has been sent to the server so it can start the background thread to check for new e-mails. Additionally, this class needs a counter of responses that have been sent and for which no reply has yet been received. As soon as all open replies have been handled, it should again notify the POP3Polling object to stop checking for those e-mails.

This class provides a method, `RegisterPolling()`, that has to be called for each registered channel to create the POP3Polling object. This method first checks whether the same username/hostname combination has already been registered. If this is not the case, it creates the new object and stores a reference to it in a Hashtable.

If the same combination has been registered before, this method first checks whether the new registration request is for a server-side channel and in this case switches the already known POP3Polling object into server mode. It also checks the polling intervals of the old and the new object and takes the lower value. Finally, it calls the POP3Polling object's `CheckAndStartPolling()` method to enable the background thread if it is in server mode.

```
using System;
using System.Collections;
using System.Threading;

namespace SMTPChannel
{
    public class POP3PollManager
    {
        // dictionary of polling instances
        static IDictionary _listeners = Hashtable.Synchronized(new Hashtable());

        // number of sent messages for which no response has been received
        private static int _pendingResponses;
        private static int _lastPendingResponses;
```

```
public static void RegisterPolling(String hostname, String username,
    String password, int pollInterval, bool isServer)
{
    String key = username + "|" + hostname;

    // check if this combination has already been registered
    POP3Polling pop3 = (POP3Polling) _listeners[key];
    if (pop3 == null)
    {
        // create a new listener
        pop3 = new POP3Polling(hostname,username,password,
            pollInterval,isServer);

        _listeners[key]= pop3;
    }
    else
    {
        // change to server-mode if needed
        if (!pop3._isServer && isServer)
        {
            pop3._isServer = true;
        }

        // check for pollInterval => lowest interval will be taken
        if (! (pop3._pollInterval > pollInterval))
        {
            pop3._pollInterval = pollInterval;
        }
    }
    pop3.CheckAndStartPolling();
}
```

Two other methods that are provided in this class have to be called to notify all registered POP3Polling objects that the remoting framework is waiting for a reply or that it has received a reply:

```
internal static void RequestSent()
{
    _pendingResponses++;
    if (_lastPendingResponses<=0 && _pendingResponses > 0)
    {
        IEnumerator enmr = _listeners.GetEnumerator();
        while (enmr.MoveNext())
```

```
        {
            DictionaryEntry entr = (DictionaryEntry) enmr.Current;
            POP3Polling pop3 = (POP3Polling) entr.Value;
            pop3._needsPolling = true;
            pop3.CheckAndStartPolling();
        }
    }
    _lastPendingResponses = _pendingResponses;
}

internal static void ResponseReceived()
{
    _pendingResponses--;
    if (_pendingResponses <=0)
    {
        IEnumerator enmr = _listeners.GetEnumerator();
        while (enmr.MoveNext())
        {
            DictionaryEntry entr = (DictionaryEntry) enmr.Current;
            POP3Polling pop3 = (POP3Polling) entr.Value;
            pop3._needsPolling = false;
        }
    }
    _lastPendingResponses = _pendingResponses;
}
```

Connecting to .NET Remoting

What you've seen until now has been quite protocol specific, because I haven't yet covered any connections between the underlying protocol to .NET Remoting. This task is handled by the SMTPHelper class. This class holds three synchronized Hashtables containing the following data:

- Objects that are waiting for a response to a given SMTP message id. These can be either Thread objects or SMTPChannel.AsyncResponseHandler objects, both of which are shown later. These are stored in _waitingFor.

- The server-side transport sink for any e-mail address that has been registered with a SMTPServerChannel in _servers.

- The reccived responses that will be cached while waking up the thread that
  has been blocked is stored in _responses. This is a short-term storage that
  is only used for the fractions of a second it takes for the thread to wake up
  and fetch and remove the response.

This class also starts with a method that transforms the .NET Remoting-
specific information in the form of a stream and an ITransportHeaders object
into an e-mail message. This method writes the standard e-mail headers, adds
the remoting-specific headers from the ITransportHeaders object, encodes the
stream's contents to Base64, and ensures a maximum line length of 73 characters.
Finally, it sends the e-mail using the SMTPConnection helper class:

```
using System;
using System.Text;
using System.IO;
using System.Collections;
using System.Runtime.Remoting.Channels;
using System.Threading;

namespace SMTPChannel
{

    public class SMTPHelper
    {

        // threads waiting for response
        private static IDictionary _waitingFor =
            Hashtable.Synchronized(new Hashtable());

        // known servers
        private static IDictionary _servers =
            Hashtable.Synchronized(new Hashtable());

        // responses received
        private static IDictionary _responses =
            Hashtable.Synchronized(new Hashtable());


        // sending messages
        private static void SendMessage(String ID,String replyToId,
            String mailfrom, String mailto, String smtpServer,
            ITransportHeaders headers,     Stream stream, String objectURI)
        {
            StringBuilder msg = new StringBuilder();
```

```
if (ID != null)
{
    msg.Append("Message-Id: ").Append(ID).Append("\r\n");
}
if (replyToId != null)
{
    msg.Append("In-Reply-To: ").Append(replyToId).Append("\r\n");
}
msg.Append("From: ").Append(mailfrom).Append("\r\n");
msg.Append("To: ").Append(mailto).Append("\r\n");
msg.Append("MIME-Version: 1.0").Append("\r\n");
msg.Append("Content-Type: text/xml; charset=utf-8").Append("\r\n");
msg.Append("Content-Transfer-Encoding: BASE64").Append("\r\n");

// write the remoting headers
IEnumerator headerenum = headers.GetEnumerator();
while (headerenum.MoveNext())
{
    DictionaryEntry entry = (DictionaryEntry) headerenum.Current;
    String key = entry.Key as String;
    if (key == null || key.StartsWith("__"))
    {
        continue;
    }
    msg.Append("X-REMOTING-").Append(key).Append(": ");
    msg.Append(entry.Value.ToString()).Append("\r\n");
}

if (objectURI != null)
{
    msg.Append("X-REMOTING-URI: ").Append(objectURI).Append("\r\n");
}

msg.Append("\r\n");
MemoryStream fs = new MemoryStream();

byte[] buf = new Byte[1000];
int cnt = stream.Read(buf,0,1000);
int bytecount = 0;
while (cnt>0)
{
    fs.Write(buf,0,cnt);
    bytecount+=cnt;
```

```
        cnt = stream.Read(buf,0,1000);
    }


    // convert the whole string to Base64 encoding
    String body = Convert.ToBase64String(fs.GetBuffer(),0,bytecount);

    // and ensure the maximum line length of 73 characters
    int linesNeeded = (int) Math.Ceiling(body.Length / 73);

    for (int i = 0;i<=linesNeeded;i++)
    {
        if (i != linesNeeded)
        {
            String line = body.Substring(i*73,73);
            msg.Append(line).Append("\r\n");
        }
        else
        {
            String line = body.Substring(i*73);
            msg.Append(line).Append("\r\n");
        }
    }

    // send the resulting message
    SMTPConnection con = new SMTPConnection (smtpServer);
    con.SendMessage(mailfrom,mailto,msg.ToString());
}
```

This method is not called directly by the framework, but instead the class provides two other methods that are made for this purpose. The first one, named SendRequestMessage(), generates a message id that is later returned using an out parameter and then calls SendMessage() to send the e-mail via SMTP. It next calls the POP3PollManager's RequestSent() method so that the background thread will start checking for incoming reply mails.

The second method, SendReplyMessage(), takes a given message id and sends a reply:

```
internal static void SendRequestMessage(String mailfrom, String mailto,
    String smtpServer, ITransportHeaders headers, Stream request,
    String objectURI, out String ID)
{
```

```
    ID = "<" + Guid.NewGuid().ToString().Replace("-","") + "@REMOTING>";
    SendMessage(ID,null,mailfrom,mailto,smtpServer,headers,request,objectURI);
    POP3PollManager.RequestSent();
}

internal static void SendResponseMessage(String mailfrom, String mailto,
    String smtpServer, ITransportHeaders headers, Stream response,
    String ID)
{
    SendMessage(null,ID,mailfrom,mailto,smtpServer,headers,response,null);
}
```

The more complex part of mapping the underlying protocol to the .NET
Remoting Framework is the handling of responses. As the combination of SMTP
and POP3 is asynchronous in its nature, whereas most .NET calls are executed
synchronously, you have to provide a means for blocking the underlying thread
until the matching response has been received. This is accomplished by the following method that adds the waiting thread to the _waitingFor Hashtable and
suspends it afterwards. Whenever a response is received (which is handled by
another function running in a different thread), the response is stored in the
_responses Hashtable and the thread awakened again. It then fetches the value
from _responses and return it to the caller:

```
internal static POP3Msg WaitAndGetResponseMessage(String ID)
{
    // suspend the thread until the message returns
    _waitingFor[ID] = Thread.CurrentThread;

    Thread.CurrentThread.Suspend();

    // waiting for resume
    POP3Msg pop3msg = (POP3Msg) _responses[ID];
    _responses.Remove(ID);
    return pop3msg;
}
```

The previous method showed you the handling of synchronous .NET
Remoting messages, but you might also want to support asynchronous delegates.
In this case, a callback object is placed in _waitingFor and the method that handles incoming POP3 messages simply invokes the corresponding method on this
callback object.

```
internal static void RegisterAsyncResponseHandler(String ID,
    AsyncResponseHandler ar)
{
    _waitingFor[ID] = ar;
}
```

One of the most important methods is MessageReceived(), which is called by POP3Polling as soon as an incoming message has been collected from the server. This method attempts to map all incoming e-mails to .NET Remoting calls.

There are two quite different types in e-mails: requests that are sent from a client to a server and reply messages that are sent back from the server. The distinction between these is that a reply e-mail includes an In-Reply-To header, whereas the request message only contains a Message-Id header.

If the incoming message is a request message, the MessageReceived() method checks the _servers Hashtable to retrieve the server-side sink chain for the destination e-mail address. It will then call HandleIncomingMessage() on this SMTPServerTransportSink object.

For reply messages, on the other hand, the method checks whether any objects are waiting for an answer to the contained In-Reply-To header. If the waiting object is a thread, the POP3Msg object will be stored in the _responses Hashtable and the thread will be awakened. For asynchronous calls, the waiting object will be of type AsyncResponseHandler. In this case the framework will simply call its HandleAsyncResponsePop3Msg() method. Regardless of whether the reply has been received for a synchronous or an asynchronous message, POP3PollManager.ResponseReceived() will be called to decrement the count of unanswered messages and to eventually stop polling if all replies have been received.

```
internal static void MessageReceived(POP3Msg pop3msg)
{
    // whenever a pop3 message has been received, it
    // will be forwarded to this method

    // check if it's a request or a reply
    if ((pop3msg.InReplyTo == null) && (pop3msg.MessageId != null))
    {
        // it's a request

        String requestID = pop3msg.MessageId;

        // Request received
```

```
            // check for a registered server
            SMTPServerTransportSink snk = (SMTPServerTransportSink)
                _servers[GetCleanAddress(pop3msg.To)];

            if (snk==null)
            {
                // No server side sink found for address
                return;
            }

            // Dispatch the message to serversink
            snk.HandleIncomingMessage(pop3msg);

        }
        else if (pop3msg.InReplyTo != null)
        {
            // a response must contain the in-reply-to header
            String responseID = pop3msg.InReplyTo.Trim();

            // check who's waiting for it
            Object notify = _waitingFor[responseID];

            if (notify as Thread != null)
            {
                _responses[responseID] = pop3msg;

                // Waiting thread found. Will wake it up
                _waitingFor.Remove(responseID );
                ((Thread) notify).Resume();
                POP3PollManager.ResponseReceived();
            }
            else if (notify as AsyncResponseHandler != null)
            {
                _waitingFor.Remove(responseID);
                POP3PollManager.ResponseReceived();
                ((AsyncResponseHandler)notify).HandleAsyncResponsePop3Msg(
                    pop3msg);
            }
            else
            {
                // No one is waiting for this reply. Ignore.
            }
        }
    }
}
```

Another method is employed to map a POP3Msg object onto the objects that
.NET Remoting needs: Stream and ITransportHeader. ProcessMessage() does this
by taking all custom remoting headers starting with X-REMOTING- from the
e-mail and putting them into a new ITransportHeader object. It then converts
back the Base64-encoded payload into a byte array and creates a new
MemoryStream that allows the remoting framework to read the byte array.
It also returns the message id as an out parameter.

```
internal static void ProcessMessage(POP3Msg pop3msg,
    out ITransportHeaders headers, out Stream stream, out String ID)
{
   // this method will split it into a TransportHeaders and
   // a Stream object and will return the "remoting ID"

   headers = new TransportHeaders();


   // first all remoting headers (which start with "X-REMOTING-")
   // will be extracted and stored in the TransportHeaders object
   String tmp = pop3msg.Headers;
   int pos = tmp.IndexOf("\nX-REMOTING-");
   while (pos >= 0)
   {
      int pos2 = tmp.IndexOf("\n",pos+1);
      String oneline = tmp.Substring(pos+1,pos2-pos-1);

      int poscolon = oneline.IndexOf(":");
      String key = oneline.Substring(11,poscolon-11).Trim();
      String headervalue = oneline.Substring(poscolon+1).Trim();
      if (key.ToUpper() != "URI")
      {
         headers[key] = headervalue;
      }
      else
      {
         headers["__RequestUri"] = headervalue;
      }
      pos = tmp.IndexOf("\nX-REMOTING-",pos2);
   }
```

```
    String fulltext = pop3msg.Body ;
    fulltext = fulltext.Trim();
    byte[] buffer = Convert.FromBase64String(fulltext);
    stream=new MemoryStream(buffer);

    ID = pop3msg.MessageId;
}
```

There's also a method called `RegisterServer()` in SMTPHelper that stores a server-side sink chain in the _servers Hashtable using the e-mail address as a key:

```
public static void RegisterServer(SMTPServerTransportSink snk,
    String address)
{
    // Registering sink for a specified e-mail address
    _servers[address] = snk;
}
```

The last two methods in the helper class are of a more generic nature. The first parses a URL in the form smtp:someone@somedomain.com/URL/to/object and returns the e-mail address separated from the object's URI (which is /URL/to/object in this case) as out parameters:

```
internal static void parseURL(String url, out String email,
    out String objectURI)
{
    // format:    "smtp:user@host.domain/URL/to/object"

    // is splitted to:
    //      email = user@host.domain
    //      objectURI = /URL/to/object
    int pos = url.IndexOf("/");
    if (pos > 0)
    {
        email = url.Substring(5,pos-5);
        objectURI = url.Substring(pos);
    }
    else if (pos ==-1)
    {
        email = url.Substring(5);
        objectURI ="";
    }
```

```
    else
    {
        email = null;
        objectURI = url;
    }

}
```

The second method is used to parse an e-mail address for an incoming request. It accepts addresses in a variety of formats and returns the generic form of user@domain.com:

```
public static String GetCleanAddress(String address)
{
    // changes any kind of address like "someone@host"
    // "<someone@host>" "<someone@host> someone@host"
    // to a generic format of "someone@host"

    address = address.Trim();
    int posAt = address.IndexOf("@");
    int posSpaceAfter = address.IndexOf(" ",posAt);
    if (posSpaceAfter != -1) address = address.Substring(0,posSpaceAfter);

    int posSpaceBefore = address.LastIndexOf(" ");

    if (posSpaceBefore != -1 && posSpaceBefore < posAt)
    {
        address = address.Substring(posSpaceBefore+1);
    }

    int posLt = address.IndexOf("<");
    if (posLt != -1)
    {
        address = address.Substring(posLt+1);
    }

    int posGt = address.IndexOf(">");
    if (posGt != -1)
    {
        address = address.Substring(0,posGt);
    }

    return address;
}
```

Implementing the Client Channel

Before looking into the implementation of the client-side SMTPClientChannel, I show you how it will later be used in a configuration file:

```
<channel
    name="smtpclient"
    type="SMTPChannel.SMTPClientChannel, SMTPChannel"
    senderEmail="client_1@localhost"
    smtpServer="localhost"
    pop3Server="localhost"
    pop3User="client_1"
    pop3Password="client_1"
    pop3PollInterval="1"
>
```

All of these parameters are mandatory, and I explain their meanings in Table 10-2.

Table 10-2. Parameters for SMTPClientChannel

PARAMETER	DESCRIPTION
name	Unique name for this channel.
senderEmail	The value for the e-mail's From: header. The server will reply to the address specified here.
smtpServer	Your outgoing e-mail server's name.
pop3Server	Your incoming mail server's name.
pop3User	The POP3 user account that is assigned to this client application.
pop3Password	The password for the application's POP3 account.
pop3PollInterval	Interval in seconds at which the framework will check for new mail at the server.

A client channel has to extend BaseChannelWithProperties and implement IChannelSender, which in turn extends IChannel. These interfaces are shown in Listing 10-3.

Listing 10-3. IChannel and IChannelSender

```
public interface IChannel
{
    // Properties
    string ChannelName { get; }
    int ChannelPriority { get; }

    // Methods
    string Parse(string url, ref String objectURI);
}

public interface IChannelSender: IChannel
{

    // Methods
    IMessageSink CreateMessageSink(string url, object remoteChannelData,
        ref String objectURI);
}
```

Let's have a look at the basic implementation of a channel and the IChannel interface first. Each channel that is creatable using a configuration file has to supply a special constructor that takes two parameters: an IDictionary object, which will contain the attributes specified in the configuration file (for example, smtpServer); and an IClientChannelSinkProvider object, which points to the first entry of the chain of sink providers specified in the configuration file.

In the case of the SMPTClientChannel, this constructor will store those values to member variables and call POP3PollManager.RegisterPolling() to register the connection information:

```
using System;
using System.Collections;
using System.Runtime.Remoting.Channels;
using System.Runtime.Remoting;
using System.Runtime.Remoting.Messaging;

namespace SMTPChannel
{
    public class SMTPClientChannel: BaseChannelWithProperties, IChannelSender
    {
        IDictionary _properties;
        IClientChannelSinkProvider _provider;
        String _name;
```

```
            public SMTPClientChannel (IDictionary properties,
                        IClientChannelSinkProvider clientSinkProvider)
    {
        _properties = properties;
        _provider = clientSinkProvider;
        _name = (String) _properties["name"];

        POP3PollManager.RegisterPolling(
            (String) _properties["pop3Server"],
            (String) _properties["pop3User"],
            (String) _properties["pop3Password"],
            Convert.ToInt32((String)_properties["pop3PollInterval"]),
            false);
    }
```

The implementation of IChannel itself is quite straightforward. You basically have to return a priority and a name for the channel, both of which can be either configurable or hard coded. You also have to implement a Parse() method that takes a URL as its input parameter. It then has to check if the given URL is valid for this channel (returning null if it isn't) and split it into its base URL, which is the return value from the method, and the object's URI, which is returned as an out parameter:

```
public string ChannelName
{
    get
    {
        return _name;
    }
}


public int ChannelPriority
{
    get
    {
        return 0;
    }
}


public string Parse(string url, out string objectURI)
{
    String email;
    SMTPHelper.parseURL(url, out email, out objectURI);
```

```
        if (email == null || email=="" || objectURI == null || objectURI =="")
        {
            return null;
        }
        else
        {
            return "smtp:" + email;
        }
}
```

The implementation of IChannelSender consists only of a single method:
CreateMessageSink(). This method will *either* receive a URL *or* a channel data
store as parameters and and will return an IMessageSink as a result and the destination object's URI as an out parameter.

When no URL is specified as a parameter, you should cast the channel data
store (which is passed as object) to IChannelDataStore and take the first URL
from it instead. You then have to check if the URL is valid for your channel and
return null if it isn't. Next you add the client channel's transport sink provider at
the end of the provider chain and call CreateSink() on the first provider. The
resulting sink chain is then returned from the method:

```
public IMessageSink CreateMessageSink(string url, object remoteChannelData,
        out string objectURI)
{

    if (url == null && remoteChannelData != null &&
            remoteChannelData as IChannelDataStore != null )
    {
        IChannelDataStore ds = (IChannelDataStore) remoteChannelData;
        url = ds.ChannelUris[0];
    }

    // format:    "smtp:user@host.domain/URI/to/object"
    if (url != null && url.ToLower().StartsWith("smtp:"))
    {
        // walk to last provider and this channel sink's provider
        IClientChannelSinkProvider prov = _provider;
        while (prov.Next != null) { prov = prov.Next ;};

        prov.Next = new SMTPClientTransportSinkProvider(
                (String) _properties["senderEmail"],
                (String) _properties["smtpServer"]);
```

```
            String dummy;
            SMTPHelper.parseURL(url,out dummy,out objectURI);

            IMessageSink msgsink =
                    (IMessageSink) _provider.CreateSink(this,url,remoteChannelData);

            return msgsink;
        }
        else
        {
            objectURI =null;
            return null;
        }
    }
}
```

Creating the Client's Sink and Provider

Even though this sink provider is called a transport sink provider, it is in fact
a straightforward implementation of an IClientChannelSinkProvider, which
you've encountered in Chapter 9. The main difference is that its CreateSink()
method has to parse the URL to provide the transport sink with the correct information regarding the destination e-mail address and the object's URI. It also
doesn't need to specify any special constructors, as it will not be initialized from
a configuration file. The complete sink provider is shown in Listing 10-4.

Listing 10-4. The SMTPClientTransportSinkProvider

```
using System;
using System.Collections;
using System.Runtime.Remoting.Channels;
using System.Runtime.Remoting;
using System.Runtime.Remoting.Messaging;

namespace SMTPChannel
{
    public class SMTPClientTransportSinkProvider: IClientChannelSinkProvider
    {

        String _senderEmailAddress;
        String _smtpServer;
```

```
    public SMTPClientTransportSinkProvider(String senderEmailAddress,
            String smtpServer)
    {
        _senderEmailAddress = senderEmailAddress;
        _smtpServer = smtpServer;
    }

    public IClientChannelSink CreateSink(IChannelSender channel,
        string url, object remoteChannelData)
    {
        String destinationEmailAddress;
        String objectURI;
        SMTPHelper.parseURL(url,out destinationEmailAddress,out objectURI);

        return new SMTPClientTransportSink(destinationEmailAddress,
            _senderEmailAddress,_smtpServer, objectURI);
    }

    public IClientChannelSinkProvider Next
    {
        get
        {
            return null;
        }
        set
        {
            // ignore as this has to be the last provider in the chain
        }
    }
  }
}
```

When relying on the helper classes presented previously, the client-side sink's implementation will be quite simple as well. First, you have to provide a constructor that allows the sender's and the recipient's e-mail address, the object's URI, and the SMTP server to be set:

```
using System;
using System.Runtime.Remoting.Channels;
using System.Runtime.Remoting;
using System.Runtime.Remoting.Messaging;
using System.IO;
```

```
namespace SMTPChannel
{

    public class SMTPClientTransportSink: BaseChannelSinkWithProperties,
        IClientChannelSink, IChannelSinkBase
    {

        String _destinationEmailAddress;
        String _senderEmailAddress;
        String _objectURI;
        String _smtpServer;

        public SMTPClientTransportSink(String destinationEmailAddress,
            String senderEmailAddress, String smtpServer, String objectURI)
        {
            _destinationEmailAddress = destinationEmailAddress;
            _senderEmailAddress = senderEmailAddress;
            _objectURI = objectURI;
            _smtpServer = smtpServer;
        }
```

The key functionality of this sink is that ProcessMessage() and AsyncProcessMessage() cannot just forward the parameters to another sink, but instead have to send it by e-mail to another process. ProcessMessage() parses the URL to split it into the e-mail address and the object's URI. Those values are then used to call SMTPHelper.SendRequestMessage(). As this method has to block until a response is received, it also calls SMTPHelper.WaitAndGetResponseMessage(). Finally, it hands over the processing of the return message to the ProcessMessage() method of SMTPHelper to split it into a stream and an ITransportHeaders object that have to be returned from ProcessMessage() as out parameter.

```
public void ProcessMessage(IMessage msg,
    ITransportHeaders requestHeaders, Stream requestStream,
    out ITransportHeaders responseHeaders,
    out Stream responseStream)
{
    String ID;
    String objectURI;
    String email;

    // check the URL
    String URL = (String) msg.Properties["__Uri"];
    SMTPHelper.parseURL(URL,out email,out objectURI);
```

```
    if ((email==null) || (email == ""))
    {
        email = _destinationEmailAddress;
    }


    // send the message
    SMTPHelper.SendRequestMessage(_senderEmailAddress,email,_smtpServer,
            requestHeaders,requestStream,objectURI, out ID);

    // wait for the response
    POP3Msg popmsg = SMTPHelper.WaitAndGetResponseMessage(ID);

    // process the response
    SMTPHelper.ProcessMessage(popmsg,out responseHeaders,out responseStream,
        out ID);
}
```

The AsyncProcessMessage() method does not block and wait for a reply, but instead creates a new instance of AsyncResponseHandler (which I introduce in a bit) and passes the sink stack to it. It then registers this object with the SMTPHelper to enable it to forward the response to the underlying sinks and finally to the IAsyncResult object that has been returned from the delegate's BeginInvoke() method:

```
public void AsyncProcessRequest(IClientChannelSinkStack sinkStack,
    IMessage msg, ITransportHeaders headers, Stream stream)
{
    String ID;
    String objectURI;
    String email;

    // parse the url
    String URL = (String) msg.Properties["__Uri"];
    SMTPHelper.parseURL(URL,out email,out objectURI);

    if ((email==null) || (email == ""))
    {
        email = _destinationEmailAddress;
    }

    // send the request message
    SMTPHelper.SendRequestMessage(_senderEmailAddress,email,_smtpServer,
        headers,stream,objectURI, out ID);
```

```
    // create and register an async response handler
    AsyncResponseHandler ar = new AsyncResponseHandler(sinkStack);
    SMTPHelper.RegisterAsyncResponseHandler(ID, ar);
}
```

The rest of the SMTPClientTransportSink is just a standard implementation of the mandatory parts of IClientChannelSink. As these methods are not expected to be called for a transport sink, they will either return null or throw an exception:

```
public void AsyncProcessResponse(IClientResponseChannelSinkStack sinkStack,
object state, ITransportHeaders headers, Stream stream)
{
    // not needed in a transport sink!
    throw new NotSupportedException();
}


public Stream GetRequestStream(System.Runtime.Remoting.Messaging.IMessage msg,
System.Runtime.Remoting.Channels.ITransportHeaders headers)
{
    // no direct way to access the stream
    return null;
}


public System.Runtime.Remoting.Channels.IClientChannelSink NextChannelSink
{
    get
    {
        // no more sinks
        return null;
    }
}
```

The last thing you have to implement before you are able to use this channel is the AsyncResponseHandler class that is used to pass an incoming reply message to the sink stack. Its HandleAsyncResponsePop3Msg() method is called by SMTPHelper.MessageReceived() whenever the originating call has been placed by using an asynchronous delegate. It calls SMTPHelper.ProcessMessage() to split the e-mail message into a Stream object and an ITransportHeaders object and then calls AsyncProcessResponse() on the sink stack that has been passed to AsyncResponseHandler in its constructor:

```
using System;
using System.Runtime.Remoting.Channels;
using System.Runtime.Remoting;
using System.IO;
using System.Runtime.Remoting.Messaging;

namespace SMTPChannel
{
    internal class AsyncResponseHandler
    {
        IClientChannelSinkStack _sinkStack;

        internal AsyncResponseHandler(IClientChannelSinkStack sinkStack)
        {
            _sinkStack = sinkStack;
        }

        internal void HandleAsyncResponsePop3Msg(POP3Msg popmsg)
        {
            ITransportHeaders responseHeaders;
            Stream responseStream;
            String ID;

            SMTPHelper.ProcessMessage(popmsg,out responseHeaders,
                    out responseStream,out ID);

            _sinkStack.AsyncProcessResponse(responseHeaders,responseStream);
        }
    }
}
```

Well, that's it! You've just completed your first client-side transport channel.

Implementing the Server Channel

As with the client channel, I show you how the server channel will be used before diving into the code. Basically, it looks exactly like the SMTPClientChannel did:

```
<channel
        name="smtpserver"
        type="SMTPChannel.SMTPServerChannel, SMTPChannel"
        senderEmail="server_1@localhost"
```

```
            smtpServer="localhost"
            pop3Server="localhost"
            pop3User="server_1"
            pop3Password="server_1"
            pop3PollInterval="1"
    >
```

The parameters for this channel are shown in Table 10-3.

Table 10-3. Parameters for SMTPServerChannel

PARAMETER	DESCRIPTION
name	Unique name for this channel.
senderEmail	The value for the e-mail's From: header. The server will reply to the address specified here.
smtpServer	Your outgoing e-mail server's name.
pop3Server	Your incoming mail server's name.
pop3User	The POP3 user account that is assigned to this client application.
pop3Password	The password for the application's POP3 account.
pop3PollInterval	Interval in seconds at which the framework will check for new mail at the server.

The basic difference between the SMTPClientChannel and the SMTPServerChannel is that the latter registers itself with the POP3PollManager as a server. This means that the POP3Polling instance will constantly check for new e-mails.

The server-side channel has to implement IChannelReceiver, which in turn inherits from IChannel again. These interfaces are shown in Listing 10-5.

Listing 10-5. IChannel and IChannelReceiver

```
public interface IChannel
{
    string ChannelName { get; }
    int ChannelPriority { get; }

    string Parse(string url, ref String objectURI);
}
```

```
public interface IChannelReceiver: IChannel
{
    object ChannelData { get; }

    string[] GetUrlsForUri(string objectURI);
    void StartListening(object data);
    void StopListening(object data);
}
```

The implementation of SMTPServerChannel itself is quite straightforward. Its constructor checks for the attributes specified in the configuration file and assigns them to local member variables. It also creates a ChannelDataStore object, which is needed for CAOs to communicate back with the server (that is, when creating a CAO using this channel, the server returns the base URL contained in this ChannelDataStore object).

It then creates the sink chain and adds the SMTPServerTransportSink on top of the chain. This is different from the client-side channel, where the constructor only creates a chain of sink providers. This is because on the server-side there is only a single sink chain per channel, whereas the client creates a distinct sink chain for each remote object. Finally the constructor calls StartListening() to enable the reception of incoming requests:

```
using System;
using System.Collections;
using System.Runtime.Remoting.Channels;
using System.Runtime.Remoting;
using System.Runtime.Remoting.Messaging;

namespace SMTPChannel
{

    public class SMTPServerChannel: BaseChannelWithProperties,
        IChannelReceiver,
        IChannel
    {
        private String _myAddress;
        private String _name;
        private String _smtpServer;
        private String _pop3Server;
        private String _pop3Username;
        private String _pop3Password;
        private int _pop3Pollingtime;
```

```
private SMTPServerTransportSink _transportSink;
private IServerChannelSinkProvider _sinkProvider;
private IDictionary _properties;

private ChannelDataStore _channelData;

public SMTPServerChannel(IDictionary properties,
        IServerChannelSinkProvider serverSinkProvider)
{
  _sinkProvider = serverSinkProvider;
  _properties = properties;
  _myAddress = (String) _properties["senderEmail"];
  _name = (String) _properties["name"];
  _pop3Server = (String) _properties["pop3Server"];
  _smtpServer = (String) _properties["smtpServer"];
  _pop3Username = (String) _properties["pop3User"];
  _pop3Password = (String) _properties["pop3Password"];
  _pop3Pollingtime =
      Convert.ToInt32((String) _properties["pop3PollInterval"]);


  // needed for CAOs!
  String[] urls = { this.GetURLBase() };
  _channelData = new ChannelDataStore(urls);

  // collect channel data from all providers
  IServerChannelSinkProvider provider = _sinkProvider;
  while (provider != null)
  {
     provider.GetChannelData(_channelData);
     provider = provider.Next;
  }

  // create the sink chain
  IServerChannelSink snk =
     ChannelServices.CreateServerChannelSinkChain(_sinkProvider,this);

  // add the SMTPServerTransportSink as a first element to the chain
  _transportSink = new SMTPServerTransportSink(snk, _smtpServer,
     _myAddress);

  // start to listen
  this.StartListening(null);
}
```

The constructor calls GetURLBase(), which provides a way for this channel to return its base URL:

```
private String GetURLBase()
{
    return "smtp:" + _myAddress;
}
```

You also have to implement IChannel's methods and properties: Parse(), ChannelName, and ChannelPriority. The implementation itself looks exactly the same as it did for the client-side channel:

```
public string Parse(string url, out string objectURI)
{
    String email;
    SMTPHelper.parseURL(url, out email, out objectURI);
    if (email == null || email=="" || objectURI == null || objectURI =="")
    {
        return null;
    }
    else
    {
        return "smtp:" + email;
    }
}

public string ChannelName
{
    get
    {
        return _name;
    }
}

public int ChannelPriority
{
    get
    {
        return 0;
    }
}
```

The single most important method of a server-side channel is StartListening(). Only after it is called will the server be able to receive requests and to handle them.

In the SMTPServerChannel, this method registers its connection as a server with the POP3PollManager. It next registers the server-side transport sink and its e-mail address with the SMTPHelper. This last step will enable the helper to dispatch requests based on the destination e-mail address:

```
public void StartListening(object data)
{
    // register the POP3 account for polling
    POP3PollManager.RegisterPolling(_pop3Server,_pop3Username,
        _pop3Password,_pop3Pollingtime,true);

    // register the e-mail address as a server
    SMTPHelper.RegisterServer(_transportSink,_myAddress);
}

public void StopListening(object data)
{
    // Not needed ;-)
}
```

To enable CAOs to work correctly, you must implement the method GetUrlsForUri() and the property ChannelData. The first allows the framework to convert a given object's URI into a complete URL (including the protocol-specific part, such as smtp:user@host.com). The second returns the channel data object that is used by the framework to provide the complete URL for a client-activated object:

```
public string[] GetUrlsForUri(string objectURI)
{
    String[] urls;
    urls = new String[1];
    if (!(objectURI.StartsWith("/")))
        objectURI = "/" + objectURI;

    urls[0] = this.GetURLBase() + objectURI;
    return urls;
}
```

```
public object ChannelData
{
   get
   {
      return _channelData;
   }
}
```

Creating the Server's Sink

A server-side transport sink has to implement IServerChannelSink, which in turn extends IChannelSinkBase. You might already know the interfaces shown in Listing 10-6 from Chapter 9, where they were used to extend the remoting infrastructure.

Listing 10-6. IChannelSinkBase and IServerChannelSink

```
public interface IChannelSinkBase
{
    IDictionary Properties { get; }
}

public interface IServerChannelSink : IChannelSinkBase
{
    IServerChannelSink NextChannelSink { get; }

    ServerProcessing ProcessMessage(IServerChannelSinkStack sinkStack,
            IMessage requestMsg, ITransportHeaders requestHeaders,
            Stream requestStream, ref IMessage responseMsg,
            ref ITransportHeaders responseHeaders, ref Stream responseStream);

    void AsyncProcessResponse(IServerResponseChannelSinkStack sinkStack,
            object state, IMessage msg, ITransportHeaders headers,
            Stream stream);

    Stream GetResponseStream(IServerResponseChannelSinkStack sinkStack,
            object state, IMessage msg, ITransportHeaders headers);

}
```

The implementation of SMTPServerTransportSink is a little bit different from classic channel sinks. First and foremost, it is not created by a sink provider but instead directly by the channel that passes the reference to the next sink, the SMTP server's address and the server's own address to the newly created SMTPServerTransportSink.

Additionally, you'll need a private class to hold state information about the origin of the request and its message ID to process the asynchronous replies:

```
using System;
using System.IO;
using System.Runtime.Remoting.Channels;
using System.Runtime.Remoting;
using System.Runtime.Remoting.Messaging;

namespace SMTPChannel
{

    public class SMTPServerTransportSink: IServerChannelSink

    {
        // will be used as a state object for the async reply
        private class SMTPState
        {
            internal String ID;
            internal String responseAddress;
        }

        private String _smtpServer;
        private String _myAddress;
        private IServerChannelSink _nextSink;

        public SMTPServerTransportSink(IServerChannelSink nextSink,
                String smtpServer, String myAddress)
        {
            _nextSink = nextSink;
            _smtpServer =smtpServer;
            _myAddress = myAddress;
        }
```

One of the main differences between a server-side transport sink and a "conventional" channel sink is that the latter receives its parameters via the ProcessMessage() method. The transport sink instead does not define a specific way to receive the incoming request from the underlying transport mechanisms.

In the case of the SMTPServerTransportSink, it receives a POP3Msg object from the SMTPHelper and processes it in HandleIncomingMessage(). It first splits the e-mail message into a Stream object and an ITransportHeaders object. It then creates a new state object of type SMTPState and populates its properties from the e-mail's values.

Next, it creates a ServerChannelSinkStack and pushes itself and the newly created state object onto it before handing over the processing to the next sink in its chain. When this method is finished, it returns a ServerProcessing value. This indicates whether the message has been handled synchronously, asynchronously, or as a one-way message.

The SMTPServerTransportSink now behaves accordingly. If the request has been handled synchronously, it generates and sends a response message. For asynchronous calls, it waits for the framework to call its AsyncProcessResponse() method. For one-way calls, it does nothing at all:

```
public void HandleIncomingMessage(POP3Msg popmsg)
{
    Stream requestStream;
    ITransportHeaders requestHeaders;
    String ID;

    // split the message in Stream and ITransportHeaders
    SMTPHelper.ProcessMessage(popmsg,out requestHeaders,
        out requestStream, out ID);

    // create a new sink stack
    ServerChannelSinkStack stack = new ServerChannelSinkStack();

    // create a new state object and populate it
    SMTPState state = new SMTPState();
    state.ID = ID;
    state.responseAddress = SMTPHelper.GetCleanAddress(popmsg.From );

    // push this sink onto the stack
    stack.Push(this,state);

    IMessage responseMsg;
    Stream responseStream;
    ITransportHeaders responseHeaders;

    // forward the call to the next sink
    ServerProcessing proc = _nextSink.ProcessMessage(stack,null,requestHeaders,
            requestStream, out responseMsg, out responseHeaders,
            out responseStream);
```

```
// check the return value.
switch (proc)
{
    // this message has been handled synchronously
    case ServerProcessing.Complete:
        // send a response message
        SMTPHelper.SendResponseMessage(_myAddress,
            state.responseAddress,_smtpServer,responseHeaders,
            responseStream,state.ID);
        break;

    // this message has been handled asynchronously
    case ServerProcessing.Async:
        // nothing needs to be done yet
        break;

    // it's been a one way message
    case ServerProcessing.OneWay:
        // nothing needs to be done yet
        break;
}
}
```

AsyncProcessResponse() is called when the framework has completed
the execution of an underlying asynchronous method. The
SMTPServerTransportSink in this case generates a response message and
sends it to the client:

```
public void AsyncProcessResponse(
    IServerResponseChannelSinkStack sinkStack, object state,
    IMessage msg, ITransportHeaders headers, System.IO.Stream stream)
{

    // fetch the state object
    SMTPState smtpstate = (SMTPState) state;

    // send the response e-mail
    SMTPHelper.SendResponseMessage(_myAddress,
        smtpstate.responseAddress,_smtpServer,headers,
        stream,smtpstate.ID);
}
```

What's still left in SMTPServerTransportSink is the implementation of the other mandatory methods and properties defined in IServerChannelSink. Most of them will not be called for a transport sink and will therefore only return null or throw an exception:

```
public IServerChannelSink NextChannelSink
{
   get
   {
      return _nextSink;
   }
}


public System.Collections.IDictionary Properties
{
   get
   {
      // not needed
      return null;
   }
}


public ServerProcessing ProcessMessage(
   IServerChannelSinkStack sinkStack, IMessage requestMsg,
   ITransportHeaders requestHeaders, Stream requestStream,
   out IMessage responseMsg, out ITransportHeaders responseHeaders,
   out Stream responseStream)
{
   // will never be called for a server side transport sink
   throw new NotSupportedException();
}


public Stream GetResponseStream(
   IServerResponseChannelSinkStack sinkStack, object state,
   IMessage msg, ITransportHeaders headers)
{
   // it's not possible to directly access the stream
   return null;
}
```

Great! You have now finished implementing your own transport channel!

Wrapping the Channel

As you've seen with the default .NET Remoting channels, you don't have to manually create and register HTTPClientChannel and HTTPServerChannel but can
instead use the combination in the form of HTTPChannel. This isn't strictly
needed for compatibility with the .NET Remoting Framework, but it does provide
more comfort for the developers using this channel. An additional feature you
might want to implement is the default assignment of a formatter to this channel. I'm now going to show you how to do this to create an SMTPChannel class.

First, the combined channel has to extend BaseChannelWithProperties and
implement IChannelSender and IChannelReceiver. Nevertheless, there won't be
too much logic in SMTPChannel, as it will delegate most of its work to either
SMTPClientChannel or SMTPServerChannel.

To check if an application wants to act as a server for .NET Remoting
requests via SMTP, you have to introduce another attribute that can be used in
the configuration file: isServer. When this is set to "yes", the SMTPChannel will
create an SMTPServerChannel as well; otherwise it will only create an
SMTPClientChannel.

The SMTPChannel has to implement a different constructor that allows the
framework to pass both an IClientChannelSinkProvider *and* an
IServerChannelSinkProvider object to it. It will then check whether either of these
is null and create a default SOAP formatter in this case.

All other methods that have to be implemented to support the specified
interfaces will just forward their calls to the respective client or server channel.
This is shown in Listing 10-7.

Listing 10-7. The SMTPChannel

```
using System;
using System.Collections;
using System.Runtime.Remoting.Channels;
using System.Runtime.Remoting;
using System.Runtime.Remoting.Messaging;

namespace SMTPChannel
{
    public class SMTPChannel: BaseChannelWithProperties,
        IChannelSender, IChannelReceiver
    {
        SMTPClientChannel _clientchannel;
        SMTPServerChannel _serverchannel;
        String _name;
```

```csharp
public SMTPChannel (IDictionary properties,
    IClientChannelSinkProvider clientSinkProvider,
    IServerChannelSinkProvider serverSinkProvider)
{
    if (clientSinkProvider == null)
    {
        clientSinkProvider = new SoapClientFormatterSinkProvider();
    }

    // create the client channel
    _clientchannel = new SMTPClientChannel(properties, clientSinkProvider);

    if ((properties["isServer"] != null) &&
        ((String) properties["isServer"] == "yes" ))
    {
        if (serverSinkProvider == null)
        {
            serverSinkProvider = new SoapServerFormatterSinkProvider();
        }

        // create the server channel
        _serverchannel = new SMTPServerChannel( properties,
                serverSinkProvider);
    }

    _name = (String) properties["name"];
}

public IMessageSink CreateMessageSink(string url,
    object remoteChannelData, out string objectURI)
{
    return _clientchannel.CreateMessageSink(url,
        remoteChannelData, out objectURI);
}

public string Parse(string url, out string objectURI)
{
    return _clientchannel.Parse(url, out objectURI);
}

public string ChannelName
{
    get
```

```csharp
        {
            return _name;
        }
    }

    public int ChannelPriority
    {
        get
        {
            return 0;
        }

    }

    public void StartListening(object data)
    {
        if (_serverchannel != null)
        {
            _serverchannel.StartListening(data);
        }
    }

    public void StopListening(object data)
    {
        if (_serverchannel != null)
        {
            _serverchannel.StopListening(data);
        }
    }

    public string[] GetUrlsForUri(string objectURI)
    {
        if (_serverchannel != null)
        {
            return _serverchannel.GetUrlsForUri(objectURI);
        }
        else
        {
            return null;
        }
    }
```

```
    public object ChannelData
    {
        get
        {
            if (_serverchannel != null )
            {
                return _serverchannel.ChannelData;
            }
            else
            {
                return null;
            }
        }
    }

    }
}
```

Using the SMTPChannel

What you've seen previously constitutes a full-featured transport channel. It supports every .NET Remoting functionality: synchronous calls, asynchronous calls, and event notification. In addition, client-activated objects can be used with this channel. To use it on the server side, you can register it by implementing a configuration file like this:

```
<configuration>
  <system.runtime.remoting>
    <application>
      <channels>
        <channel name="smtp"
            type="SMTPChannel.SMTPChannel, SMTPChannel"
            senderEmail="server_1@localhost"
            smtpServer="localhost"
            pop3Server="localhost"
            pop3User="server_1"
            pop3Password="server_1"
            pop3PollInterval="1"
            isServer="yes" />
      </channels>
```

```
        <service>
          <wellknown mode="Singleton"
                     type="Service.SomeSAO, Service"
                     objectUri="SomeSAO.soap" />
        </service>
      </application>
    </system.runtime.remoting>
</configuration>
```

The corresponding client-side configuration file might look like this:

```
<configuration>
  <system.runtime.remoting>
    <application>

      <channels>
        <channel name="smtp"
            type="SMTPChannel.SMTPChannel, SMTPChannel"
            senderEmail="client_1@localhost"
            smtpServer="localhost"
            pop3Server="localhost"
            pop3User="client_1"
            pop3Password="client_1"
            pop3PollInterval="1"
            isServer="yes" />
      </channels>

      <client>
        <wellknown type="Service.SomeSAO, Service"
                   url="smtp:server_1@localhost/SomeSAO.soap" />
      </client>

      <client url="smtp:server_2@localhost">
        <activated type="Service.SomeCAO, Service" />
      </client>

    </application>
  </system.runtime.remoting>
</configuration>
```

In the source code download that accompanies this book online, you'll find not only the complete implementation of this channel, but also a test environment consisting of three projects (two servers and a client) that shows the following features using the SMTPChannel:

- Server-activated objects

- Client-activated objects

- Synchronous calls

- Asynchronous calls using a delegate

- Raising and handling events

- Passing references to CAOs between different applications

Preparing Your Machine

To run the samples on your machine, you'll need to have access to three e-mail accounts (two for the servers and one for the client) with SMTP and POP3. For testing purposes I therefore recommend that you download and install Mercury/32, a free e-mail server, to allow you to easily perform the configuration without having to bother any system administrators. You can get it from http://www.pmail.com.

Please create three user accounts in Mercury/32 after installing and running it (Configuration ➢ Manage local users), each having the same password as the user name: client_1, server_1, and server_2. You can see the final state in Figure 10-1.

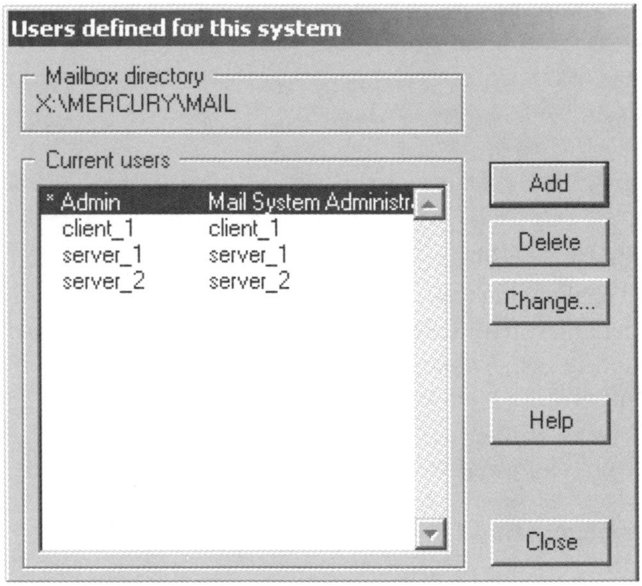

Figure 10-1. These user accounts are needed for these examples.

You also need to change to Mercury core configuration (Configuration ➤ Mercury core module) to recognize the local domain. To do this, switch to the Local domains tab and enter **localhost** in the **Local host or server** and **Internet name** text boxes as shown in Figure 10-2.

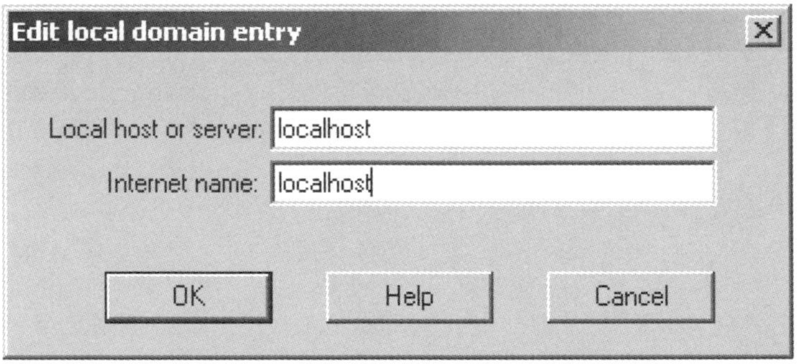

Figure 10-2. Preparing the core modules

Summary

After reading this chapter you have finally reached the level of .NET Remoting wizardship. Not only do you know how to extend the framework using custom sinks and providers, but now you can also implement a complete channel from scratch. You learned that most work in implementing a custom channel has to be expended in understanding and encapsulating the underlying protocol. Mapping an asynchronous protocol to synchronous calls and vice versa is an especially important and challenging task. You also know how to implement IChannelSender and IChannelReceiver, how to combine them into a top-level channel and how to assign default formatters to a channel.

In the next chapter, I introduce you to the possibilities of using the basic principle of .NET Remoting, which is the processing of method calls using messages instead of stack-based calling conventions in your local applications.

Context Matters

THIS CHAPTER IS ABOUT message-based processing in local applications. Here you learn how you can intercept calls to objects to route them through IMessageSinks. This routing allows you to create and maintain parts of your application's business logic at the metadata level by using attributes. You also discover why it might be a good idea to do so.

> **CAUTION**   *Everything in this chapter is 100 percent undocumented. Reliance on these techniques is not supported by either Microsoft, the publisher, or the author of this book. Use at your own risk! If your computer won't work afterwards, your toaster blows up, or your car doesn't start, I assume no liability whatsoever. You're now about to enter the uncharted territories of .NET and you do so on your own risk. I can only provide some guidance.*

Well, it's great that you're still with me after this introductory warning. So let's start with a look at some common business applications. You will quite likely have some object model that holds local data before it's committed to the database. Those classes will contain parts of your business logic. For example, assume that your application provides an instant way for employees of your company to donate various amounts of their paychecks to charity organizations. In that case you might have a data object that looks like the one shown in Listing 11-1, which allows a user to set an organization's name and the donation of a specified amount to it.

Listing 11-1. The First Version of the Organization Object

```
using System;

namespace ContextBound
{
    public class Organization
    {
        String _name;
        double _totalDonation;
```

```
        public String Name
        {
           set
           {
               _name = value;
           }
           get
           {
               return _name;
           }
        }

        public void Donate(double amount)
        {
           _totalDonation = _totalDonation + amount;
        }

    }
}
```

You might also have some database restriction or business logic that limits an organization's name to 30 characters and allows a maximum donation of $100.00. Therefore you need to extend Donate() and the setter of Name to check for this logic:

```
public String Name
{
    set
    {
        if (value != null && value.Length > 30)
        {
            throw new Exception("This field must not be longer than 30 characters");
        }

        _name = value;
    }
    get
    {
        return _name;
    }
}
```

```
public void Donate(double amount)
{
    if (amount > 100)
    {
        throw new Exception("This parameter must not be greater than 100.");
    }
    _totalDonation = _totalDonation + amount;
}
```

You're checking the business logic and your application works as expected. So far, so good. The problems only commence as soon as more developers start using your objects as the base for their applications because they don't know about those restrictions by reading the interface definition alone. As in most real-world applications, the business logic is in this case hidden inside the implementation and is not part of the metadata level. There is no way for another developer to tell that the maximum amount for a valid donation is $100.00 without looking at your source code.

If you're a well-informed developer, you already know that you can at least document those parameters using inline XML comments to automatically generate online documentation for your classes—but you still have to document and implement the logic in two separate places. If you've never, ever changed any implementation detail without updating the inline documentation, you don't need to read further—you already solved the problem.

Working at the MetaData Level

In most projects though (at least in some I've recently heard of) there is a direct proportionality between days to deadline and quality of documentation. Somehow people tend to forget to update comments as soon as their boss is reminding them that they should have shipped it yesterday.

Wouldn't it be great to just specify those checks using some source code attributes and have some "black magic" happen between the client and your objects that takes care of checking the passed values against those attributes?

In a perfect world, these methods might simply look like this:

```
public String Name
{
    [Check(MaxLength=30)]
    set
    {
        _name = value;
    }
```

```
      get
      {
         return _name;
      }
   }

   public void Donate([Check(MaxValue=100)] double amount)
   {
      _totalDonation = _totalDonation + amount;
   }
```

Now the documentation of your business logic is applied on the metadata level! You could easily use reflection to generate printed or online documentation that includes these basic business logic checks as well.

Well, unfortunately, no checks have been done yet. In fact, when using this class, you could easily set `Name` to any possible value and `Donate()` to whatever amount you'd like.

> **CAUTION**   *You're now really about to read about unsupported and undocumented features of .NET Framework. Your mileage may vary.*

What's still missing is that magic something I mentioned that would sit between the client and your object (running maybe within the same process and application) and perform those checks. This is where ContextBoundObject enters the game.

Creating a Context

When you create a class that is derived from ContextBoundObject, nothing special happens yet: by default all objects are still created in the same context. You can, however, decorate this class with an attribute that inherits from ContextAttribute and overrides the following two methods:

```
public bool IsContextOK(Context ctx, IConstructionCallMessage ctor)
public void GetPropertiesForNewContext(IConstructionCallMessage ctor)
```

When doing this, the first method is called whenever someone is creating a new instance of the target class (for example, the previous Organization class). If it returns `true`, nothing happens, and the object is created in the same context as the client. There won't be the chance to intercept a call from the client to this instance by using a message sink.

If the method returns false, on the other hand, a new "virtual" remoting boundary—the context—is created. In this case the framework will subsequently call GetPropertiesForNewContext() to allow you to add the IContextProperty objects that you want to use with this context.

The implementation of a complete attribute that will later be used to create a sink to intercept calls to this object is shown in Listing 11-2.

Listing 11-2. A ContextAttribute That Allows You to Intercept Calls

```
using System;
using System.Runtime.Remoting;
using System.Runtime.Remoting.Contexts;
using System.Runtime.Remoting.Activation;
using System.Runtime.Remoting.Messaging;

namespace ContextBound
{
    [AttributeUsage(AttributeTargets.Class)]
    public class CheckableAttribute: ContextAttribute
    {
        public CheckableAttribute(): base ("MyInterception") { }

        public override bool IsContextOK(Context ctx,
            IConstructionCallMessage ctor)
        {
            // if this is already an intercepting context, it's ok for us
            return ctx.GetProperty("Interception") != null;
        }

        public override void GetPropertiesForNewContext(
            IConstructionCallMessage ctor)
        {
            // add the context property which will later create a sink
            ctor.ContextProperties.Add(new CheckableContextProperty());
        }
    }
}
```

An IContextProperty on its own doesn't provide you with a lot of functionality, as you can see in Listing 11-3.

Listing 11-3. The IContextProperty Interface

```
public interface IContextProperty
{
    string Name { get; }

    void Freeze(Context newContext);
    bool IsNewContextOK(Context newCtx);
}
```

Freeze() is called when the context itself is frozen. This indicates that no change of context properties is allowed afterwards. IsNewContextOk() is called after all context attributes have added their context properties to allow your property to check for dependencies. If IContextProperty A can only be used together with IContextProperty B, it can check in this method if both properties are available for the newly created context. If this method returns false, an exception will be thrown.

Name simply has to return the context property's name that will be used to retrieve it by calling Context.GetProperty("*<name>*"). To be able to create a sink to intercept calls to this object, this class will have to implement one of the following interfaces: IContributeObjectSink, IContributeEnvoySink, IContributeClientContextSink, or IContributeServerContextSink. In the examples to follow, I use IContributeObjectSink, which is shown in Listing 11-4.

Listing 11-4. The IContributeObjectSink Interface

```
public interface IContributeObjectSink
{
    IMessageSink GetObjectSink(MarshalByRefObject obj, IMessageSink nextSink);
}
```

To create a new instance of CheckerSink, you can implement the IContextProperty as shown in Listing 11-5.

Listing 11-5. The CheckableContextProperty

```
using System;
using System.Runtime.Remoting;
using System.Runtime.Remoting.Contexts;
using System.Runtime.Remoting.Activation;
using System.Runtime.Remoting.Messaging;

namespace ContextBound
{
```

```csharp
public class CheckableContextProperty: IContextProperty,
    IContributeObjectSink
{
    public bool IsNewContextOK(Context newCtx)
    {
        return true;
    }

    public void Freeze(Context newContext)
    {
        // nothing to do
    }

    public string Name
    {
        get
        {
            return "Interception";
        }
    }

    public IMessageSink GetObjectSink(MarshalByRefObject obj,
        IMessageSink nextSink)
    {
        return new CheckerSink(nextSink);
    }

}
}
```

CheckerSink itself is a common IMessageSink implementation. Its first iteration is shown in Listing 11-6.

Listing 11-6. The CheckerSink's First Iteration

```csharp
using System;
using System.Reflection;
using System.Runtime.Remoting;
using System.Runtime.Remoting.Activation;
using System.Runtime.Remoting.Contexts;
using System.Runtime.Remoting.Messaging;

namespace ContextBound
{
```

```
public class CheckerSink: IMessageSink
{
    IMessageSink _nextSink;

    public CheckerSink(IMessageSink nextSink)
    {
        _nextSink = nextSink;
    }

    public IMessage SyncProcessMessage(IMessage msg)
    {
        Console.WriteLine("CheckerSink is intercepting a call");
        return _nextSink.SyncProcessMessage(msg);
    }

    public IMessageCtrl AsyncProcessMessage(IMessage msg,
        IMessageSink replySink)
    {
        Console.WriteLine("CheckerSink is intercepting an async call");
        return _nextSink.AsyncProcessMessage(msg,replySink);
    }

    publicIMessageSink NextSink
    {
        get
        {
            return _nextSink;
        }
    }
}
}
```

To enable this way of intercepting the Organization class shown at the beginning of this chapter, you have to mark it with [Checkable] and have it inherit from ContextBoundObject to create the context property.

The Organization class, which is shown in Listing 11-7, does not yet employ the use of custom attributes for checking the maximum amount of a single donation or the maximum length of the organization's name. It just demonstrates the basic principle of interception.

Listing 11-7. The Organization Now Is a ContextBoundObject

```
using System;

namespace ContextBound
{
    [Checkable]
    public class Organization: ContextBoundObject
    {
        String _name;
        double _totalDonation;

        public String Name
        {
            set
            {
                _name = value;
            }
            get
            {
                return _name;
            }
        }

        public void Donate(double amount)
        {
            Organization x = new Organization();
            x.Name = "Hello World";
            _totalDonation = _totalDonation + amount;
        }

    }
}
```

A simple client for this class is shown in Listing 11-8.

Listing 11-8. This Client Is Using the ContextBoundObject

```
using System;
using System.Runtime.Remoting.Contexts;

namespace ContextBound
{
    public class TestClient
    {
        public static void Main(String[] args) {
            Organization org = new Organization();
            Console.WriteLine("Will set the name");
            org.Name = "Happy Hackers";
            Console.WriteLine("Will donate");
            org.Donate(103);

            Console.WriteLine("Finished, press <return> to quit.");
            Console.ReadLine();
        }
    }
}
```

When this application is started, you will see the output shown in Figure 11-1.

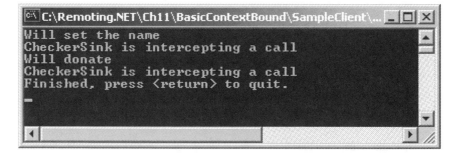

Figure 11-1. The application's output when using the ContextBoundObject

As you can see here, the CheckerSink intercepts the setting of the property Name and the call to Donate(), although it doesn't yet do anything to check the constraints I mentioned earlier.

The first step to enabling the sink to do something useful is to create a custom attribute that will later be used to designate a parameter's maximum length and maximum value. This attribute, which can be used for parameters and methods, stores the properties MaxLength, MaxValue, and NonNull as shown in Listing 11-9. Its DoCheck() method will later be called by the sink to check a given value against the attribute's definition.

Listing 11-9. The CheckAttribute

```
using System;

namespace ContextBound
{
    [AttributeUsage (AttributeTargets.Parameter | AttributeTargets.Method)]
    public class CheckAttribute: Attribute
    {
        private int _maxLength;
        private int _maxValue;
        private bool _nonNull;

        public int MaxLength {
            get {
                return _maxLength;
            }
            set {
                _maxLength = value;
            }
        }

        public int MaxValue
        {
            get
            {
                return _maxValue;
            }
            set
            {
                _maxValue = value;
            }
        }

        public bool NonNull
        {
            get
            {
                return _nonNull;
            }
```

```
            set
            {
                _nonNull = value;
            }
        }

        public void DoCheck (Object val)
        {
            // check for NonNull
            if (_nonNull && val == null)
            {
                throw new Exception("This value must not be null");
            }

            // check for MaxLength
            if (_maxLength > 0 && val.ToString().Length > _maxLength)
            {
                throw new Exception("This value must not be longer than " +
                        _maxLength + " characters");
            }

            // check for MaxValue
            if (_maxValue > 0)
            {
                if ((double) val > _maxValue)
                {
                    throw new Exception("This value must not be higher than " +
                            _maxValue );
                }

            }
        }
    }
}
```

To make use of this attribute in the organization class, you have to mark the parameter to Donate() and the set method for the Name property as shown here:

```
public String Name
{
    [Check(NonNull=true,MaxLength=30)]
    set
```

```
        {
            _name = value;
        }
        get
        {
            return _name;
        }
    }

    public void Donate([Check(NonNull=true,MaxValue=100)] double amount)
    {
        _totalDonation = _totalDonation + amount;
    }
```

Checking Parameters in an IMessageSink

Listing 11-10 shows the implementation of the CheckerSink. Calls from
SyncProcessMessage() and AsyncProcessMessage() have been added to the private DoCheck() method, which iterates over the assigned attributes and forwards
the business logic checks to CheckAttribute.DoCheck() for each parameter that is
marked with this attribute.

Listing 11-10. The CheckerSink

```
using System;
using System.Reflection;
using System.Runtime.Remoting;
using System.Runtime.Remoting.Activation;
using System.Runtime.Remoting.Contexts;
using System.Runtime.Remoting.Messaging;

namespace ContextBound
{

    public class CheckerSink: IMessageSink
    {
        IMessageSink _nextSink;
        String _mType;
        public CheckerSink(IMessageSink nextSink, String mType)
        {
            _nextSink = nextSink;
            _mType = mType;
        }
```

```csharp
public IMessage SyncProcessMessage(IMessage msg)
{
    DoCheck(msg);
    return _nextSink.SyncProcessMessage(msg);
}

public IMessageCtrl AsyncProcessMessage(IMessage msg,
    IMessageSink replySink)
{
    DoCheck(msg);
    return _nextSink.AsyncProcessMessage(msg,replySink);
}

public IMessageSink NextSink
{
    get
    {
        return _nextSink;
    }
}

private void DoCheck(IMessage imsg)
{
    // not interested in IConstructionCallMessages
    if (imsg as IConstructionCallMessage != null)  return;

    // but only interested in IMethodMessages
    IMethodMessage msg = imsg as IMethodMessage;
    if (msg == null) return;


    // Check for the Attribute
    MemberInfo methodbase = msg.MethodBase;

    object[] attrs = methodbase.GetCustomAttributes(false);

    foreach (Attribute attr in attrs)
    {
        CheckAttribute check = attr as CheckAttribute;

        // only interested in CheckAttributes
        if (check == null) continue;
```

```
            // if the method only has one parameter, place the check directly
            // on it (needed for property set methods)
            if (msg.ArgCount == 1)
            {
                check.DoCheck(msg.Args[0]);
            }
        }


        // check the Attribute for each parameter of this method
        ParameterInfo[] parms = msg.MethodBase.GetParameters();

        for (int i = 0;i<parms.Length;i++)
        {
            attrs = parms[i].GetCustomAttributes(false);
            foreach (Attribute attr in attrs)
            {
                CheckAttribute check = attr as CheckAttribute;

                // only interested in CheckAttributes
                if (check == null) continue;

                // if the method only has one parameter, place the check directly
                // on it (needed for property set methods)

                check.DoCheck(msg.Args[i]);
            }
        }

    }

  }
}
```

You can then change the sample client to demonstrate what happens when it performs an invalid operation, as shown in Listing 11-11.

Listing 11-11. This Client Does Not Honor the Business Logic Constraints

```csharp
using System;
using System.Runtime.Remoting.Contexts;

namespace ContextBound
{
   public class TestClient
   {
      public static void Main(String[] args) {
         Organization org = new Organization();
         try
         {
            Console.WriteLine("Will set the name");
            org.Name = "Happy Hackers";
            Console.WriteLine("Will donate");
            org.Donate(99);
            Console.WriteLine("Will donate more");
            org.Donate(102);
         }
         catch (Exception e)
         {
            Console.WriteLine("Exception: {0}",e.Message);
         }

         Console.WriteLine("Finished, press <return> to quit.");
         Console.ReadLine();
      }
   }
}
```

When you start this application, you will get the output shown in Figure 11-2.

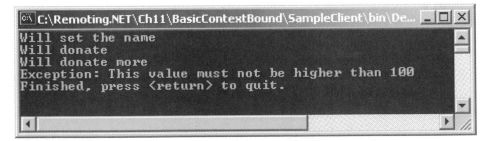

Figure 11-2. The client's illegal operation is prohibited by the CheckerSink.

Great! You are now checking your business logic constraints by using attributes that are assigned at the metadata level instead of checks that are hidden in your source code.

One interesting consideration that I have not yet mentioned is the following: what would happen if the first Organization object instantiates another Organization object and calls the `Donate()` method on the secondary object? Will this call also go through the message sink? In fact, in the current configuration it won't. This example just protects your class library from "outside" clients but doesn't affect any calls inside this context. This is because the CheckableAttribute's `IsContextOK()` only requests a new context when it's called from outside a checked context.

To make *all* calls to Organization (no matter what their origin) go through the CheckerSink, you'd have to change CheckableAttribute to return `false` from `IsContextOK()`:

```
public override bool IsContextOK(Context ctx, IConstructionCallMessage ctor)
{
    return false;
}
```

This will request a new context for each and every instance of any class that is marked with `[Checkable]` and that inherits from ContextBoundObject.

> **NOTE** *Something you should never forget when using these techniques: you are dealing with remote objects! This also means that they are lifetime-managed by leases and will time out the same way as "conventional" remote objects do. You might therefore want to add a sponsor to it as shown in Chapter 6.*

Summary

In this last chapter, I showed you some undocumented techniques to move constraints away from the implementation up to the metadata level. When using this approach together with reflection on the types of your class library, you will be able to automatically generate documentation that includes all those metadata-level checks. You learned about using different contexts in your local application and how to use IContextProperty and IContributeObjectSink to intercept calls to your objects by using IMessageSink objects.

I just want to remind you that context sinks are a great technology, but unfortunately not yet officially supported or documented by Microsoft. If you use them, it will be at your own risk! If any problems occur when doing so, you will be on your own. But isn't that the fate of anyone who's going to enter uncharted territory?

Conclusion

In this book you learned .NET Remoting from the basics to very advanced topics. In the first chapters I introduced you to the various kinds of remote objects and how to create and register them. I covered the intricacies of client-activated objects and server-activated objects. You also learned about the various ways of generating the necessary metadata to allow the .NET Remoting Framework to create transparent proxies. I showed you the deployment options for remoting servers that can be either managed applications (including console applications, Windows Services, and Windows Form applications) and IIS. I then showed you more advanced topics such as security, event handling, versioning, and lifetime management by using leases and sponsors.

In the second part of the book I showed you how .NET Remoting works internally. You were introduced to proxies, messages, transport channels, formatters, message sinks, and channel sinks. After covering those architectural basics, I showed you how to leverage the .NET Remoting Framework's extensibility model by implementing your own sinks and sink providers. At the end of the second part you finally learned how to implement a complete transport channel from scratch and how to use ContextBoundObject to intercept message calls.

You are now well prepared for the development of distributed applications using the .NET Framework—so go ahead and do your stuff!

Index

Apress Titles

ISBN	PRICE	AUTHOR	TITLE
1-893115-73-9	$34.95	Abbott	Voice Enabling Web Applications: VoiceXML and Beyond
1-893115-01-1	$39.95	Appleman	Dan Appleman's Win32 API Puzzle Book and Tutorial for Visual Basic Programmers
1-893115-23-2	$29.95	Appleman	How Computer Programming Works
1-893115-97-6	$39.95	Appleman	Moving to VB. NET: Strategies, Concepts, and Code
1-59059-023-6	$39.95	Baker	Adobe Acrobat 5: The Professional User's Guide
1-893115-09-7	$29.95	Baum	Dave Baum's Definitive Guide to LEGO MINDSTORMS
1-893115-84-4	$29.95	Baum, Gasperi, Hempel, and Villa	Extreme MINDSTORMS: An Advanced Guide to LEGO MINDSTORMS
1-893115-82-8	$59.95	Ben-Gan/Moreau	Advanced Transact-SQL for SQL Server 2000
1-893115-91-7	$39.95	Birmingham/Perry	Software Development on a Leash
1-893115-48-8	$29.95	Bischof	The .NET Languages: A Quick Translation Guide
1-893115-67-4	$49.95	Borge	Managing Enterprise Systems with the Windows Script Host
1-893115-28-3	$44.95	Challa/Laksberg	Essential Guide to Managed Extensions for C++
1-893115-39-9	$44.95	Chand	A Programmer's Guide to ADO.NET in C#
1-893115-44-5	$29.95	Cook	Robot Building for Beginners
1-893115-99-2	$39.95	Cornell/Morrison	Programming VB .NET: A Guide for Experienced Programmers
1-893115-72-0	$39.95	Curtin	Developing Trust: Online Privacy and Security
1-59059-008-2	$29.95	Duncan	The Career Programmer: Guerilla Tactics for an Imperfect World
1-893115-71-2	$39.95	Ferguson	Mobile .NET
1-893115-90-9	$49.95	Finsel	The Handbook for Reluctant Database Administrators
1-59059-024-4	$49.95	Fraser	Real World ASP.NET: Building a Content Management System
1-893115-42-9	$44.95	Foo/Lee	XML Programming Using the Microsoft XML Parser
1-893115-55-0	$34.95	Frenz	Visual Basic and Visual Basic .NET for Scientists and Engineers
1-893115-85-2	$34.95	Gilmore	A Programmer's Introduction to PHP 4.0
1-893115-36-4	$34.95	Goodwill	Apache Jakarta-Tomcat
1-893115-17-8	$59.95	Gross	A Programmer's Introduction to Windows DNA
1-893115-62-3	$39.95	Gunnerson	A Programmer's Introduction to C#, Second Edition
1-59059-009-0	$39.95	Harris/Macdonald	Moving to ASP.NET: Web Development with VB .NET
1-893115-30-5	$49.95	Harkins/Reid	SQL: Access to SQL Server
1-893115-10-0	$34.95	Holub	Taming Java Threads
1-893115-04-6	$34.95	Hyman/Vaddadi	Mike and Phani's Essential C++ Techniques
1-893115-96-8	$59.95	Jorelid	J2EE FrontEnd Technologies: A Programmer's Guide to Servlets, JavaServer Pages, and Enterprise JavaBeans
1-893115-49-6	$39.95	Kilburn	Palm Programming in Basic
1-893115-50-X	$34.95	Knudsen	Wireless Java: Developing with Java 2, Micro Edition
1-893115-79-8	$49.95	Kofler	Definitive Guide to Excel VBA
1-893115-57-7	$39.95	Kofler	MySQL
1-893115-87-9	$39.95	Kurata	Doing Web Development: Client-Side Techniques
1-893115-75-5	$44.95	Kurniawan	Internet Programming with VB

ISBN	PRICE	AUTHOR	TITLE
1-893115-38-0	$24.95	Lafler	Power AOL: A Survival Guide
1-893115-46-1	$36.95	Lathrop	Linux in Small Business: A Practical User's Guide
1-893115-19-4	$49.95	Macdonald	Serious ADO: Universal Data Access with Visual Basic
1-893115-06-2	$39.95	Marquis/Smith	A Visual Basic 6.0 Programmer's Toolkit
1-893115-22-4	$27.95	McCarter	David McCarter's VB Tips and Techniques
1-893115-76-3	$49.95	Morrison	C++ For VB Programmers
1-893115-80-1	$39.95	Newmarch	A Programmer's Guide to Jini Technology
1-893115-58-5	$49.95	Oellermann	Architecting Web Services
1-893115-81-X	$39.95	Pike	SQL Server: Common Problems, Tested Solutions
1-59059-017-1	$34.95	Rainwater	Herding Cats: A Primer for Programmers Who Lead Programmers
1-59059-025-2	$49.95	Rammer	Advanced .NET Remoting
1-893115-20-8	$34.95	Rischpater	Wireless Web Development
1-893115-93-3	$34.95	Rischpater	Wireless Web Development with PHP and WAP
1-893115-89-5	$59.95	Shemitz	Kylix: The Professional Developer's Guide and Reference
1-893115-40-2	$39.95	Sill	The qmail Handbook
1-893115-24-0	$49.95	Sinclair	From Access to SQL Server
1-893115-94-1	$29.95	Spolsky	User Interface Design for Programmers
1-893115-53-4	$44.95	Sweeney	Visual Basic for Testers
1-59059-002-3	$44.95	Symmonds	Internationalization and Localization Using Microsoft .NET
1-893115-29-1	$44.95	Thomsen	Database Programming with Visual Basic .NET
1-59059-010-4	$54.95	Thomsen	Database Programming with C#
1-893115-65-8	$39.95	Tiffany	Pocket PC Database Development with eMbedded Visual Basic
1-893115-59-3	$59.95	Troelsen	C# and the .NET Platform
1-893115-26-7	$59.95	Troelsen	Visual Basic .NET and the .NET Platform
1-59059-011-2	$39.95	Troelsen	COM and .NET Interoperability
1-893115-54-2	$49.95	Trueblood/Lovett	Data Mining and Statistical Analysis Using SQL
1-893115-16-X	$49.95	Vaughn	ADO Examples and Best Practices
1-893115-68-2	$49.95	Vaughn	ADO.NET and ADO Examples and Best Practices for VB Programmers, Second Edition
1-59059-012-0	$49.95	Vaughn/Blackburn	ADO.NET Examples and Best Practices for C# Programmers
1-893115-83-6	$44.95	Wells	Code Centric: T-SQL Programming with Stored Procedures and Triggers
1-893115-95-X	$49.95	Welschenbach	Cryptography in C and C++
1-893115-05-4	$39.95	Williamson	Writing Cross-Browser Dynamic HTML
1-893115-78-X	$49.95	Zukowski	Definitive Guide to Swing for Java 2, Second Edition
1-893115-92-5	$49.95	Zukowski	Java Collections
1-893115-98-4	$54.95	Zukowski	Learn Java with JBuilder 6

Available at bookstores nationwide or from Springer Verlag New York, Inc. at 1-800-777-4643; fax 1-212-533-3503. Contact us for more information at sales@apress.com.

Apress Titles Publishing SOON!

ISBN	AUTHOR	TITLE
1-59059-022-8	Alapati	Expert Oracle 9i Database Administration
1-59059-015-5	Clark	An Introduction to Object Oriented Programming with Visual Basic .NET
1-59059-000-7	Cornell	Programming C#
1-59059-014-7	Drol	Object-Oriented Flash MX
1-59059-033-3	Fraser	Managed C++ and .NET Development
1-59059-038-4	Gibbons	Java Development to .NET Development
1-59059-030-9	Habibi/Camerlengo/ Patterson	Java 1.4 and the Sun Certified Developer Exam
1-59059-006-6	Hetland	Practical Python
1-59059-003-1	Nakhimovsky/Meyers	XML Programming: Web Applications and Web Services with JSP and ASP
1-59059-001-5	McMahon	Serious ASP.NET
1-59059-021-X	Moore	Karl Moore's Visual Basic .NET: The Tutorials
1-893115-27-5	Morrill	Tuning and Customizing a Linux System
1-59059-020-1	Patzer	JSP Examples and Best Practices
1-59059-028-7	Rischpater	Wireless Web Development, 2nd Edition
1-59059-026-0	Smith	Writing Add-Ins for .NET
1-893115-43-7	Stephenson	Standard VB: An Enterprise Developer's Reference for VB 6 and VB .NET
1-59059-032-5	Thomsen	Database Programming with Visual Basic .NET, 2nd Edition
1-59059-007-4	Thomsen	Building Web Services with VB .NET
1-59059-027-9	Torkelson/Petersen/ Torkelson	Programming the Web with Visual Basic .NET
1-59059-004-X	Valiaveedu	SQL Server 2000 and Business Intelligence in an XML/.NET World

Available at bookstores nationwide or from Springer Verlag New York, Inc. at 1-800-777-4643; fax 1-212-533-3503. Contact us for more information at sales@apress.com.

About Apress

Apress, located in Berkeley, CA, is a fast-growing, innovative publishing company devoted to meeting the needs of existing and potential programming professionals. Simply put, the "A" in Apress stands for *"The Author's Press™"* and its books have *"The Expert's Voice™"*. Apress' unique approach to publishing grew out of conversations between its founders Gary Cornell and Dan Appleman, authors of numerous best-selling, highly regarded books for programming professionals. In 1998 they set out to create a publishing company that emphasized quality above all else. Gary and Dan's vision has resulted in the publication of over 50 titles by leading software professionals, all of which have *The Expert's Voice™*.

Do You Have What It Takes to Write for Apress?

Apress is rapidly expanding its publishing program. If you can write and refuse to compromise on the quality of your work, if you believe in doing more than rehashing existing documentation, and if you're looking for opportunities and rewards that go far beyond those offered by traditional publishing houses, we want to hear from you!

Consider these innovations that we offer all of our authors:

- **Top royalties with *no* hidden switch statements**
  Authors typically only receive half of their normal royalty rate on foreign sales. In contrast, Apress' royalty rate remains the same for both foreign and domestic sales.

- **A mechanism for authors to obtain equity in Apress**
  Unlike the software industry, where stock options are essential to motivate and retain software professionals, the publishing industry has adhered to an outdated compensation model based on royalties alone. In the spirit of most software companies, Apress reserves a significant portion of its equity for authors.

- **Serious treatment of the technical review process**
  Each Apress book has a technical reviewing team whose remuneration depends in part on the success of the book since they too receive royalties.

Moreover, through a partnership with Springer-Verlag, New York, Inc., one of the world's major publishing houses, Apress has significant venture capital behind it. Thus, we have the resources to produce the highest quality books *and* market them aggressively.

If you fit the model of the Apress author who can write a book that gives the "professional what he or she needs to know™," then please contact one of our Editorial Directors, Gary Cornell (gary_cornell@apress.com), Dan Appleman (dan_appleman@apress.com), Peter Blackburn (peter_blackburn@apress.com), Jason Gilmore (jason_gilmore@apress.com), Karen Watterson (karen_watterson@apress.com), or John Zukowski (john_zukowski@apress.com) for more information.